An Introduction to
Western Music

An Introduction to Western Music

BACH

BEETHOVEN

WAGNER

STRAVINSKY

by F. E. KIRBY

Fp THE FREE PRESS *New York*

COLLIER-MACMILLAN LIMITED *London*

this book is for
Russell,
Nicholas,
Paula,
and
Nathaniel

Preface

*t*his book is primarily intended for use in conjunction with undergraduate introductory courses in the history and literature of music, particularly those that are one term or semester in length. Since the number of books that purport in one way or another to serve this function is legion, the justification for yet another attempt in this field can lie only in a different conception of the course. The approach followed usually varies somewhat from course to course and book to book, depending on whether the material is conceived systematically, the emphasis being placed on the different genres of musical composition, or historically, with the emphasis on the chronological development of the art. Most often the approach involves both: The basic elements of the art and the different types of musical composition are presented in some sort of historical order, together with brief accounts of the leading composers and their works and with summary characterizations of the different historical periods.

A problem arises in connection with this approach: Any respectable historical survey of Western music requires some familiarity with basic elements of the art as well as with the principal forms and types of musical composition; but this familiarity is precisely what the readers are assumed to lack. The frequent result is that the approach really serves neither need, since both aspects are watered down and presented in an oversimplified and hence presumably more palatable form. For example, one much-used book of this kind contains biographical sketches of thirty-odd composers along with individual explanations of a hundred-odd compositions. One may well question what really remains of all this in the students' minds once the ten- or fifteen-week exposure has come to an end.

On the other hand, there does not appear to be a real solution to the problem, for it does not seem generally possible to do without the two elements: That some sort of historical approach accompany the introduction to music and music literature seems virtually mandatory in most cases. An approach that would deal with representative compositions *as compositions*—however attractive it might be to some—is in most instances simply not viable under the conditions that prevail generally at present.

The present book represents a compromise. Its basic idea is simple:

Preface

Instead of saying a little about a lot, it tries to say a lot about a little, at the same time (it is hoped) keeping well away from the extreme of saying a great deal about nothing. Instead of offering short discussions of all the important composers coupled with presentations of important compositions, it presents the history of Western music from the Baroque to the present, centering around (but by no means limited to) the work of four indisputably great and important composers: Bach, Beethoven, Wagner, and Stravinsky. Each composer is presented at some length and in considerable detail on the basis of representative works that for the most part are thoroughly discussed and extensively illustrated in the music examples. This principal part of the book is preceded by two chapters, the first a presentation of what has been taken to constitute the most essential elements of music theory, the other a brief survey of the most important phases in the historical development of Western music up to a time of Bach. These two chapters, like the rest of the book, are based on a number of compositions that are explained in some detail. In this fashion it has been found possible to describe, with detailed reference to individual compositions, all the principal genres of Western music. At the end of the book there are two appendixes: The first contains a bibliography along with other commentary, and the second, the full text of the Ordinary of the Mass.

It should be emphasized that there is nothing sacred about either the composers that have been chosen or the number of four. Other possibilities were considered, ranging from eight composers (adding Perotin, Machaut, Josquin, and Monteverdi) down to two (Bach and Beethoven). Or other choices could have been made: Handel, Mozart, Chopin, and Schoenberg, for instance. The possibilities are infinite. Yet it seemed better, probably for reasons that are at least partially subjective, to use the four that make up the book.

It is recognized that this approach, which was developed while teaching a course at Lake Forest College since 1965, is unusual. But it is unusual only in the context of music and music history. In connection with English literature, for example, it is quite usual to introduce students to the field by selecting a few representative works by a relatively small number of writers. In any case, the book is offered as an attempt at solving what, as already stated, appears to be an insoluble problem. It is at least hoped that others will find something in the approach that in some way meets their own needs.

For permission to reprint music under copyright, acknowledgment is made to the following publishers: Associated Music Publishers, Inc., New York; Belmont Music Publishers, Los Angeles; and Boosey and Hawkes, Inc., New York. Full particulars are given with the respective music examples.

With respect to the excerpts from the literary writings of Igor Stravinsky: The quotations from *Poetics of Music* (pp. 30–32, 37, 62, and 80–81), found on pages 382, 389–90, are reprinted by permission of Harvard University Press, Copyright 1947 by the President and Fellows of Harvard College. The quotations from *Expositions and Developments*, found on page 388, are reprinted

Preface

by permission of the publishers, Doubleday and Company, Garden City, New York. The quotations from the *Autobiography* are reprinted by permission of Igor Stravinsky.

For permission to reproduce illustrations, acknowledgment is made to the Art Institute of Chicago; Roy Bernard et Cie., Paris; the Bettmann Archive, New York; Deutsches Museum, Munich; Museum of Fine Arts, Boston; Galleria Nazionale d'Arte Moderna, Rome; German Information Center, New York; Historisches Museum der Stadt Wien, Vienna; Musée du Louvre, Paris; Museum of Modern Art, New York; National Portrait Gallery, London; Mr. and Mrs. Morton G. Neumann, Chicago; and the Trustees of Sir John Soane's Museum, London. Special thanks go to the Conn Instrument Corporation, Elkhart, Indiana, for providing pictures of the various musical instruments.

It comes as a pleasant duty to acknowledge assistance of various kinds in connection with the preparation of the book as a whole, as follows: to my students Mrs. Lillian S. Fraker, who read the entire manuscript and made numerous valuable suggestions affecting all aspects of the book, and Miss Linda Selby, who read and commented on much of it; to Mrs. Helen Hurd, who typed and edited it; to the Alexander von Humboldt-Stifung of Bad Godesberg (West Germany), the unknowing supporter of a good deal of the work, since the first writing-down of the book took place in 1966 at odd moments here and there during the course of research on a completely different problem, while the author, under the sponsorship of the Humboldt Foundation, was in residence at the University of Hamburg; to the Library of the School of Music, Northwestern University; to Lake Forest College, to its administration, which provided numerous services and facilities, and to the students of Music 21 over the past few years, who provided much of the incentive for the project; and, finally, to my wife and family, who suffered along with all of it.

F. E. K.

Lake Forest College

Contents

Music Examples

Music Examples

Music Examples

Music Examples

Music Examples

Illustrations

Chapter One

Music as an Art

*M*an's urge to understand is as basic as his urge to act. The ancient Greeks expressed this clearly by the twofold division they recognized between the practical and the theoretical, the former involving actually doing something, the latter dealing with explanations. This concern for understanding very early embraced the field of art in general and of individual artworks in particular, thus establishing the field of inquiry we call aesthetics. An early approach to the problem of the nature and purpose of the artwork was made by the philosopher Aristotle, who in his *Poetics* laid down the principle of *mimesis*, that art is the imitation of nature. But the exact relation that exists between the artwork and nature has been much disputed in philosophical and aesthetic writings over the centuries, and the solutions given have varied a good deal. It seems clear that the realms of art and nature are fundamentally different from one another: An artwork is made by man, whereas something existing in nature is the work of a higher power. This distinction was explicit in the Middle Ages, when the artwork was said to be *artificial*, a term that meant the same as our *artistic*, as opposed to *natural*, meaning the world of nature. At the same time, an individual artwork often represents man's attempt to show homage to, or in some manner to approach, this higher power; and thus art has always occupied an important position in human culture.

An artwork, then, is in some way or other a man-made imitation or representation of nature. Nature provides the raw materials, which are adapted by the artist in an infinite number of ways to make an artwork of some kind, which in turn may suggest or symbolize something that exists in the world of nature. The important thing is that the artwork is made, fashioned, by the artist: This is the original sense of the word *poetics* or *poesis* —something that is made by man.

The materials with which the artist works will, of course, vary with his chosen artistic medium. That is to say, while the painter is most fundamentally engaged in the organization of lines and colors on a flat area, the sculptor organizes a volume either by modeling clay or by carving down a block of stone. We might say, then, that while the painter works in the dimension of plane surface, the sculptor's work is in the realm of three-dimensional space.

1

Similarly with the other arts, the writer is engaged in the organization of words to produce a literary work (as Hemingway said, "the right words in the right order," or the French poet Valéry, "it is not with ideas that one makes a sonnet, but with words"), and the dancer utilizes bodily motions and gestures. And where does music fit in? The dimension in which a piece of music necessarily exists is *time*: Music is simply the organization of sounds in time as perceived by one or more listeners. Music is time made audible—time lived or experienced through sounds.

Returning to our earlier line of argument, a piece of music is made out of sounds by an artist (either worked out beforehand, composed, or else simply performed, sung or played). In music we have to deal with temporal succession, sounds occurring after one another in time. Stravinsky, in his *Poetics of Music*, defines a musical composition simply as "a speculation in sound and time." That is to say, sounds are deployed through a stretch of passing time, the entire process controlled by the speculative powers of the human intellect, by reason. The composer has greater control over the way his work organizes time than does the writer, because the very realization, the presentation, of his work must take place in time; once this process is started, time and music become inseparable, and time is filled with music. The French philosopher Henri Bergson has laid great stress on the importance of time in music. Naturally the composer remains at the mercy of the performers, who often obscure and distort his original conception. But nonetheless, since music cannot exist without time, the composer's grasp of this elusive element is greater than that of his colleagues in the other arts.

When one attempts to apply to music Aristotle's idea of art as the imitation of nature, one immediately runs into difficulties, since direct musical imitations, as of a thunderstorm or a barnyard scene, are not really characteristic of the art at its best, whereas other so-called imitations, as of a water lily, a sunset or sunrise, are not so definite that the listener would make the proper association unless he sees the title of the piece printed on his program. Music therefore lacks the precise denotative quality that obtains in the other arts.

If we use as a basis the broad definition of music given by Stravinsky (a musical piece is a speculation in sound and time), we obtain the two basic areas in the world of nature that require investigation if we are to gain an understanding of the elements of the art of music: the physical world of sound and the phenomenon or dimension of time. It will be seen that each of these broad areas is adapted, adjusted as it were, to provide the basis for the art of music; for each, appropriate systems of definite relationships have been established. Although each culture has its own preferences for how this is done, we are here concerned only with what is found in the West. We have, therefore, to examine each of these two areas, sound and time, to see how each has been adapted for purposes of the art of music.

Sound: The Organization of Pitch

From the standpoint of physics, a sound is caused when molecules in the air or water are set in motion by the vibration of some object. As the object moves rapidly back and forth it causes a series of *vibrations* in the air, called *sound waves*, which radiate from it in all directions unless some means of directing them is employed. Mere *noise* obtains when these vibrations are irregular, uneven, and erratic; a *tone* results when they are organized, controlled, and regular. Although there have been instances of the use of noise in musical compositions—especially in the twentieth century—most Western music has been based on tones.

A sound wave producing a musical tone has three principal physical characteristics:

1. *Frequency.* The frequency is the speed of the vibrations, measured in cycles per second (cps) or vibrations per second (vps). This determines the *pitch*, whether the tone is high or low; the more rapid the frequency, the higher the pitch. The frequency is also a function of the length of the sound source: The shorter the length of the vibrating string, air column, or whatever, the greater the frequency and the higher the pitch. The range used in music generally extends from 30 cps (lowest tone on the organ) to around 20,000 cps (the highest sounds audible to the human ear).

2. *Amplitude.* The size of the vibrations, the amplitude, determines the *loudness* of the tone; the greater the amplitude, the louder the tone. The exact determination of relative loudness or intensity is complicated by the fact that the amplitude necessary to produce a certain degree of loudness varies for tones of different pitch, bass tones generally requiring larger amplitudes than treble tones.

3. *Partial vibrations* (*partials, partial tones, overtones,* or *harmonics*). Every object or substance producing a musical tone vibrates not only as a whole but also in parts. The pitch produced when it vibrates as a whole is the loudest, and this determines the pitch at which the tone is heard; this is called the *fundamental.* But the object or substance also vibrates in parts, in halves, thirds, quarters, fifths, and so on, so that higher pitches are also produced, which are not separately heard, but which blend in with the fundamental. Taken together, these are known as the *overtone series* (see Example 1-15). Every voice and musical instrument, every tone-producing agent, has its own particular pattern of fundamental and partials, and it is this particular pattern of partials that determines the *tone color*: the *quality* or *timbre* of the tone generated. For example, the viola and the clarinet are two instruments whose range from top to bottom is roughly the same, and yet the pattern of partials produced on a viola, a bowed string instrument, is completely different from that produced by a clarinet, a woodwind instrument. Some tones, such as that

produced by a tuning fork, are relatively free of partials, but a tone completely lacking them, a sine-wave tone, may be generated only electronically.

In the series of partial tones there is to be seen a relationship of paramount importance for all music, that between the fundamental and its first partial tone. Let us take as an example a string whose fundamental pitch is 440 cps, a pitch known as *concert A*, to which our musical instruments are generally tuned. The vibrations produced as each half of the string vibrates go twice as fast, or at 880 cps. If the fundamental tone (440 cps) is sounded simultaneously with the higher (880 cps), the two will be found to have a certain affinity: They blend, go together, and seem to belong to one another. These two tones constitute what is called an *octave* (discussed later), and this agreement between them is the "miracle of the octave"—it makes our whole system of music possible. Whenever the frequency of a pitch is doubled, or cut in half, or quadrupled or whatever (as long as it goes by multiples of two), we will be hearing octaves.

The acoustical phenomenon of the octave, two tones whose frequencies stand in the ratio 2:1 (or multiples thereof), is inherent in the natural world of sound. All music avails itself of this phenomenon. Differences arise in how this is done—that is to say, in what way the octave is subdivided to gain additional pitches. But once the octave is subdivided and all pitches thus established are arranged in order, usually from the lowest to the highest, we then speak of a *scale* (from the Latin *scala*, ladder). Many different scales have been used in the West and elsewhere. Here we will present the essentials of the Western scale system in its fully developed form, as it has been in use since the late seventeenth century.

An *interval* is defined as the distance between any two tones, or notes (the terms from now on will be used interchangeably), of different pitch; usually one thinks of an interval as less than an octave, but an interval can exceed the distance of an octave. The smallest interval used in the traditional scale system of Western music is the *semitone*, or half step, which can best be visualized from the piano keyboard, on which the semitone obtains between any two immediately adjacent tones. Generally speaking, it represents the smallest interval clearly and readily perceptible to our ears, although it must be said that custom plays a large role in this and that in other cultures, such as those of India, Arabia, and China, as well as in our own twentieth-century music, intervals smaller than the semitone have been employed. Two semitones make up a *tone*, or whole step. These two smallest intervals, the tone and the semitone, are used to subdivide the octave, and seven of them are needed to do this, five tones and two semitones. When these seven are played successively in ascending or descending sequence and according to any of several fixed arrangements (see later), there results what is called a *diatonic* (through the notes, i.e., using all seven) scale. These seven notes have been named according to the first seven letters of the alphabet: A, B, C, D, E, F, G,

Sound: The Organization of Pitch

after which one can begin again, having reached the octave, with A and can continue.

Although the tone and the semitone may be regarded in a sense as the basic intervals, larger intervals are possible. The size of these larger intervals depends on how far one skips; for instance, the interval from A to B is called a second (since two notes, or letter names, are involved); from A to C would be a third (since three notes, or letter names, are involved, A, B, and C), from C to F a fourth (four, C, D, E, F), from C to G a fifth (C, D, E, F, G), and so on up from A to A, called the octave, since eight notes are involved. We will return to the question of intervals later in the discussion.

The system of naming and notating (writing down) the musical pitches in Western music is dependent on the diatonic scale of seven notes. These seven notes are represented by the lines and spaces on the *staff*, which usually consists of five lines and four spaces in which small round figures called *notes* may be written. In order to show what pitches the various lines and spaces represent, there are *clefs* (from the Latin *clavis*, key) placed at the beginning. Three clefs are in common use: the *treble* clef (also known as the G clef, violin clef, and soprano clef), which has the second line from the bottom as G; the *bass* clef, in which the second line from the top is F; and the *alto* clef (or the viola clef), in which the middle line is C. In all three clefs it is possible to continue up above the staff or down below it, indicating lines and spaces by short lines (ledger lines) drawn through the note or its stem. The one note

EXAMPLE 1-1

NOTES: THE STAFF, CLEFS, AND LEDGER LINES

treble clef   bass clef   tenor clef   ledger lines

that has the same form in either treble or bass clef is middle C, which is also represented by the middle line in the viola clef.[1]

EXAMPLE 1-2

MIDDLE C

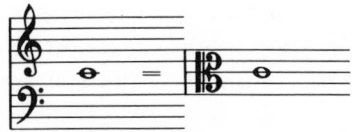

---

[1] The C clef is movable; i.e., it may be placed on any line, but it usually appears on the middle line.

There are a number of diatonic scales. First we will describe the most important of them, the *major* scale. The major scale is made by moving from the lower note of the octave to the upper, using the following succession of tones (T) and semitones (S): T, T, S, T, T, T, S; or, beginning with the note C, playing only the white notes on the piano keyboard.

EXAMPLE 1-3

THE MAJOR SCALE ON C

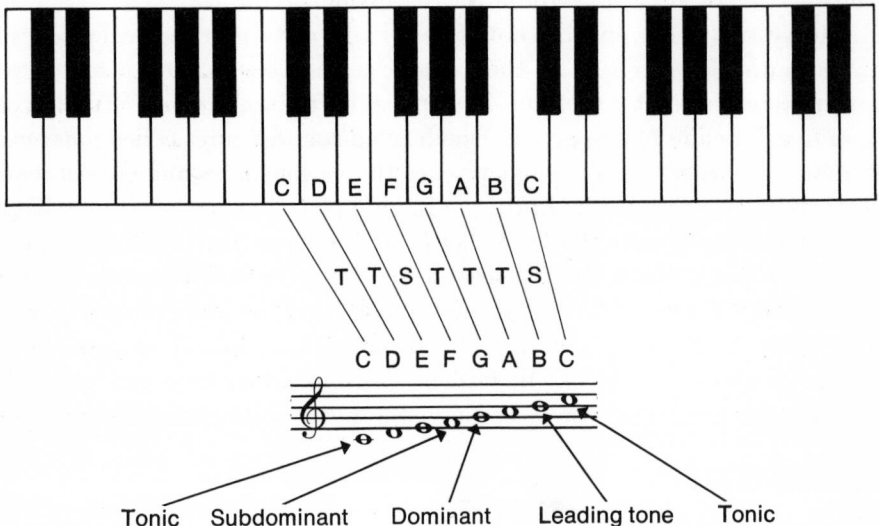

Each of the notes in such a scale has a name and in the context of a traditional piece of music exercises a particular function. The note on which the scale begins and ends is the most important, for it is the one around which all the other notes are oriented; it is called the *tonic*. Next in importance, especially in connection with harmony (see later), is the fifth of the scale (in the case of the major scale beginning on C, this will be G), called the *dominant*, and the note immediately below it, the fourth, in this case, F, called the *sub-dominant* (which, alternatively, lies a fifth below the tonic, hence "subdomi-nant" in the sense of dominant from underneath). The other important note or degree in the major scale is the seventh, known as the *leading tone* because it lies a semitone below the tonic (in the C major scale, the note B); in the con-text of melodic writing, it is often used to lead up to the point of stability that is attained when one continues up from the last semitone and reaches the tonic.

The next most important diatonic scale is the *minor*, which exists in three different forms. The first of these is the *natural* minor scale, which can

Sound: The Organization of Pitch

be obtained, analogous to the C major scale, by using only the white keys of the piano, but moving stepwise from A to A, thus producing the succession of tones and semitones: T, S, T, T, S, T, T. This, however, was regarded as unsatisfactory, because instead of the interval of the semitone between the leading tone and the tonic (seventh and eighth steps of the scale, G and A) there was a tone, so that the effect of the leading-tone relationship was lost. This shortcoming was remedied by sharping (raising by a semitone, indicated by the sign ♯) the seventh tone (from G to G sharp), which restores the leading-tone relationship and which produces the second of the three forms of the minor scale, the *harmonic*. In doing this, however, another difficulty arose because the interval between F and G sharp is a very large "tone" consisting of three semitones instead of the usual two (an interval known as an augmented second); as such an interval has a pronounced coloristic effect (Oriental in quality), and hence was felt undesirable in most of our music, a compromise was adopted whereby both F and G are sharped when the melodic line ascends, and they are sung naturally (indicated by ♮) when it descends. This third form of the minor scale is called the *melodic*.

EXAMPLE 1-4

THE NATURAL, HARMONIC, AND MELODIC FORMS OF THE MINOR SCALE

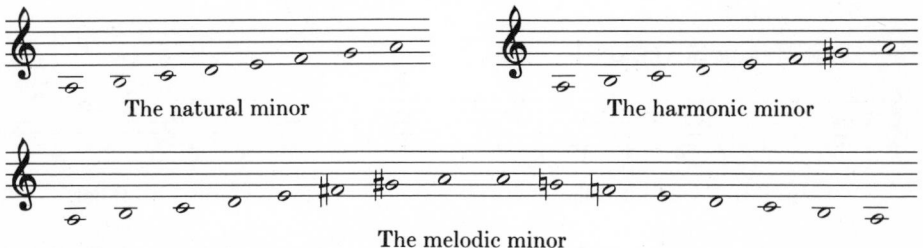

The natural minor   The harmonic minor

The melodic minor

There are still other forms of scales that have been used in Western music. Other diatonic (seven-note) scales are the so-called *church modes* (or Gregorian modes, ecclesiastical modes: the term *mode* means the same as *scale*) used in the Middle Ages and Renaissance, such as the Dorian (on the piano using the white keys, from D to D), Phrygian (E to E), Lydian (F to F), Mixolydian (G to G), and a number of others. But not all scales are diatonic: There is the scale consisting exclusively of semitones, hence containing twelve different notes, called the *chromatic* scale; and the scale consisting exclusively of tones, containing only six different notes, the *whole-tone* scale; and the five-note or *pentatonic* scale, the most common form of which is produced by playing just the black notes on the piano keyboard. A diatonic scale, let it be repeated, is one that uses seven different notes, one for each of the first seven letters of the alphabet according to one of the proper arrangements of the five tones and the two semitones.

Let us return to the major scale with its characteristic succession of tones and semitones (T, T, S, T, T, T, S) and assume that we have a singer who for some reason does not wish to begin on the note C, but rather on the note G. If, on the piano, we begin on G and move on up the white notes, it will be seen that the succession of tones and semitones works out except for the last two, from E to F and from F to G, which are S and T, respectively; in effect the leading-tone relationship is gone. To produce the proper succession of tones and semitones for the major scale, the F must be sharped (raised a semitone). On the other hand, if our singer wants to begin on the note F and to make a major scale, we will find that to obtain the characteristic succession of tones

EXAMPLE 1-5

THE MAJOR SCALE ON G

Without the F sharp   Proper form, with the F sharp

and semitones it is necessary to flat (lower by a semitone, indicated by the sign ♭) the fourth note, B.

EXAMPLE 1-6

THE MAJOR SCALE ON F

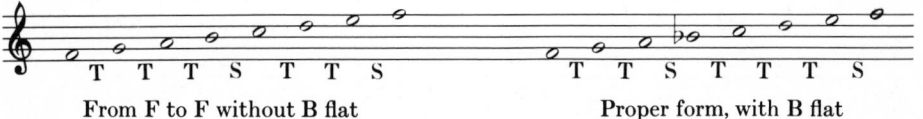

From F to F without B flat   Proper form, with B flat

One can build a major scale on any note and, by adding the appropriate sharps or flats, obtain the necessary succession of tones and semitones; but in every diatonic scale each note (letter name) appears once and once only.

This process of moving the major scale (or any other fixed sequence of notes) around, maintaining the succession of tones and semitones but beginning on different pitches, is known as *transposition*. The scale (major) remains the same, but the tonic, the note on which it begins, the *key*, is changed. In a musical composition, moving from one key (tones from a scale related to one tone as tonic) to another key (tones from a scale related to a different note as tonic) is called *modulation*.

The system of keys (major scales) is best seen in its completeness from the "circle of fifths": Every time one moves up a perfect fifth[2] in building major

---

[2] A perfect fifth must have its outside notes five degrees apart (C to G, D to A, etc.) and must embrace three tones and one semitone: Thus from B to F would be too small, and the B must be flatted or the F sharped.

scales (from C to G), one will add a new sharped note (always the seventh degree); and every time one moves down a perfect fifth (from F to B flat, B flat to E flat, etc.), one will have a new flatted note (always the fourth

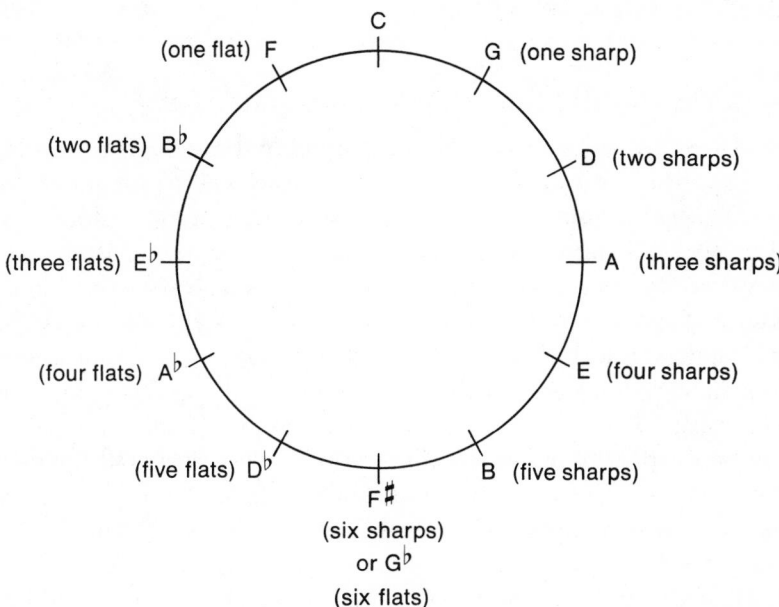

The circle of fifths (major keys).

degree). Two notes that have different names but the same pitch (D flat and C sharp) are said to be in *enharmonic* relationship to each other.

In practice the sharps and flats characteristic of a particular key are not written in when needed, but are presented at the beginning of the piece right after the clef, in what is called the *key signature.*

EXAMPLE 1-7

SOME COMMON KEY SIGNATURES

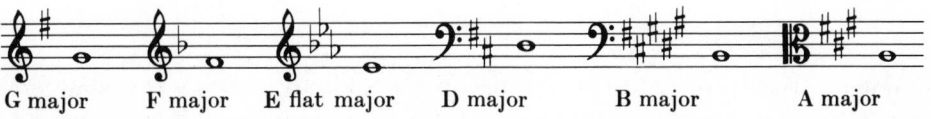

G major   F major   E flat major   D major   B major   A major

The minor scales (it is only the natural form of the minor scale that we need to consider) work the same way, and can be derived from the circle of fifths for the major keys: The minor scale with the same key signature as a major scale will lie a third below this major scale—i.e., C and A (no sharps, no flats), G and E minor (one sharp), E major and C-sharp minor (three sharps), F major and D minor (one flat), A-flat major and F minor (four flats), and so on. Such keys, major and minor, with the same key signature are said to be related: A minor is the *relative minor* to C major. On the other hand, C major is the *parallel major* to C minor.

Time: Metrical and Rhythmical Organization

Such, then, are the raw materials of sound as they have been adapted by musicians in the West for use in the art of music. There remains the other fundamental aspect of music, the dimension of time. Here we will once again observe the rationalizing power of the human intellect. Time at the least is very difficult to describe and explain and at the most very mysterious. To paraphrase St. Augustine in his *Confessions*, "as long as you do not ask me to explain it, I understand time very well." In general we perceive time as events, experiences in chronological succession, as constantly moving on, moving forward, the future becoming the present, the present becoming the past. But there is another aspect to our perception of time: We perceive it, not as mere undifferentiated succession, but rather as marked off, separated into pieces, in which the element of periodicity, of cyclic recurrence, is prominent. This is basic in our experience: The earth revolves on its axis, the moon goes around the earth, the earth goes around the sun, and so on. In the individual human being there are also cyclic occurrences connected with the operation of the vital functions, as breathing, the pulse, activity and sleep, the fertility cycle in the female, and so forth.

This cyclic or periodic aspect in our perception of time is exploited in the art of music. An example sometimes used to demonstrate this is the leaky faucet that one may hear at night: drip . . . drip . . . drip. The passing of time is marked off by the periodic drips. But one can take these equal and undifferentiated drips and mentally organize them into groups, either of two drips or of three:

drip	drip		drip	drip		drip	drip
⌊1	2⌋		⌊1	2⌋		⌊1	2⌋

drip	drip	drip		drip	drip	drip		drip	drip	drip
⌊1	2	3⌋		⌊1	2	3⌋		⌊1	2	3⌋

Although other types of organization are possible, it is these two simplest kinds that provide the basis for temporal organization in music. Let us, instead of drips, speak in terms of beats, a series of pulsations, some of which may be strong, others weak, but all equal in duration. These beats may be organized in groups of two or multiples thereof, or in groups of three or multiples there-

Time: Metrical and Rhythmical Organization

of: In the first case we would have *binary* or *duple* meter, and in the second we would have *ternary* or *triple* meter. Each unit, be it of two beats or of three or whatever, is called a *measure* or *bar* and is separated from the others in musical notation by a vertical line, called the *bar line*.

In an actual musical composition, however, instead of tones equal in duration, we find tones that differ in duration: Some are the same length as the beat, others are longer than the beat, still others are shorter. Thus we have *rhythm*, the actual arrangement of various durations in a piece of music. Rhythm is measured by the meter, the arbitrary grouping of beats by twos or by threes (hence, "meter," from the Latin *metrum*, to measure). The note value that most often represents a single beat is the quarter note, ♩. Two quarter notes constitute a half note, ♪(two beats), and two half notes make up a whole note, ○ (four quarter-note beats); on the other hand, half of a quarter note is an eighth note, ♪, and half of that a sixteenth note, ♬, and so on. There also exist signs to denote silence, pauses of specific lengths, called *rests*, which correspond to the notes:

EXAMPLE 1-8

RESTS AND THE CORRESPONDING NOTE VALUES

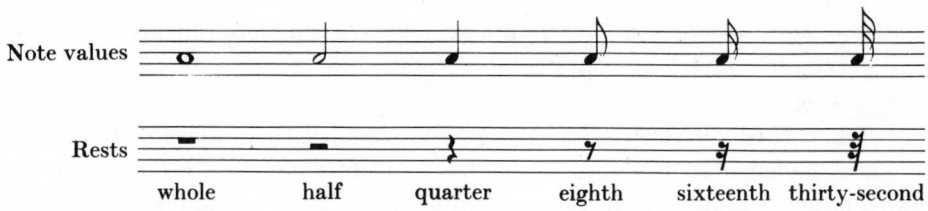

Note values	whole	half	quarter	eighth	sixteenth	thirty-second

If a note is to be held over a bar line, a *slur* or *tie* is used to indicate that the second note is not to be struck. Another mensural sign that should be mentioned is the *dot* (known as the dot or point of augmentation), which increases the value of the note it follows by one half. Rhythms using the dot are, not unnaturally, known as *dotted rhythms*.

EXAMPLE 1-9

THE TIE AND THE DOT

The tie   The dot

The metrical facts of a composition—the number of beats in a bar and the note value that receives one beat—are indicated by the *time signature* which appears at the beginning, in the form of two numerals, one written above the other. The upper numeral tells what the meter is (how many beats in a bar), the lower what note value is equivalent to a beat.

EXAMPLE 1-10

SOME COMMON TIME SIGNATURES

The speed with which the beats of the meter move is called the *tempo*. This speed has since the eighteenth century been imprecisely designated by Italian terms, which often give an indication of the expressive character of the piece as well as the tempo:

Very slow: *grave, largo, adagio.* Or *largo con gran' espressione* (largo, with great expression), *adagio cantabile* (lyric or singing adagio)

Moderate: *andante* (from *andare*, to walk), *moderato*

Fast: *allegretto, allegro, vivace.* Or *allegro molto* (very much allegro), *allegro moderato* (moderate allegro), *allegro con fuoco* (allegro, with fire)

Very fast: *presto, prestissimo*

Since 1816, composers have frequently availed themselves of the *metronome*, a device that produces beats the speed of which can be regulated by controlling the number of beats per minute. Thus, largo would fall within 40 to 77 beats per minute, andante between 126 and 152, allegro between 152 and 176, and presto between 176 and 208. Designations for a gradual change in tempo may appear during a piece: *ritard* or *ritardando* (slow down) and *accelerando* or *stretto* (speed up).

So much, then, for meter and the different kinds of metrical organization and how they and their varieties are represented in musical notation. Although meter is of basic importance in our musical system, what strikes us in a musical composition is not so much its meter but its *rhythm*; and by rhythm, as already stated, is meant the specific patterns and combinations in which notes of varying duration appear. In most instances the rhythm of a piece exists within the context of one of the basic meters. But the meter is a standardized and generalized pattern, abstract, something given, whereas the rhythm is individual to the particular musical composition. In the famous Allegretto of Beethoven's Symphony in A major (No. 7, Op. 92) we may observe the following:

Time: Metrical and Rhythmical Organization

EXAMPLE 1-11

METER AND RHYTHM IN THE ALLEGRETTO FROM BEETHOVEN'S SYMPHONY IN A MAJOR (OP. 92)

Here the rhythm follows the simple metric pattern closely, subdividing only the second beat of the odd-numbered bars. In the Finale of the same symphony we see:

EXAMPLE 1-12

METER AND RHYTHM IN THE ALLEGRO CON BRIO FROM BEETHOVEN'S SYMPHONY IN A MAJOR (OP. 92)

In it the relation between meter and rhythm is again fairly close. But in the first movement we see the following:

EXAMPLE 1-13

METER AND RHYTHM IN THE VIVACE FROM BEETHOVEN'S SYMPHONY IN A MAJOR (OP. 92)

It has been said that in a piece of music, once it gets under way, you know the meter, but you cannot precisely tell what will happen with respect to the rhythm; in short, one can predict the meter, but not the rhythm.

A common device for creating variety in rhythm is *syncopation*. This depends on the firm establishment of a rhythm with regularly recurring accents in accordance with a common meter; then when an accent fails to appear where it should, on a "strong" beat, in accordance with the metric pattern, or when it comes on what should be a "weak" beat, according to that pattern, we have a syncopation. A particularly clear example is found in Mozart's Symphony in D major (the *Prague Symphony*), where a passage in the last movement appears in both its "normal" and a syncopated form.

EXAMPLE 1-14

SYNCOPATION IN THE ALLEGRO FROM MOZART'S SYMPHONY IN D MAJOR (K. 504)—PRINCIPAL THEME

A few other notational signs may be explained here:

The accent: >
The staccato (sharp attack, quick release): $\dot{\textbf{J}}$
The fermata (indefinite hold): ⊙
Sign of repetition: :‖
Signs connected with dynamics:
    piano (soft), *p*; softer, pianissimo, *pp*; and so on, *ppp* . . .
    forte (loud), *f*; louder, fortissimo, *ff*; and so on, *fff* . . .
    Both moderated
      by
    m: *mp*, mezzo-piano (less soft) or *mf*, mezzo-forte (less loud)
    crescendo (gradually getting louder): ⊂
      or
    diminuendo or *decrescendo* (gradually getting softer): ⊃

Elements of Harmony

We have established the first principles of sound and time in music. It is necessary now to look somewhat further into the element of sound, the musical tones and their relationships. The characteristic music of the West is *polyphonic*, i.e., many-voiced; musical tones of different pitches are sounded simultaneously. The arrangement of the various musical pitches that sound simultaneously and the rules governing these relationships are the subject of *harmony* (from the Greek *harmonia*, reconciliation of opposites; concord). We must survey some of the leading principles of this discipline.

Elements of Harmony

The fundamental unit in harmony consists simply of two tones of different pitches, an *interval*. When the second note of the interval follows the first, we speak of a *melodic* interval, but when they are sounded simultaneously, of a *harmonic* interval. Intervals are grouped according to *consonance* and *dissonance*. A consonance is usually understood to represent a stable sound, from which one need not move, where one could stop, whereas a dissonance is unstable, requiring progression to a consonance to *resolve* the dissonance. It is clear that this idea has but limited validity for much twentieth-century music. The meaning of consonance and dissonance may also be explained in terms of the series of partial tones (see pages 3–4): The most consonant intervals (known as the perfect consonances) come toward the beginning of the series, the less consonant intervals (the secondary or imperfect consonances) next, and the dissonances come later, further removed from the fundamental note.

EXAMPLE 1-15

THE NATURAL SERIES OF PARTIAL TONES, FROM C

Fundamental

The intervals, then, are grouped as follows:

EXAMPLE 1-16

INTERVALS

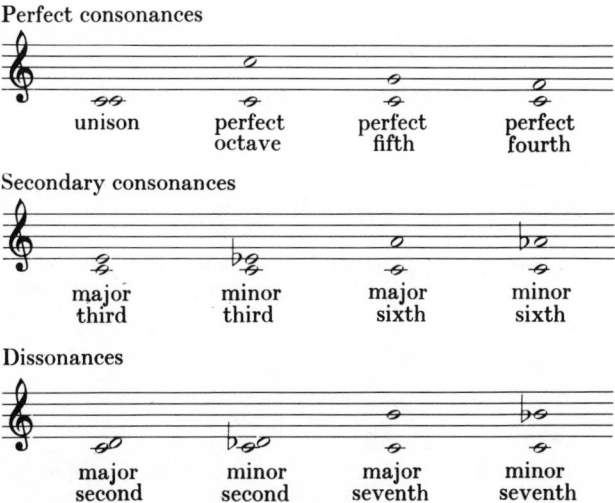

Perfect consonances

unison   perfect octave   perfect fifth   perfect fourth

Secondary consonances

major third   minor third   major sixth   minor sixth

Dissonances

major second   minor second   major seventh   minor seventh

It will be noted that the imperfect or secondary consonances and the dissonances, with one exception, each exist in two forms, *major* and *minor*, the minor a semitone smaller than the major. This is not true of the perfect or primary consonances; should they be made larger or smaller by a semitone, we would speak of augmentation and diminution. That is to say, to be perfect a fifth must embrace three tones (whole steps) and one semitone (half step); a perfect fourth must consist of two tones and one semitone. In this what counts is how the interval is spelled, not how it sounds; that is, the minor third from C extends to E flat, but will sound exactly the same as the augmented second from C, which goes to D sharp, since D sharp and E flat are enharmonically equivalent; but depending on the context, one will be preferred to the other. The exception is the augmented fourth or diminished fifth, also known as the *tritone*, which consists of three tones. In the Middle Ages this interval was known as *diabolus in musica* (the devil in music) because it caused difficulties in singing and in harmony.

The most important element in the Western system of harmony, however, is not the interval (a complex of two notes only), but the *chord* (a complex of more than two notes sounding simultaneously). The basic chord in our Western music, the *triad*, consists of three notes, the two outermost a fifth apart, the middle note a third from each of the two outer notes. Each triad is named by its lowest, or bass, note which is said to be the *root* of the chord. There are four different kinds of triads: If the interval between the root and the middle note (or third) is a major third, the triad is said to be *major*; if it is a minor third, the triad is said to be *minor*; if the top note (or fifth) of a major triad is raised a semitone, the triad is said to be *augmented*; and if the top note of a minor triad is lowered a semitone, the triad is said to be *diminished*.

EXAMPLE 1-17

AUGMENTED AND DIMINISHED INTERVALS

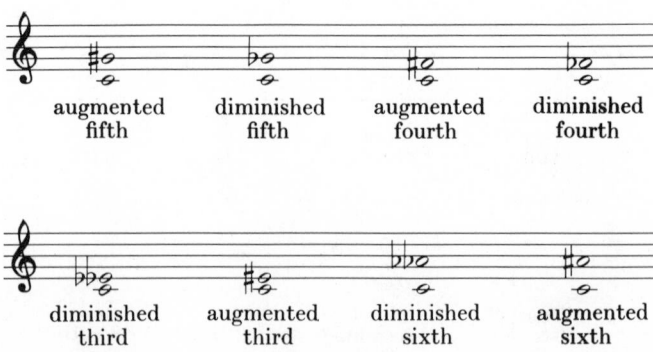

augmented fifth	diminished fifth	augmented fourth	diminished fourth

diminished third	augmented third	diminished sixth	augmented sixth

EXAMPLE 1-18

TRIADS

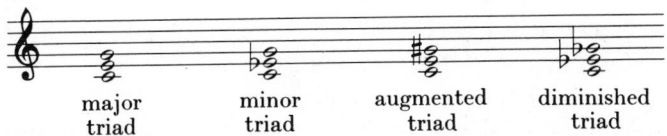

| major triad | minor triad | augmented triad | diminished triad |

One can make other chords built in thirds by adding notes above the fifth of a triad. Adding a note a third above the fifth of a major triad makes a *seventh chord*, whereas adding a third to a seventh chord makes a *ninth chord*, both of which may be major, minor or diminished, depending on the size of the seventh or ninth and the third. Still other chords are possible—eleventh and thirteenth chords, and so on.

EXAMPLE 1-19

SEVENTH AND NINTH CHORDS

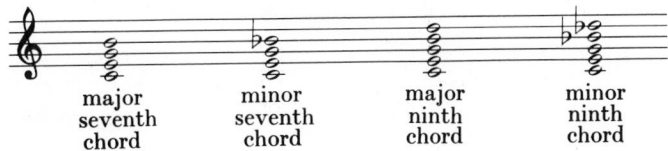

| major seventh chord | minor seventh chord | major ninth chord | minor ninth chord |

In all the examples given up to now, the chords, triads, seventh chords, ninth chords, and so on, have been given in *root position*, the root of the chord being the lowest note. But they may just as easily appear with some other note as the lowest note, in which case we speak of *inversions* of the chord. In the case of triads, two inversions are possible: In the *first inversion* the root goes to the top, and the third becomes the lowest note; in the *second inversion* the fifth is the lowest note, the root is in the middle, and the third on top.

EXAMPLE 1-20

INVERSIONS OF A TRIAD

C major triad

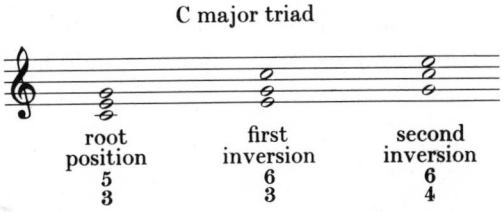

| root position 5 3 | first inversion 6 3 | second inversion 6 4 |

Counting from the bass note, in a triad in root position, the top note is a perfect fifth and the middle a major third above this note, so the triad is called a 5/3 chord; similarly, in a triad in first inversion, the bottom and top notes are a sixth apart, the bottom and middle notes a third apart, so the triad is known as a 6/3 chord (or simply as a sixth chord); and the second inversion triad, with a sixth between the outer notes and a fourth between the bottom and the middle notes, is called a 6/4 chord. The same applies to seventh and ninth chords, except, of course, that three inversions are possible for seventh chords and theoretically four for ninth chords.

All the examples of chords (root position and inversions) that have been given up to now have also been in *close position*—i.e., the notes are as close together as possible (as in Example 1-20). In an actual musical composition they will most often not be arranged this way, but will be in *open position*, spaced out, depending upon what effect the composer desires. But no matter how far apart the notes are spaced, they may still be regarded as chords, and for purposes of analysis the notes are always brought together into close position.

EXAMPLE 1-21

OPEN POSITION

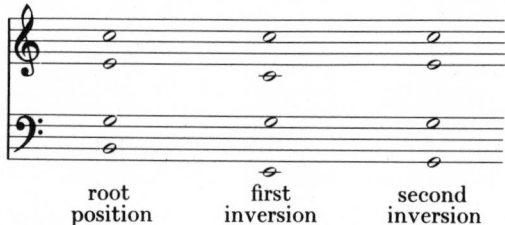

root
position

first
inversion

second
inversion

Constituent notes of a triad may be used more than once in a chord—i.e., they may be *doubled*. Finally, in actual music, chords do not usually appear as simple blocks of simultaneously sounding notes, but are more apt to be broken up or decorated by notes that do not belong to the chord proper. It is this that helps give Western music its great variety, its seemingly infinite possibilities for expression.

The triad, then, is the prime constituent of our system of harmony. The triads belonging in any key are those built on the different degrees of the scale beginning on that particular tonic. In C major we would have:

EXAMPLE 1-22

TRIADS IN THE KEY OF C MAJOR

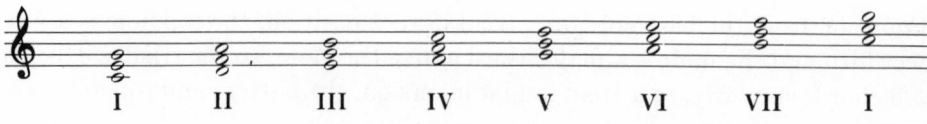

I   II   III   IV   V   VI   VII   I

Elements of Harmony

It will be seen that major triads are found on I, IV, and V; minor triads on II, III, and VI; and on VII the triad is diminished: This will be true of any major key. The most important triads are those whose roots are on the most important degrees of the scale: I (tonic), IV (subdominant), and V (dominant) (VII, the leading tone, which has a diminished triad, is usually associated with the dominant). By using merely these three principal triads it is possible, rather crudely to be sure, to "harmonize," put chords to, almost any popular melody. The minor triads belonging to the key (those built on II, III, and VI) may be used to provide variety and harmonic color. The same melody could be harmonized using some of these other triads as well.

EXAMPLE 1-23

Au clair de la lune—SIMPLE HARMONIZATION

EXAMPLE 1-24

Au clair de la lune—MORE ELABORATE HARMONIZATION

The system works in the same way for the minor keys, as may be seen from C minor:

EXAMPLE 1-25

TRIADS IN THE KEY OF C MINOR

Here the triads on I, IV, and V are minor; those on III, VI, and VII are major; and II is diminished (unless the harmonic minor, which is common, is used, in which case V is major, or the melodic form, in which both IV and V would be major). Again, many common melodies in the minor may be successfully harmonized by using only the I, IV, and V triads in the key.

In our system of harmony great importance attaches to the relation between the tonic and the dominant (I and V). The most important means of pointing up the tonic is by the succession V–I (dominant–tonic). This is especially so in *cadences*, concluding passages or chord progressions (from the Latin *cadere*, to fall), which may appear either at the end of a piece or internally to mark a stopping place or caesura.[3] There are several standard types of cadence: the *authentic* or *full* cadence, from V to I; the *half* cadence, not coming to a full stop, from I to V; and the *plagal* cadence, IV to I, familiar from the "Amen" at the end of hymns. Yet another type is used for variety to obtain a certain effect, to make the listener think there is going to be a simple authentic cadence, but instead of going from V to I, the progression is from V to VI (VI being, in a major key, a minor triad); this is known as the *deceptive* cadence.

EXAMPLE 1-26

CADENCES IN C MAJOR

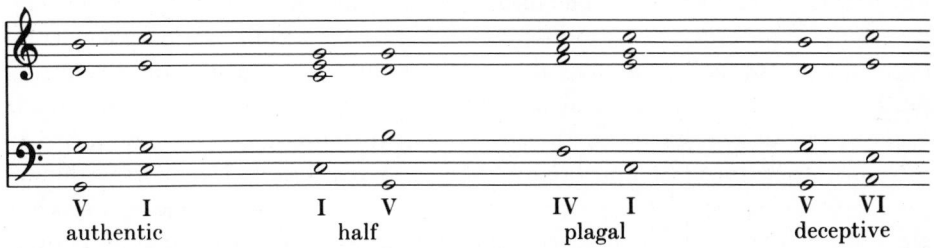

V	I	I	V	IV	I	V	VI
authentic		half		plagal		deceptive	

Most of the elaborations in harmony appear as dominant chords, to enhance and intensify the dominant preparatory to the resolution to the tonic. The most common example of this is the *dominant seventh chord*, which is nothing but the seventh chord constructed on the dominant degree of the scale; but the addition of the dissonant extra note, the seventh, makes the chord less stable and thus makes it drive more toward resolution. The same thing is true of dominant ninth chords, major and minor, which were extensively used in the music of the late nineteenth century.

This system of chords and their relationships has governed the main tradition of Western art music at least since the seventeenth century, and in

EXAMPLE 1-27

DOMINANT SEVENTH AND NINTH CHORDS IN THE KEY OF C MAJOR

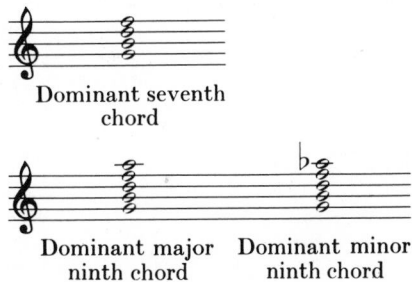

Dominant seventh
chord

Dominant major   Dominant minor
ninth chord   ninth chord

[3] Cadences may be melodic or harmonic, but the term is usually employed with reference to harmony.

some respects its principles go back at least to the Renaissance. That it is not, however, the only possible system is apparent from the music of other cultures, as well as from our own twentieth-century music, in which its basic premises are frequently denied, others being set forth and used instead. Some of these new principles will be dealt with later on.

Texture

It is conventional to distinguish two different kinds of *texture* (ways in which voices or voice-parts are used): *monophonic* and *polyphonic*, the second with two subdivisions, *contrapuntal* and *homophonic*. We have monophonic music when there is but a single melody being sung, whether it be a song sung by a folk singer or a college alma mater sung in a stadium by thirty thousand enthusiastic football fans. But if there is more than one melodic line being performed at the same time, we speak of polyphonic music. Polyphonic music is said to be contrapuntal[4] if the component melodic lines are to be heard as melodies in themselves, and homophonic if they are not. Usually in a homophonic composition the uppermost melodic line is the most important, while the others form a harmonic accompaniment, usually consisting of chords. A good example of homophonic pieces is the hymns sung by the congregation in church. The accompanying schematic diagram may illustrate the types of textures.

In contrapuntal music, we are conscious of several different melodic lines being performed at the same time, and it is this *linear* aspect that is important. See Example 1–28 for a passage in which four voice-parts are combined in this fashion.

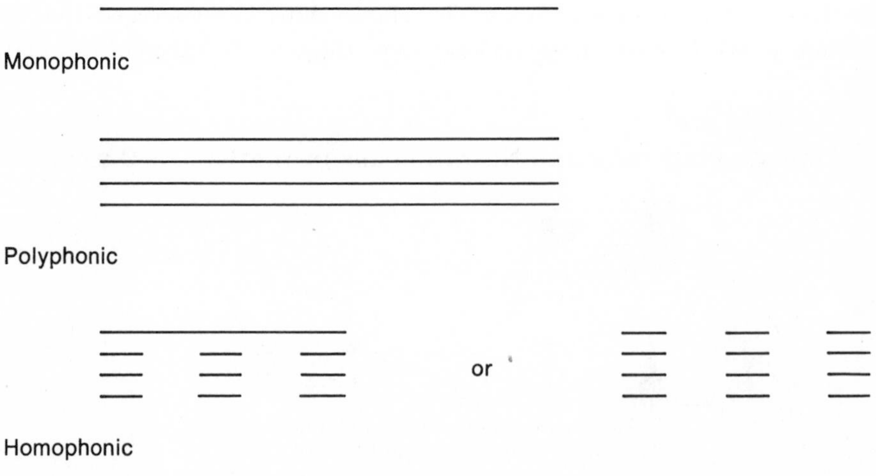

Monophonic

Polyphonic

or

Homophonic

Textures.

[4] The derivation of this term will be explained later. It should be pointed out that the term *polyphonic* is often used for *contrapuntal* to denote this type of music.

Texture

EXAMPLE 1-28

OCKEGHEM: KYRIE I, FROM *Mass Mi Mi*

Most contrapuntal music, however, is not of this type. More common is to have the same pattern of notes occur in all the voice-parts, a procedure known as *imitation* (also imitative counterpoint or imitative polyphony).[5] An important type of composition depending on imitative counterpoint is the *fugue*.

EXAMPLE 1-29

ROUND (SIMPLE CANON): "Frère Jacques"

As written:

Frè - re   Jac - ques, Frè - re   Jac - ques, dor - mez vous,   dor - mez vous?

Son-nez les ma-ti - nes Son-nez les ma-ti - nes Din, din, don,   Din, din, don.

Realization as four-part round (beginning):

[5] For illustrations of imitative counterpoint, see Examples 2-16, 3-7 (No. 2), and 4-1.

Musical Instruments

The strictest form of imitation is called *canon*, and in the common meaning of the term each voice-part has the same notes all the way through. The most well-known example of this is the simple *round*, such as "Frère Jacques." But canonic music can be extremely complex, as will be seen in the late work of Bach and Stravinsky.

Musical Instruments

The final topic to be taken up in connection with the element of sound in music has to do with how musical tones are in fact produced: the *instruments* of music. Since there are both instrumental and vocal music, the human voice as a means of producing musical tones must also be considered. Generally, human voices are classified according to their *range*, or *tessitura*, the highest and lowest pitches an individual voice can negotiate and all the pitches in between. The four principal tessituras are called soprano, alto, tenor, and bass, and their normal ranges are as follows:

EXAMPLE 1-30

TESSITURAS

| soprano | alto | tenor | bass |

Tessituras lying above, below, or in between are often distinguished: mezzo-soprano (between soprano and alto), or the very high coloratura soprano, and the baritone (a high bass, but not a tenor), or the very deep *basso profondo*.

The instruments proper are classified according to how the tone is produced. Four basic types of tone-producing agents are distinguished: *chordophone* (vibrating string), *aerophone* (vibrating air column), *membranophone* (vibrating membrane), and *idiophone* (whole body of instrument vibrates). More commonly we speak of stringed instruments, wind instruments, and percussion instruments, which would include membranophones and idiophones. Within each classification the various instruments are grouped in accordance with their tessitura just as were the human voices.

Most important for the art music of the West are the bowed string instruments. The highest, or soprano, member of the family is the *violin*, next comes the *viola*, then the *violoncello* or simply *cello*, and finally the largest and deepest, the *double bass* or *violone*. Their principal ancestors in the Renaissance were the members of the viol family. The principle of operation of the bowed string instruments is roughly this: Usually there are four strings, tuned in fourths and fifths, running from lowest to highest. By stopping a string—

The bowed string instruments: violin, viola, violoncello, double bass. (COURTESY
CONN INSTRUMENT CORPORATION, ELKHART, INDIANA.)

pressing it down hard against the instrument and thus shortening the length
that is free to vibrate—the pitch it gives off is raised; and the player is free to
move from string to string. The instrument is normally played with a bow
(*arco*) held in one hand which moves back and forth across the string(s), while
the other hand stops the strings in the appropriate places; occasionally the
instrument is played without the bow, the hand simply plucking the strings
(*pizzicato*).

Other string instruments are not bowed, but plucked: the *guitar*, the
banjo, the *dulcimer* (actually struck rather than plucked), the *lute*, the *harp*,
and so on. But again the principle remains the same: Each instrument has a
number, usually four or more, of strings tuned to different pitches, and the
strings must be appropriately stopped—depressed by a finger—thus varying
the length that is free to vibrate.

In the wind instrument family, two large divisions are distinguished: the
woodwinds and the *brass* instruments. To take up the woodwind instruments
first, from the highest to the lowest there are the *flute*, the *oboe*, the *clarinet*,

The woodwind instruments: flute, oboe, clarinet, bassoon. (COURTESY CONN INSTRUMENT CORPORATION, ELKHART, INDIANA.)

and the *bassoon.* Some of these exist in more than one form: for instance, the *piccolo* (or *flauto piccolo*), a small and hence very high-pitched flute; the *English horn,* much like the oboe; the *bass clarinet,* a large and deep form of clarinet; and the *contrabassoon,* a large deep bassoon; the *saxophone,* which comes in several sizes, is in operation similar to the clarinet. In all wind instruments, the principle of operation is to shorten the length of a vibrating air column, thus raising its pitch. This is done by opening, or uncovering, holes in the side of a cylindrical pipe, which has the effect of shortening the length of the column in which the air can vibrate. However, while the flute operates as a simple pipe or whistle, each of the other woodwind instruments uses a *reed,* a small thin piece of wood which is put into vibration as the player blows into the mouthpiece.

The brass instruments, in descending order of tessitura, are the *trumpet,* the *French horn,* the *trombone,* and the *tuba;* a somewhat smaller variant of the trumpet is the *cornet.* The principle of operation is the same as with the

The brass instruments: trumpet, French horn, trombone (above), *tuba*. (COURTESY CONN INSTRUMENT CORPORATION, ELKHART, INDIANA.)

woodwinds, except that in the trombone the length of the pipe is controlled by a sliding or telescoping arrangement, so that the instrument is often called the slide trombone.

Out of many different percussion instruments a few may be mentioned here. Among the drums we have the *timpani* (two to four differently tuned drums), the *snare drum*, and the large untuned *bass drum*. Other percussion instruments are the *cymbals*, the *triangle*, the *glockenspiel*, the *tambourine*, and the *gong*.

A large category of instruments remains, the keyboard instruments. Here the instruments are grouped not according to how the sound is produced, but according to how the instrument is played—i.e., by the keyboard. In most of them the mechanism actuated by means of the keyboard involves vibrating strings; but in the *organ*, the keyboard actuates a mechanism that forces air through pipes. An important difference between keyboard instruments and those previously discussed is that the keyboard instruments—with the excep-

Musical Instruments

tion of a small form of organ, the *portative* or *organetto*—are capable of producing polyphonic music all by themselves. In general, this is not possible on string and wind instruments, with the exception of some of the plucked string instruments. For this reason the keyboard instruments are more complex in their operation than the other instruments.

To deal with the stringed keyboard instruments first, the *harpsichord* (also called *cembalo, clavicembalo, clavecin*, and *Kielflügel*) and the *clavichord* are the oldest, having existed at least since the fourteenth century. Of the two, the clavichord is the simpler. When the key is struck, a thin light blade of wood, the *tangent*, is pushed up against the string, causing its (the string's) undamped section, between where the tangent strikes and the front of the instrument, to vibrate. In the case of the harpsichord, a larger instrument which comes in various sizes and kinds, the strings are plucked. The long thin piece of wood that holds the plectrum is called the *jack*. When the key is depressed, the jack is pushed up and the plectrum plucks; on the return a movable tongue withdraws the plectrum so that no plucking takes place as the jack falls back into position. Both the harpsichord and the clavichord have extremely light and transparent sounds, the clavichord being particularly soft. Very little dynamic variation is possible on these instruments, except on the larger harpsichords equipped with several different sets of strings, but even then it is impossible to produce much in the way of a crescendo or decrescendo. Hence in the middle of the eighteenth century, when such dynamic variation became an important element in music, these instruments gave way to one that was capable of such dynamic variation, the *piano* or *pianoforte* (originally *cembalo piano e forte*), whose very name reflects its salient quality. The keyboard actuates a hammer action, so that the string is forcibly struck: The harder the key is struck, the greater the force with which the hammer strikes the string and the louder the tone produced. The mechanism to do all this is much more complex than that used in either the harpsichord or the clavichord.

The organ is by far the oldest of the keyboard instruments, being traceable back to Greek, Roman, and Hebrew antiquity, and having a continuous existence in one form or another down to the present. The basic elements in an organ are the pipes, a steady supply of wind (air under pressure) and a key mechanism to control which pipes sound and which do not. Basically, the type of tone color depends upon the pipes, of which there are two principal kinds, *flue* and *reed*. The former work as simple whistles, and the latter have thin tongues of wood that set the air column in vibration. The reed pipes have a sharper, more coloristic tone quality than do the flue pipes. It is possible in many different ways to vary the tone quality produced by organ pipes, and the more common musical instruments are often imitated by different organ pipes. Usually an organ is a composite of several systems of pipes, each of which could serve as a small organ in its own right, usually with a coupling arrangement so that the organist can employ all or as many divisions of the organ as he pleases at the same time. In many cases the composer does not specify the tone colors to be used in the performance of a work, so that this determination becomes often an important part of what the organist has to do.

Elements of Composition

We have now surveyed the raw materials that make up the art of music. Although it has been necessary to discuss each of them separately, in a musical composition they appear in combination. It is therefore necessary to give a brief introduction to some of the leading elements and principles of musical composition so that we find some basis on which to gain an understanding of actual musical works. Odd as it may seem, it is possible from the examination of a simple melody to show the first principles of this art. In the first place, a *melody* may be defined as an organized sequence of musical tones or notes. How the notes are organized, however, depends on a number of factors. Usually a melody is not one continuous strain which goes on and on without pauses; rather there are caesuras, pauses, points of repose. A passage from one such caesura and ending at the next is called a *phrase*. The phrase is primarily to be associated with the need for a singer to breathe. The same applies to music for wind instruments. In the case of the bowed string instruments, such caesuras are provided by the strokes of the bow. Only the keyboard and the plucked string instruments are exempt from such caesuras, resulting from the normal operation of the instruments. In any case, a melody is usually divided into a number of phrases, much as a paragraph is divided into a number of sentences.

The manner in which these phrases are put together, the relationships that may exist among them, determines the organization of the melody as a whole. For instance, there are melodies in which none of the phrases is exactly the same, each brings something new, as in "My Country, 'Tis of Thee." Such

EXAMPLE 1-31

"My Country, 'Tis of Thee"

a melody is called *through-composed*. But unity here is provided by a rhythmic pattern, a sequence of rhythmic values, which organizes all the phrases except the last:

Elements of Composition

More often the phrases will not all be different from one another, but some will be the same. As an example, let us consider the well-known melody "All Through the Night." Here the first phrase (*A*) is immediately repeated; then comes a contrasting phrase (*B*), after which the first phrase is repeated in full, thus producing the scheme of repetitions, *A A B A*. (This scheme of repetitions is found in innumerable song melodies, as for example, *Au clair de la lune* [Examples 1-23 and 1-24] or the "Londonderry Air" and "Flow Gently, Sweet Afton.") The phrase *A* is characterized by dotted rhythm (once in each bar except the last) and by the leap of a third. In phrase *B* the range is higher (F to E), the motion stepwise, and the notes equal in rhythmic value, except for the end, which recalls the end of *A*. The *B* part of the melody thus provides an element of contrast with the *A* part.

EXAMPLE 1-32

"All Through the Night"

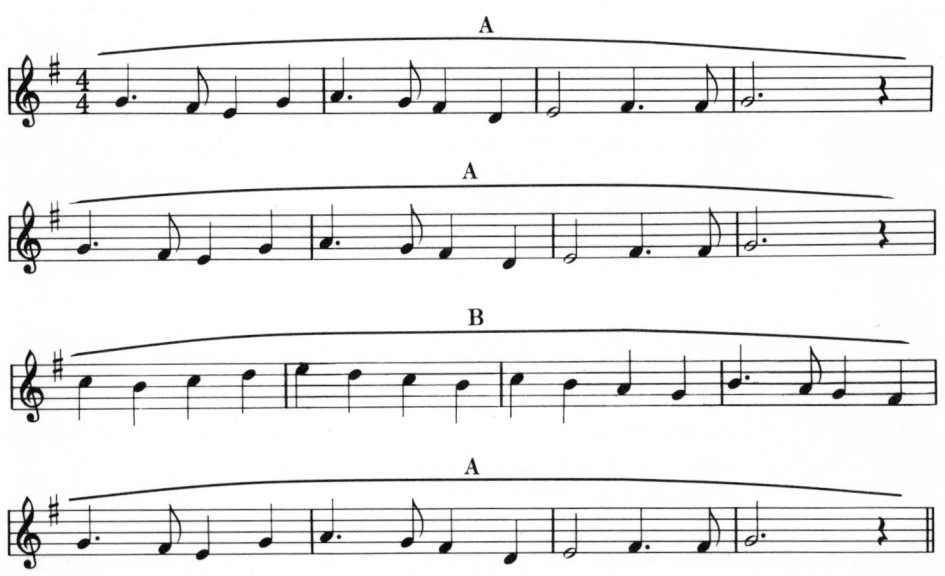

Apart from a repeated rhythmic pattern, such as we found in "My Country, 'Tis of Thee," a means of providing consistency or coherence in a melody or other composition is by the use of a small, simple melodic fragment, usually two or three notes in length, but characterized by a striking interval or rhythmic pattern; such a fragment or particle is called a *motive*. An example of a melody using a motive is the famous Largo from Dvořák's Symphony in E minor (*From the New World*).

EXAMPLE 1-33

DVOŘÁK: LARGO (THEME FROM THE SECOND MOVEMENT OF SYMPHONY
IN E MINOR [NO. 9 *From the New World*])—MELODY

Here the pattern of phrases is *a a'b b a a"* or *A B A'*. This represents a
common musical form known as *three-part form*. As in "All Through the Night,"
the range of the *B* part lies higher than that of the *A* part. The motive that
runs throughout providing coherence is simply ♪♩ ♩ and is mainly rhythmic
in its effect; it plays an important part in the variations or transformations of
the *A* phrase that take place at the end of the melody. The melody also exhi-
bits the use of the pentatonic scale. There are melodies, particularly from the
Baroque period, compounded largely of the repetition of a single motive; as an
example:

EXAMPLE 1-34

BACH: ALLEGRO, FROM CONCERTO GROSSO IN G MAJOR (*Brandenburg
Concerto, No. 3*)—BEGINNING (MAIN MELODIC LINE)

To return to Dvořák's Largo, we can see how the composer employs the
resources of harmony in his composition. It would be possible to harmonize
the melody quite simply, using only the I, IV, and V triads in the key D-flat
major. Dvořák, however, has added harmonic color by the use of the augmented form of the I triad in the first repetition of the opening phrase:

Elements of Composition

EXAMPLE 1-35

HARMONIZATION OF DVOŘÁK'S LARGO

Finally, orchestration plays an important part in the effect of the Largo, which in its original context is part of a larger composition, a movement of a symphony. It opens with solemn chromatic chords, pianissimo, in the woodwinds and brass, after which the melody proper begins, assigned to the plaintive English horn, with subdued accompaniment by the strings. Details of the accompaniment, however, contribute to the overall effect: When the first phrase of the melody reappears after the *B* part, the accompaniment begins to move in quarter notes, which provides impetus moving to the climax toward the end. It is thus possible, from this one short and comparatively simple example, to see in a nutshell some of the most important principles of organization used in the art music of the West.

A distinction must be drawn between a melody and a *theme*. Here the difference lies not in the essential nature of the two, but rather in the context in which each appears. It must, however, be realized that the terminology is not always strictly adhered to and that the two are not invariably properly distinguished. Generally speaking, a melody is complete in itself, existing by itself, in itself and for itself, independently, as "The Star-Spangled Banner" or any national anthem, hymn, or folk song. A theme, on the other hand, is part of a larger musical work and thus is not complete and independent in and of itself; the larger musical work may, and usually does, employ more than one theme. This is the basic distinction. Of course, one could take a melody, a folk song, for instance, and use it as part of a larger work, as was often done in the late nineteenth and early twentieth centuries, so that a melody would become a theme; and conversely many, but by no means all, themes can be satisfactorily separated from the larger work of which they are a part and presented as complete in themselves, so that a theme would become a melody (this was the case with Dvořák's Largo, previously discussed). A theme, however, need not be a completely organized melody; it may consist of a motive, or perhaps of a phrase or two. The terms *theme* and *thematic*, therefore, refer to melodic materials employed in the context of a larger musical composition.

To return once more to some of the basic aspects of composition, a number of additional points may be introduced in connection with melody.

We have already mentioned the overall form, the relationships among the component phrases, the role of the motive, the use of rhythmic patterns, the importance of harmony and of instrumentation. Other features that can cause a melody or a musical passage to have a certain character are the use of intervals and, for a vocal melody, how the text is set. A melody may move primarily by tones and semitones (whole and half steps), which is felt as "natural"; such a melody is said to proceed in *conjunct* or *stepwise motion*. Examples of this would be the "Joy" theme from Beethoven's Ninth Symphony (see Example 4-19). On the other hand, the melody could proceed by leaps, thirds, fourths, fifths, and so on, or by *disjunct motion*, as in "The Star-Spangled Banner." Most melodies exhibit the use of both conjunct and disjunct motion. The range of a melody is also an important factor: whether its notes are high or low, or whether the compass of notes used is small (less than a fifth) or great (more than an octave). Still another point concerns the way the syllables of a text are set to music. In most well-known song melodies, hymns and the like, there will usually be one note of the melody for each syllable of the text: This is called *syllabic* declamation or text setting; both "My Country, 'Tis of Thee" and "The Star-Spangled Banner" are examples of this, which is regarded as usual and "normal." The other possibility is to have a number of notes to a syllable of the text, in which case the declamation or text setting is said to be *melismatic*: This is found generally in music intended for professional singers, operatic and cantata arias, and the like. A well-known Christmas carol with melismatic writing is "Angels We Have Heard on High," at the end, on the

EXAMPLE 1-36

MELISMATIC TEXT DECLAMATION, "Angels We Have Heard on High"—
CLOSING PART

word "Gloria." Once again, it is not uncommon to find the two types of declamation in one and the same composition. Putting a melisma to a word or syllable of a word usually has the effect of heightening, of enhancing, its position in the composition. Much the same thing is accomplished by the use of a melodic leap where the line had been moving primarily in conjunct motion, or by a sudden change in the harmony, a new tempo or meter and rhythm.

We have, then, in a general way established the elements and some of the most basic procedures of the art of music. The manner in which they are selected and employed in a particular musical composition determines what we call the *style* of the piece. This will depend not only upon the individual composer but also upon the way music was regarded and practiced in the time when the particular composition was created. In the proper study of a musical artwork, therefore, these elements must be assessed, both singly and collectively, in order to arrive at the proper interpretation of the composition. The following chapters provide an introduction to this subject.

Chapter Two

The Historical Background

*t*here are four principal topics around which a discussion of the development of music as an art in Western civilization may conveniently be centered: the ancient Greeks, Gregorian chant, the secular monophonic music of the Middle Ages, and the development of polyphony. Each of these will be dealt with in turn.

Music in Greek Antiquity

In the study of Greek music we are confronted with an unusual situation: Although there are a number of treatises (theoretical writings) explaining the basis of Greek music, along with numerous references to music found in philosophical writings, very little actual music—about twelve pieces in all, some of them fragmentary—has come down to us. Although the Greeks had methods of notating music, this was done only exceptionally, since to them music was essentially an improvisatory art; this is true of Oriental music as well. For this reason there is no way of determining exactly how what is explained at length in the treatises was applied in actual musical compositions. In any case, the term *music* (*mousiké*) had a much broader meaning to the Greeks than it does to us now. It denoted to them the complex of literature, music, and even dance, and was seen as comprising three parts: *logos* (the literal meaning of the words), *rhythmos* (metrical and rhythmic organization of the words and melodic line), and *harmonia* (pitch organization). It seems that the cultivation of music was widespread throughout Greek culture, especially in conjunction with religious observances, dramatic performances, and athletic contests.

Music was held by the Greeks to be a gift of the gods, and as such it appears frequently in Greek mythology and prehistory. The old epics, the *Iliad* and the *Odyssey*, were chanted by bards or rhapsodists until one of their number, known as Homer, took the trouble to write down at least the words. In these epics we find references to the sensuous song of the sirens, the singing of Achilles, Agamemnon listening to the distant music for Hector's funeral. By all odds the most celebrated musician of Greek mythology was Orpheus, the singer and lute player from Thrace, who ventured down into the Underworld and through the power of his music wrested his wife Eurydice from Hades' grasp, only to lose her upon his return. This legend has provided the subject for many operas and dramatic works as well as countless allusions in literary works. We say "legend" and rightly so; but at the same time one can go to Greece today and see on display what purports to be the lyre of Orpheus. So one can at least wonder.

Apart from the association with mythology, the other important aspect of Greek music is the link with mathematics. This is especially clear from the work of Pythagoras of Samos (6th century B.C.), who is famous as a mathematician for the so-called Pythagorean theorem of plane geometry. But Pythagoras is important also for having established the mathematical basis of the different musical intervals. A legend has him passing a most unusual blacksmith's shop from which emanated sonorous musical concords as the hammers banged on the anvils. Like a true experimentalist, Pythagoras went in and investigated, discovering that the anvils by weight[1] were proportionately related to each other, 1:2, 2:3, 3:4, and thus produced the basic primary musical consonances, the octave, the perfect fifth and the perfect fourth. Pythagoras then worked out the mathematical ratios for the other musical intervals, and his name is thus prominent in the history of music theory.

Since the Greeks believed that numerical relationships were the basis of all phenomena, the art of music, in which these ratios were clearly and concretely exemplified, became, as it were, the key or the sounding symbol of all reality. This notion is found all through Greek antiquity and finds perhaps its best-known exposition and summary in the work of Boethius (c. 480–525), who was connected with the court of Theodoric the Ostrogoth and whose most famous writing was *The Consolation of Philosophy*. In his *De institutione musica* (*Concerning the Institution of Music*), Boethius distinguished three different kinds of music: *musica mundana*, *musica humana*, and *musica instrumentalis*. All deal essentially with the manifestation of these mathematical ratios: in *musica instrumentalis* it is how they appear in the whole realm of audible sound, including the art of music (the term, then, does not mean "instrumental music"); in *musica humana* it is how they are related in the constitution of the human body and soul; whereas in the last, *musica mundana*, it is how they operate with respect to the motions of the heavenly bodies. The expression "music of the spheres" is related to this conception. As another example, there is Plato's *Timaeus*, a late work of the philosopher's, in which the creation of the universe is presented in mathematical-musical terms. It may be mentioned that the idea is clearly present in the general curriculum for the study of philosophy (the liberal arts) in the medieval school: The seven liberal arts, or disciplines, comprised the *quadrivium*, the four mathematical disciplines, and

---

[1] We know that this would not work; it would be the size that would determine pitch, not weight.

*Drinker playing aulos
(c. 6th century* B.C.*).*
(COURTESY MUSEUM
OF FINE ARTS, BOSTON,
PIERCE FUND)

Kithara players.
(COURTESY GERMAN
MUSEUM, MUNICH)

the *trivium*, the three rhetorical disciplines, and music took its place among the mathematical arts, along with arithmetic, astronomy, and geometry;[2] but this, of course, was not music as a performing art, but rather the study of the mathematical ratios underlying the musical intervals. This link between music, mathematics, and astronomy reappears every now and then in philosophical and other treatises, such as Johann Kepler's *Harmonices mundi* (1619), Marin Mersenne's *L'Harmonie universelle* (1637), or the recent study of imagery in English poetry based on this idea, John Hollander's *The Untuning of the Sky* (1961).

If in the Greek conception music was regarded as being the audible symbol of the order of the universe and of all things, it follows that music, or a musical composition, operating with these basic ratios would possess great powers. And this indeed was the Greek view. We have already mentioned instances from mythology of the power attributed to music and musicians, to build cities, to bring about political stability and tranquillity, to cure illness, even to wake the dead. The power of music over human emotions—known as *ethos*—is of great historical importance. As examples we may follow the lead of the nineteenth-century philosopher and philologist Friedrich Nietzsche and select two opposing types of music out of the many that existed, each of which had its own particular scale, emotional and religious connotations, and musical instruments. On the one hand there was the *Dorian* music, associated primarily with Apollo, the god of light, reason and order, performed on the *kithara* (or lyre); on the other hand, the *Phrygian* music from the East, associated with Dionysius and the Dionysian rituals, extreme, orgiastic, intoxicating, and played usually on the *aulos* (a double-reed wind instrument). The pipes of Pan, for instance, are doubtless to be associated with this Phrygian music. The polarity of these two kinds of music emerges clearly from Plato's *Republic* and Aristotle's *Politics* when the question of the role of music in the commonwealth is taken up: The Dorian music is always favored by Plato and Aristotle because it is strong, forthright, masculine and, character-building, whereas the Phrygian music is lascivious, provocative, and debilitating, and hence to be rejected.

Dorian and Phrygian, then, appear to have denoted something more than scales or keys in our understanding of these terms. Rather, each must have comprised not only an octave filled with a certain succession of smaller intervals (tones and semitones) and a certain note serving as tonic, but also a set of characteristic melodic patterns or phrases, or motives, in which particular intervals or combinations of intervals played a determinant role. These set melodic patterns, then, were respectively associated with particular emotional connotations. Furthermore, there existed certain rhythmic patterns, each of which likewise possessed special emotional powers. It might be pointed out

---

[2] In the trivium: grammar, rhetoric, and dialectic.

The Historical Background

EXAMPLE 2-1

GREEK SCALES*

Dorian

Phrygian

* Greek scales were thought of as descending in pitch.

that similar features are to be found in Oriental music, as for instance the *ragas* (scales and melodic patterns) and *talas* (rhythmic patterns) of Indian music, or the *maqam* of Arabian music. Finally, we should mention the *nomos*, or law, a term that seems to refer to a large and purely instrumental perform- ance (one hesitates to use the term *composition*, since the *nomos* in all prob- ability was improvised), which was in a specific scale and with particular connotations.

So far as we know, Greek music was monophonic—that is to say, purely melodic. In some of the variations in the scale system, *microtones* (intervals smaller than the semitone) were used. This is also true of Oriental music. It would seem that this refinement and sophistication with respect to musical intervals goes hand in hand with a monophonic music; at least it has been foreign to most Western music until recently.

The Gregorian Chant

Another corpus of monophonic music, one that unlike Greek music has been preserved (although probably not in its original form), is the medieval liturgical music of the Christian (Catholic) Church, known as Gregorian chant or plainsong.[3] It has been named for St. Gregory the Great who was Pope from 590 to 604, and who brought about a standardization of the liturgy which in- cluded assembling the music and codifying its use. Gregory is in no way the composer of this music, a small part of which goes back to the chants of the Hebrew synagogues and to the first few centuries A.D. A good deal more was composed in the Middle Ages.

Before introducing the repertory of the Gregorian chant, the system of scales, or modes, used in this music must be explained, since it provided the basis for Western music until the seventeenth century. Although Greek

[3] The meaning of the term *plainsong* will become clear later on.

terminology is employed to name the different scales, the Gregorian modes differ from their Greek counterparts. For the Gregorian scales see Example 2–2. It will be noted that for each authentic mode there is a corresponding plagal mode, the range of which is a fourth below that of the authentic mode; but each mode in a pair has the same tonic. The idea of having a tonic in the middle of a scale, as in the plagal modes, goes back to the Greek scale system. As far as is known, the Greek associations connected with the Dorian and Phrygian modes, for example, are not taken up in this system.

At the heart of the Gregorian chant is the idea of providing music for the recitations from the Bible, especially that part associated with lyric poetry and song, the *psalms*. A psalm may be described simply as a lyric poem, with no norms concerning the number of lines or strophic organization. The musical settings of psalms in the repertory of Gregorian chant proceed line by line. In a simple setting of a complete psalm, the melody is of the greatest simplicity, displaying syllabic declamation, conjunct melodic motion and many repeated notes; it is, in the full sense of the word, a chant rather than a melody. A simple melodic phrase is invented and used for each verse (line) of the psalm. This simple melodic phrase, known as a *psalm tone* or *recitation tone*, is associated with a particular scale or mode, each of which had its own set of such psalm tones. In performance there are two principal possibilities: *antiphonal* performance, which exploits the fact that each line of a psalm usually falls into two equal halves, and employs two small choral groups which sing the halves of a verse in alternation; and *responsorial* performance, in which a soloist alternates with a chorus (the chorus is thought of as responding to the

EXAMPLE 2-2

THE SCALE SYSTEM OF GREGORIAN CHANT

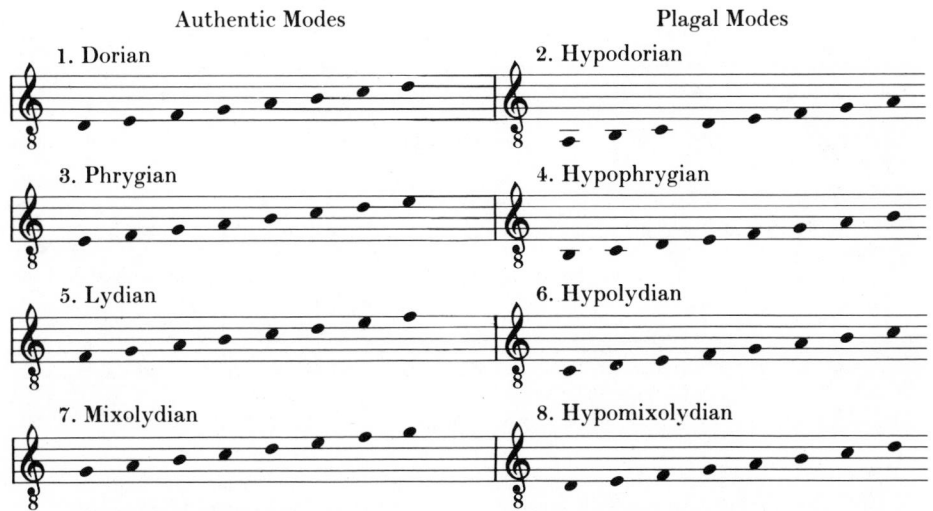

soloist). The verses of the psalm are preceded and followed by a short musical piece called an *antiphon,* which is written primarily for the chorus and the text of which comes from another psalm or from elsewhere in the Bible. The order, then, in the performance of a psalm is antiphon—all verses of psalm sung to psalm tone (repeated)—antiphon. Presented as an example is Psalm 113 together with the antiphon *Laus Deo patri.*[4] The remaining verses of the psalm are chanted to the same recitation formula.

EXAMPLE 2-3

GREGORIAN CHANT: ANTIPHON *Laus Deo patri* WITH PSALM 113, *Laudate pueri*—BEGINNING

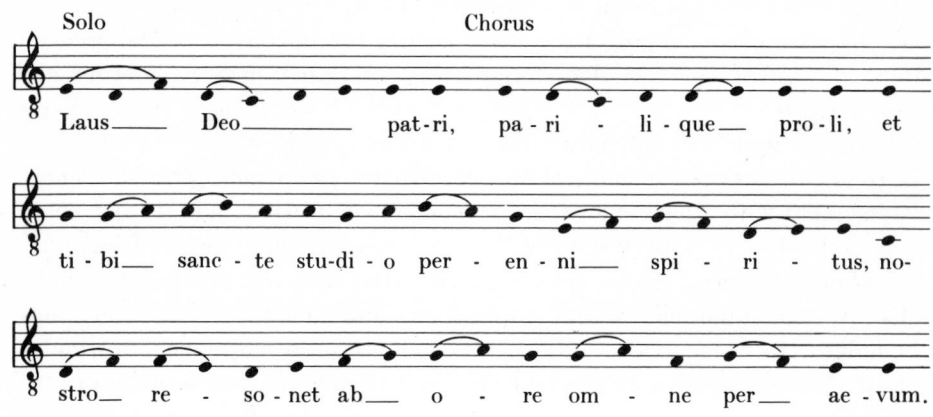

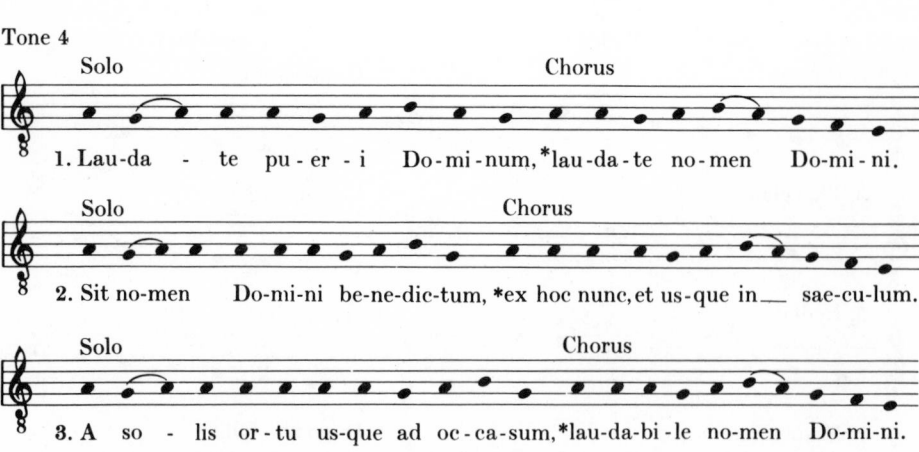

---

[4] The notation and rhythmic aspects of Gregorian chant are explained on page 47.

The Gregorian Chant

EXAMPLE 2-3 (*continued*)

TEXT AND TRANSLATION (MODIFIED FROM THE KING JAMES VERSION):

ANTIPHON
Laus Deo patri, parilique proli, et tibi sancte studio perenni spiritus, nostro resonet ab ore omne per aevum.

Let praise resound from our mouths to God the Father and to the Son, His equal, and to Thee, Holy Spirit, with increasing zeal through all eternity.

PSALM
Laudate pueri Dominum, laudate nomen Domini.

Praise, O ye servants of the Lord, praise the name of the Lord.

Sit nomen Domini benedictum, ex hoc nunc, et usque in saeculum.

Blessed be the name of the Lord from this time forth and for ever more.

A solis ortu usque ad occasum, laudabile nomen Domini.

From the rising of the sun unto the going down of the same the Lord's name is to be praised.

Excelsus super omnes gentes Dominus, et super caelos gloria ejus.

The Lord is high above all nations, and His glory above the heavens.

Quis sicut Dominus Deus noster, qui in altis habitat, et humilia respicit in caelo et in terra?

Who is like unto the Lord our God, who dwelleth on high, who humbleth Himself to behold all things that are in heaven, and in the earth?

Suscitans a terra inopem, et de stercore erigens pauperem,

He raiseth up the poor out of the dust, and lifteth the needy out of the dunghill,

Ut collocet eum cum principibus, cum principibus populi sui.

That He may set him with princes, even with the princes of his people.

Qui habitare facit sterilem in domo, matrem filiorum laetantem.

He maketh the barren woman to keep house, and to be a joyful mother to children.

LESSER DOXOLOGY
Gloria patri, et Filio, et Spiritui Sancto.

Glory be to the Father, and to the Son, and to the Holy Ghost.

Sicut erat in principio, et nunc, et semper, et in saecula saeculorum.

As it was in the beginning, is now, and ever shall be, world without end.

Amen.

Amen.

The Historical Background

This represents the simplest and basic form of psalmodic recitation or chanting. It is short; the verses are set to what may be termed a melodic recitation formula. As such it appears in the daily services celebrated by the monks which make up the *Officium* or *Canonical Hours*. But this simple form provides the model for more elaborate compositions based on psalm texts that are reserved for more important services, the most distinguished among the Canonical Hours (Matins and Vespers particularly) and the principal public service, the *Mass*, which indeed is the central act in the entire liturgy. For these the most ornate kind of responsorial performance is called upon, using a trained soloist, as is well reflected in the highly melismatic way in which the text is set. It will be noted that although in such pieces only the first line of the psalm is included (often a line is taken from elsewhere in the Bible to serve as a verse), the setting is considerably more elaborate than was the antiphon already discussed (Example 2-3). In this respect, the modern practice of performing this music primarily by chorus completely obscures the original intent. Example 2–4 is such a composition, a response of the type called a *Gradual*,[5] from the Mass on Christmas morning, *Viderunt omnes*, together with the psalm verse *Notum fecit*, after which the response is repeated.

EXAMPLE 2-4

GREGORIAN CHANT: *Viderunt omnes*, GRADUAL FOR CHRISTMAS

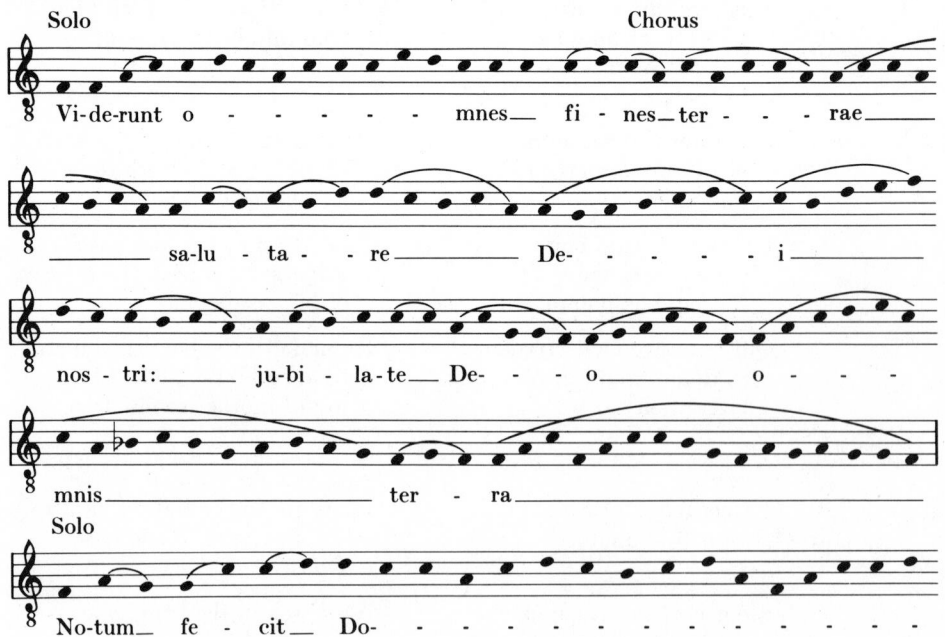

[5] The designation *Gradual* arises from the circumstance that originally this responsorial psalm was performed by a soloist standing on the steps (*gradus*) of the altar.

The Gregorian Chant

EXAMPLE 2-4 (*continued*)

TRANSLATION OF TEXT (KING JAMES VERSION, FROM PSALM 98, VERSES 3 AND 5):

RESPOND

All the ends of the earth have seen the salvation of our God. Make a joyful noise unto the Lord, all the earth.

VERSE

He hath remembered His mercy and His truth toward the house of Israel: all the ends of the earth have seen the salvation of our God.

The musical portions of the Mass are divided into two sections, the *Proper* and the *Ordinary.* The distinction between the two is based on their texts: The Ordinary of the Mass consists of those sections whose texts are invariable throughout the year, whereas the Proper of the Mass consists of those sections whose texts change in accordance with the liturgical character of the day, be it Christmas, Epiphany, Good Friday, Easter, St. Michael's Day, or whatever. The items of the Proper, for the most part, exemplify the elaborate responsorial type of psalmody, and the Gradual *Viderunt omnes,* just quoted, is part of the Proper of the Mass for Christmas. The five sections making up the Ordinary of the Mass, those portions most often set by composers since the fifteenth century, are as follows:[6]

---

[6] Full text and translation appear in Appendix Two.

> *Kyrie:* a plea for mercy from God and Christ
> *Gloria:* the Greater Doxology
> *Credo:* the Nicene Creed
> *Sanctus* and *Benedictus:* the three-times Holy and the Eucharist itself
> *Agnus Dei:* a plea for mercy from the Lamb of God

None of these is related to the psalms. Many of the Gregorian melodies used for these were written quite late in the Middle Ages. The Gloria and Credo, having the longest texts, are set in a simple syllabic fashion, whereas the other three are melismatic.

EXAMPLE 2-5

GREGORIAN CHANT: KYRIE *Cunctipotens genitor Deus*

One other form in the Gregorian chant repertory is the *hymn.* This represents a wholly medieval contribution to the Canonical Hours. A Gregorian hymn is essentially the same as a Protestant hymn or chorale except that it is not part of the public service and hence not sung by the congregation. Otherwise both employ strophic poems as texts, and this strophic form is respected in the musical setting; that is to say, each strophe has the same music, which is sung over and over again until all the strophes have been completed. As would be expected in a choral piece from this repertory, the declamation is primarily syllabic.

EXAMPLE 2-6

GREGORIAN CHANT: *Exsultet orbis gaudiis*, HYMN FOR COMMON OF
APOSTLES AND EVANGELISTS—STROPHES I AND II

1. Ex - sul - tet _ or - bis gau - di - is _____ Cae-lum _ re - sul - tet
2. Vos _ sae - cu - lo - rum ju - di - ces _____ Et ve - ra _ mun-di

lau-di - bus _____ A - pos - to - lo-rum glo-ri - am _____
lu - mi-na _____ Vo-tis_ pre-ca-mur cor-di - um _____

Tel - lus_ et _____ as - tra _____ con-ci - nunt. _____
Au - di - te _____ vo - ces _____ sup-pli - cum. _____

TRANSLATION OF TEXT:

Let heaven rejoice,
The skies resound in praise;
To the glory of the apostles
Sing the earth and the stars.

Ye judges of the centuries
And the true lights of the world,
We pray from our hearts,
Hear our supplicating voices.

Gregorian chant in the earlier Middle Ages was transmitted by *oral
tradition*: It was not written down, but was simply handed down by rote from
one generation of singers to the next. By the ninth century, however, this oral
tradition for some reason began to weaken, so that a method for the notation
of musical pitches had to be devised. The first step is represented by various
signs, called *neumes*, consisting of different kinds of dots (*punctus*) and
groups of connected dots (*ligatures*), which were used in connection with the
liturgical texts as a mnemonic device to aid in the performance of the melodies.
This imprecise notation was superseded in the eleventh century by the invention
of the staff, usually attributed to Guido of Arezzo. As far as we know, the
element of rhythm, the precise durations of the different notes, was not expressed in this notation at all. In most medieval treatises dealing with the
subject there will be found the explanation that all the notes of this music are
to be regarded as rhythmically equivalent, and it is this circumstance that
gives rise to the name *plainsong* (from *cantus planus*). This idea provides the
point of departure for the work of the monks in Solesmes, France, who in the
nineteenth century worked to revive the use of chant in the Catholic Church

and who are responsible for many modern editions of the repertory of Gregorian chant. But it should be kept in mind that the original rhythmic interpretations have not come down to us.

Other Monophonic Music in the Middle Ages

The close association between music and poetry which we observed in ancient Greece has maintained itself in Western civilization, and we will have occasion every now and then to make reference to it. The link is particularly strong in the Middle Ages. There is, for instance, a large body of secular poetry in Latin, much of which is associated with the wandering scholars (the monks who wandered from monastery to monastery, and from university to university, also known as goliards); but frequently only the texts have been preserved, since the music is notated in a way that we are not able to transcribe: such is the large collection written at the Bavarian monastery of Benedikt-beuern, the so-called *Carmina burana* (now in Munich). Also of importance were additions—textual, musical, or both—to the musical parts of the liturgy, a practice generally known as *troping*, such an addition being called a *tropus* or *trope*. These are of various kinds. An important liturgical form that emerged from this practice was the *prose* or *sequence*, characterized by its use of paired phrases (*aa*, *bb*, *cc*, etc.). Of some interest are tropes in dialogue form, which ultimately grew into large works known as liturgical dramas; two of these, the *Play of Daniel* and the *Play of Herod*, have recently become well known. Most tropes were abolished by the Council of Trent between 1545 and 1563.

Toward the year 1050 poetry in the vernacular began to make its appearance, first in the south of France (in Provence) in the hands of a group of nobility that has come to be known as the *troubadours*.[7] Many of these poems, unlike the Latin poems just mentioned, appear together with music; but, again, the exact reading of the rhythm is impossible to establish. All sorts of poems appear in this large repertory: topical songs (Crusade songs, war songs, songs commemorating political events, treaties, victories, death), love songs, religious songs, dance songs; and it may be assumed that the epic poems set down by members of the group (the *chansons de geste*) were also put to music, but for these the music has not come down. The poet Dante Aligheri has given us an account of the musical forms used by the troubadours in his treatise *De vulgari eloquentia*. From this it appears that all the forms were strophic, but from the musical standpoint there were basically two kinds of strophe: the *oda continua*, which was through-composed, and the *pedes cum cauda*, which used the repetitive phrase structure *aab*, consisting, in Dante's

---

[7] The derivation of the term is not without interest: *trouba*, related to *trouver* (to find or invent) is also related to the Latin *tropus* (trope) and thus, in meaning at least, to the Greek *poesis* (to make or invent). All refer to the inventive, that is, creative, work of the artist.

terminology, of two *pedes* (feet) and a *cauda* (tail or coda). But this distinction is not reflected in the two main poetic types, *canzo* and *vers*. As an example of this free and refined art, we give a *canzo*, or love song, by Gace Brulé in the *pedes cum cauda* form.

EXAMPLE 2-7

GACE BRULÉ: *Je ne puis pas si loing*

TRANSLATION OF TEXT:

I cannot flee so far
That I forget my lady.
Since she will not deign to keep me
I do not know where to go.

Together my heart and my desire
And my sorrows and loving too much
And all that I cannot hide from her
Have killed me, so I can suffer
no more.

Another group appeared in the north of France somewhat later, known as the *trouvères*. The topics handled in their compositions are similar to those found in the troubadour repertory, but the musical forms, fixed repetitive patterns (the *formes fixées*), became much stricter. These in general are based on the refrain principle. Using different letters for the various lines of texts and the corresponding phrases of music (capital letters mean same text and same music; lower case letters mean different text but same music), the following schemes result for the form of the single strophes:

Rondeau: *A B a A a b A B*
Virelai: *A b b a A*
Ballade: *a a b*

Repertories of monophonic secular songs using fixed forms existed in the other countries of Europe. In Germany there were the *minnesinger*, known especially for their treatment of the old Germanic epics (the *Nibelungenlied,* or *Song of*

EXAMPLE 2-8

ENGLISH MONOPHONIC SONG: *Worldes blis*

World - es ___ blis ne last no ___ thro - we, Hit wit ant ___ wend a - - wey a - non. _ The leng - ur that hich ___ hit i - - kno - we, _ The lasse hic ___ find-e ___ pris ther - on ___ For al hit ___ is i - - meynd wyd ___ ka - re, _ Mid so - re - we ant wid ___ u - vel ___ fa - re, _ Ant at the last - e poue - re ant _ ba - re ___ Hit let mon wen hit gin - net a - gon. Al the blis-se, this ___ he - re ant ___ the - re ___ Bi - lou - keth at ___ hend - e ___ wop ant ___ mon. _

TRANSLATION OF TEXT:

> Worldly joy lasts hardly at all.
> It fades away almost at once.
> The longer I know it
> The less it is worth to me.
> For it is all mixed with troubles,
> With sorrow and misfortune,
> And, at the end, it leaves a man poor and naked
> When it begins to pass away.
> All joy, both here and there, is but weeping and sorrow.

The Development of Polyphony

the *Nibelungs*; *Parsifal* by Wolfram von Eschenbach, and *Tristan und Isolde* by Gottfried von Strassburg); and much later, in the fifteenth and sixteenth centuries, their counterparts, the *meistersinger*, who were no longer nobles but tradesmen, brought the tradition of German monophonic music to its end.

In Italy, to return to the Middle Ages proper, we have the penitential songs (the flagellant, or *Geissler*, songs) of the thirteenth century, in Spain the lyrical *Cantigas* in praise of Mary by King Alfonso X (ruled 1252–1284, known as *El Sabio*, the Wise), and a number of monophonic compositions from England, such as the one in Example 2–8.

The Development of Polyphony

All the music discussed up to now has been monophonic—that is to say, purely melodic. But the most characteristic music of the West, in sharp contrast to that found elsewhere, is polyphonic; and the growth and development of polyphonic music, especially since the twelfth century, did much to eclipse and virtually to eliminate the older monophonic art.

At the same time, polyphonic music in the West took its point of departure from monophonic music. It is not known exactly when the practice of polyphony began in Europe. Many statements in writings of various sorts beginning as early as the sixth century which have been interpreted as meaning polyphony are by no means unequivocal: As an example, Cassiodorus, in his *Institutiones* (c. 555), defines an interval as the "fusion" of a high and low tone, which may refer to polyphony or may not. At all events, by the eighth and ninth centuries there had arisen the practice of performing simple polyphonic settings based on the melodies of the Gregorian chant, a practice known as *organum*.[8] The procedure is explained in several musical treatises, among them the *Musica Enchiriadis* from the late ninth or early tenth century and the *Micrologus* by Guido of Arezzo (eleventh century), both of which are simple introductions to the art of music, handbooks for choir singers. In no case is organum presented as anything new or extraordinary; it is regarded simply as a method of enhancing certain Gregorian melodies.

The procedure in this earliest kind of organum is as follows: While one singer sings the melody from the Gregorian chant, at the same time another sings the same melody a fourth below or a fifth below, and they proceed then in parallel motion throughout the piece. In such a setting the Gregorian chant is known as the *vox principalis*, the added part as the *vox organalis*. For each *punctus* (point or note) of the *vox principalis* (the chant melody) there corresponds a *punctus* of the *vox organalis* (the added part). It is from this *punctus contra punctum* (or *nota contra notam*, note against note) that our term *counterpoint* comes. Each of these two parts may also be sung simultaneously at the octave by other singers, so that a four-voice setting is the result:

[8] While the derivation of this word, which is accented on the first syllable, is uncertain, it is generally assumed to have nothing to do with the organ.

EXAMPLE 2-9

PARALLEL ORGANUM: *Sit gloria Domini*, FROM THE *Musica Enchiriadis*

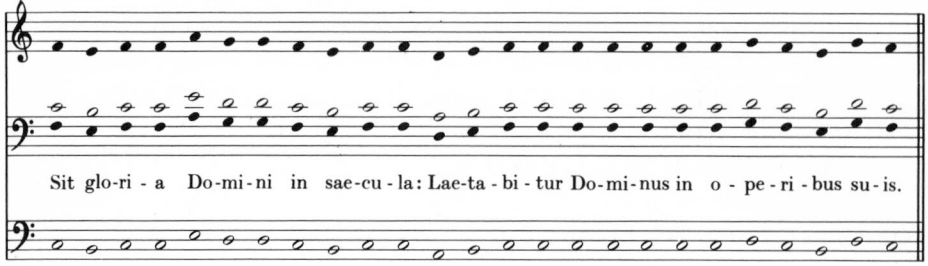

Sit glo-ri - a   Do-mi-ni   in   sae-cu - la: Lae-ta - bi - tur Do-mi-nus in   o - pe - ri - bus su - is.

Note: The *vox principalis* is written in white notes, the *vox organalis* in black notes.

TRANSLATION OF TEXT:

Glory be to the Lord: in eternity the Lord will rejoice in His works.

The only examples of this early organum, known as *parallel* or *primitive organum*, that we have are found in these instruction manuals, where they serve merely as illustrative examples. Once one has learned how to perform organum, one may apply the same procedure to any chant melody. Organum at this stage, then, was an improvisation, albeit an improvisation with very strict rules.

The development from this simple and rigid type of polyphony proceeded along two lines: first, a freeing from the strict parallel motion, and second, a move away from the strict *punctus contra punctum* relationship between the two parts. It is impossible to say which of these took place first. It soon became the practice to have the *vox principalis* as the lower voice and the *vox organalis* as the upper voice, and this remained the rule. But the strict parallelism of motion was abandoned, so that the added voice was free to move in *contrary* (opposite) or *similar* (same direction but a different interval) motion to the Gregorian chant, provided that it formed, most of the time, primary consonances with it. Along with this went the growing rhythmic independence of the two voices, whereby the *vox organalis* may have several notes to one note of the *vox principalis*. A change in terminology is associated with this step: Instead of *vox principalis* the Gregorian chant is called *tenor*, either because it "holds" the borrowed melody or because its notes are "held" longer than are those of the added part, which becomes known as the *duplum* (second part). Two-part organum, then, goes under the name *organum duplum*. This particular type of organum—called either *melismatic organum* (because of the melismatic nature of the duplum) or organum in *sustained-tone style* (because of the held notes in the tenor)—was cultivated extensively at the monastery of St. Martial in Limoges in the early twelfth century (see Example 2-10).

The Development of Polyphony

Such a piece is no longer a simple improvisation according to strict rules, as was the case with the earlier forms of organum. Rather we may speak of composition in the usual sense of the term.

The decisive development in the relatively new polyphonic art of organum took place in the last half of the twelfth and the early thirteenth century at Notre Dame in Paris. We have the names of the two composers who exercised leadership here: Leonin and Perotin. The principal aspect of their work involved the development of a means of representing rhythmic values in musical notation.

This system of representing rhythmic values in musical notation is analogous to the organization of classical metrics, which was *quantitative* (long and short syllables) rather than *qualitative* (strong and weak syllables).

EXAMPLE 2-10

ORGANUM DUPLUM: *Benedicamus Domino*, FROM THE SCHOOL OF ST. MARTIAL—BEGINNING

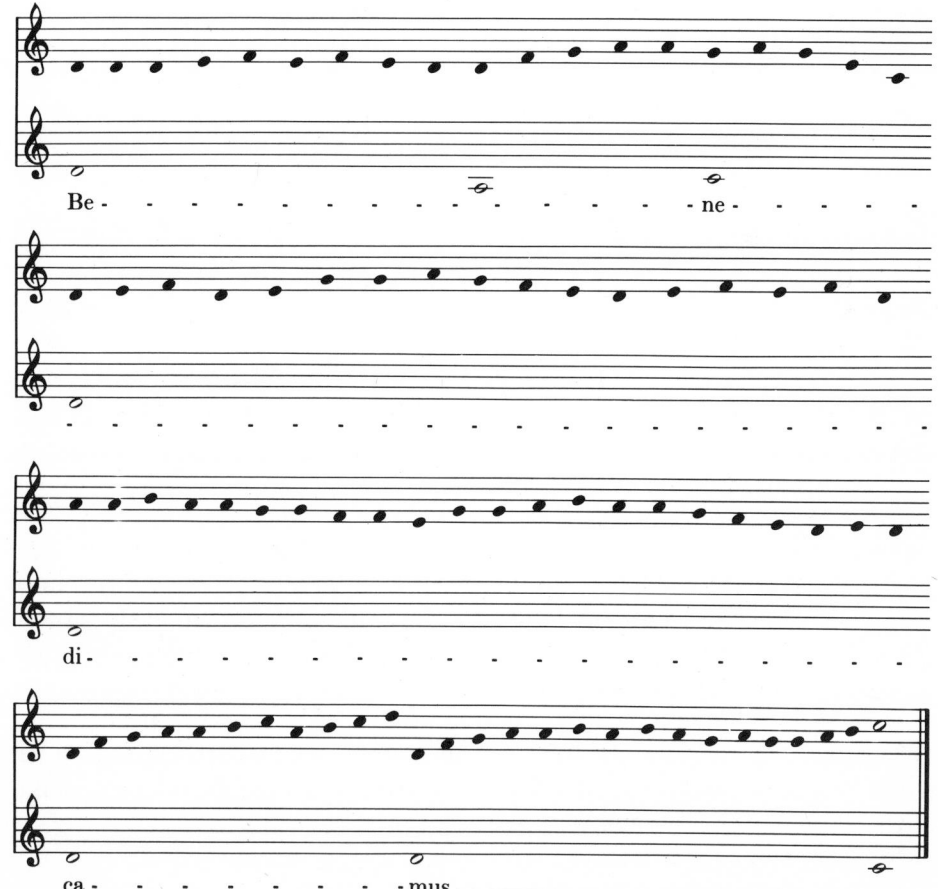

The Historical Background

Two values are fundamental: the *longa* (long) and the *brevis* (short), with two breves equal to one longa. On this basis it is possible to make musical equivalents to the feet of classical metrics: The trochee (long-short) becomes ♩ ♪, the iambus (short-long) becomes ♪ ♩, and so on. Generally speaking, a piece employs the same rhythmic pattern, called a *rhythmic mode*, throughout. The mode to be used was indicated, not by a time signature, but by certain combinations of groups of notes (ligatures) at the beginning: e.g., a group of three (a three-note ligature) followed by an indefinite number of groups of two (two-note ligatures) signified the trochaic or first mode, by far the most common, whereas groups of two followed by a three-note ligature signified the second, or iambic, mode. In all, six different modes were recognized. Rests were indicated by short vertical strokes. There was also provision for rhythmic variations: Lengthening the *longa* and breaking the *longa* into *breves*, breaking the *breves* in turn into smaller units called *semibreves*, and so forth. The whole system is generally known as *modal notation* or *modal rhythm*.

EXAMPLE 2-11

MELODIC LINE IN THE FIRST RHYTHMIC MODE

Ligatures:

Modern notes:

Whereas Leonin's work consisted entirely of *organum duplum* (two-voice organum), Perotin composed organum also for three and four voices (*organum triplum* and *organum quadruplum*). In general his works reveal a greater degree of rhythmic organization than do those of Leonin. Apart from the rhythmic organization, however, these Notre Dame works are not dissimilar in their technique to those composed earlier at St. Martial: The tenor (the Gregorian chant melody) is in the lowest voice and proceeds often in very slow, long-held notes; above this the upper voices, using the modal rhythms and moving much faster, are added by the composer one after the other. Nonetheless, there are places—usually in the original chant a melisma appears —where the notes of the tenor are speeded up, usually to simple *longae*; such passages are said to be in *discant* style and were called *clausulas*. Harmonically, the perfect consonances are the most important, particularly at the major divisions of a composition, but other consonances, and even dissonances, make their appearance every now and then.

The organum continued to be regarded as an enhancement of the chant and hence was reserved for the most important festivals of the church year.

The Development of Polyphony

Such a festival was Christmas, for which we have a large four-voice organum by Perotin, the Gradual for the Mass of Christmas morning, *Viderunt omnes*. Here the Gregorian Chant is the tenor, the lowest voice, while the others, after a held *longa* of indefinite duration, show the characteristic trochaic rhythm of the first rhythmic mode. Since the piece is long, only its beginning is reproduced here.[9] The effect of the short, incessantly repeated rhythmic pattern along with the lean sound of the perfect consonances and dissonant sevenths is striking.

EXAMPLE 2-12

PEROTIN: *Viderunt omnes*, GRADUAL FOR CHRISTMAS—BEGINNING

Two other forms of polyphony may also be associated with the school of Notre Dame: The *motet* and the *conductus*. The former began as an elaboration of and a development from the organum: A portion of organum in discant style is excerpted, taken out of context, with new and different texts being

9 For the chant itself, see Example 2-4.

given to its upper voices, thus making a motet. The motet, then, is a poly-textual form. Indeed the texts do not even have to be in the same language. Motets completely independent of the organum then became dominant. It will be seen that there is some similarity between this idea and the practice of troping (the addition of texts and music to previously existing musical composition; see page 48). A new term may conveniently be introduced here: *cantus firmus*, which means any previously existing melody that is used in a polyphonic composition, hence in this period much the same thing as "tenor." In the following three-voice motet each of the two upper voices has its own

EXAMPLE 2-13

MOTET: *En non Diu—Quant voi—Eius in oriente*—BEGINNING

The Development of Polyphony

EXAMPLE 2-13 *(continued)*

TRANSLATION OF TEXTS:

TRIPLUM

Now truthfully! Whatever we are told, when the grass is green and the weather clear, and the nightingale is singing, then my dainty love begs me sweetly to sing a pretty tale of love: "Marion, let Robin be my love!" Truly I must try to please her and wear a wreath of flowers for so sweet a lover when I see the roses budding, the grasses green and the weather clear.

MOTETUS

When I see the roses budding, the grass green and the weather clear, and the nightingale is singing, then my dainty love begs me to rejoice with her and play, for he who does not love does not live either; for this only one should live: to love his sweetheart, to serve and honor her forever. Now truthfully: whatever we are told, my heart is full of the sorrows of love.

text (both, however, are in French) while the tenor or cantus firmus is a portion of the plainsong Alleluia *Vidimus stellam* (for Epiphany), the melisma on the words "Eius in oriente." It will be noted that the upper voices move more rapidly than the tenor.

The conductus represents the earliest polyphonic form in which all the voices are freely invented by the composer; there is no cantus firmus. Stylistically the conductus is like a motet without a tenor; it displays discant style, and all the voices are subject to the patterns of modal rhythm. But, unlike the motet, in a conductus all the voices have the same Latin text. Although the declamation is mainly syllabic, melismatic passages are often found at the beginning and end. A good example is a three-voice conductus attributed to Perotin, *Salvatoris hodie.*

By the early fourteenth century a number of developments had taken place. The rigid short repetitive patterns of the rhythmic modes gave way to a more varied and flexible system in which both duple and triple meter were possible and in which the rhythmic value of a given note was indicated by its shape, much as is the case with our conventional system of notation. The repertory of musical forms expanded a good deal. The old art of the organum, however, was not perpetuated, and in its place came motets, conductus, polyphonic compositions for the Mass, as well as many secular-vernacular forms. All of this together is known as *ars nova* (new art). Contributions came from all over Europe; France, Italy, and England were the leaders.

Representative is the foremost French composer of the time, Guillaume de Machaut (c. 1300–1377), who worked in most of the forms available in the repertory, sacred as well as secular. One of his most celebrated compositions is the *Mass of Notre Dame*, composed around 1365, which represents the first complete polyphonic setting of the Ordinary of the Mass by one man. The procedure followed in this work is essentially the same as what we found in the organum: The Gregorian chant appears as cantus firmus in the middle voice (not the lowest), to which the other three voices are added, and as before the principal intervals used are the perfect consonances.[10] Rhythmically, however, there is greater complexity. This can be seen most readily from the tenor, which is organized by an elaborate rhythmic pattern which is repeated over and over again, a procedure known as *isorhythm*.

EXAMPLE 2-14

ISORHYTHMIC PATTERN IN THE TENOR OF THE SANCTUS OF MACHAUT'S MASS

The rhythmic pattern

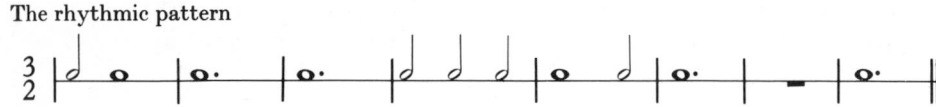

Excerpt from the Gregorian chant

(Do-) mi - nus __ De - - - -us Sa - - - - -ba - - -oth

Excerpt from the tenor part

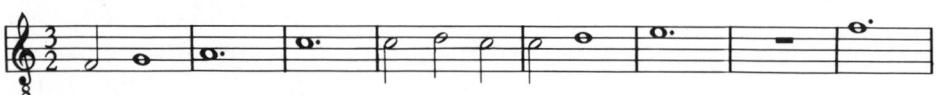

Although essentially concerned with repetitions of a rhythmic pattern, isorhythm can involve melody as well and can appear in the upper voices. Rhythm, indeed, is the most important aspect of the composition. The rhythms are angular and striking; and one of the most characteristic features is to have rests in one voice alternating against notes in another, producing a back-and-forth effect known as *hocket*. In the tenor part of the Sanctus of Machaut's Mass (Example 2-15), the isorhythm begins in bar 17.

It will be observed that there are two basic characteristics in the medieval polyphonic music discussed up to this point. First, we have the idea of adding voices to a given melody, a cantus firmus, which usually comes from Gregorian chant; this procedure results in what may be called *successive* composition, the different voices invented one after the other to go along with a given melody.[11] This gives much of this music a strongly linear, layered quality; indeed it often seems as if the composer intended to make each voice as different from the others as possible. Second, the principal development that takes place in these

---

[10] Here the voice with the cantus firmus is the tenor. Against it come two voices, each called countertenor, one above (*contratenor altus*), the other below (*contratenor bassus*); the uppermost part is known variously as *cantus* or *discantus* and *superius*, the latter being the Latin of the Italian *soprano*.

[11] It should be pointed out that the secular polyphonic forms of the time, although also composed successively, do not make use of cantus firmi.

The Development of Polyphony

EXAMPLE 2-15

MACHAUT: SANCTUS, FROM THE MASS—BEGINNING

EXAMPLE 2-15 (*continued*)

EXAMPLE 2-15 (*continued*)

centuries affects rhythmic rather than harmonic organization: rhythm becomes increasingly more elaborate, while the harmonic basis remains essentially unchanged.

With the fifteenth century, the coming of the Renaissance and, with it,
humanism, all this underwent a change. There were two important elements
in this change. First, we have the increased knowledge of Greek art and the
rediscovery of Aristotle's *Poetics* with its dictum of *mimesis*, that art should
imitate nature. Closely allied with this was a second idea, that an artwork
should be pleasing to the senses. In painting, for example, we may observe a
new interest in the realistic portrayal of persons, objects, and landscapes;
and it is no accident that the means of representing perspective, creating the
illusion of depth and thereby enhancing the viewer's pleasure, was developed

at this time. In music there are two parallel developments. The first of these involved harmonic organization. Up to now the perfect consonances had been dominant and their "perfection," as we have seen, was largely mathematical: They were formed by the simpler numerical ratios. The change came in the recognition and more general use of the secondary consonances, because they sounded more pleasing, euphonious, sweet. The pleasing of the ear, then, became more important than the use of the long-sanctioned perfect consonances. The second idea was bound up with the Aristotelian dictum that art imitates nature. Although the position of music in such a conception is not immediately clear, it was decided then that music should imitate human passions, emotions, or affections: Thus expression became important in music. It will be noted that there is some similarity between this idea and the Greek doctrine of ethos.

In connection with these new ideas came a new technique in composition in which all the voices in a work are unified by sharing the same thematic material. The linear character of medieval music, in which each of the voices is different in character from the others, is overcome, and all voices participate equally in the presentation of the thematic material.

Josquin des Prez. Contemporary woodcut.

These new features—the new euphony, the idea of music as expressive, and the new technique of composition—appear in the work of composers from the northwestern part of Europe, a group conveniently if somewhat inaccurately known as the Netherlands School. Although the fundamentals of the new music were established by the middle of the fifteenth century in the work of Guillaume Dufay (c. 1400–1474), the first important wholly characteristic representative of the group is Josquin des Prez (c. 1445–1521), whose works remained in the repertory throughout the sixteenth century.

The forms of sacred music, the Mass and the motet, stand in the center of the new Netherlands music. It is to the latter, the motet, that Josquin devoted particular attention, providing it with a form that has been associated with the genre ever since. The motet of the Renaissance is different in several important respects from its medieval predecessor: No longer is it necessarily a cantus firmus composition, but it still remains by and large liturgical. Furthermore, the plurality of texts found in the medieval form of the motet disappears; in most Renaissance motets there is but one text. Finally, it is in the motet, apparently, that the new technique of composition (already mentioned) first became established; at all events, the new technique dominates the motets of Josquin. This new procedure is an application of the principle of imitative counterpoint (see page 24): The composer takes the text that is to be set to music, conceives it as divided into suitable sections (sentences or phrases), and then devises for each of these a suitable musical phrase or theme. The first of these themes is then presented and treated in imitation in all the voices; then the next is handled in the same way, and so on, until the entire text has been disposed of. This procedure is known as *through-imitation* (the awkward but generally accepted translation of the German *Durchimitation*). It is in the creation of musical themes for particular phrases of the text that the element of musical expression comes in, for Josquin sought by his musical phrases to enhance, to express qualities inherent in the text, both rhythmic and expressive. The old linear quality, associated with the technique of successive composition (see page 58), has given way to a homogeneity among the voices, since in the imitative contrapuntal style all voices participate equally in the presentation of the thematic material. This gives the music a greatly different, more unified, aspect. Indeed, it seems as if the voices could no longer have been composed successively, but must have been conceived simultaneously.

As an example let us take the first half of a setting for four voices of a penitential psalm, *De profundis* (Psalm 129, King James Version No. 130) by Josquin. The text appears in the motet as follows:

De profundis clamavi ad te
  Domine:
	Out of the depths have I cried
	  unto Thee, O Lord:

Domine, exaudi vocem meam.	Lord, hear my voice.
Fiant aures tuae intendentes	Let thine ears be attentive
In vocem deprecationis meae.	To the voice of my supplication.

Si iniquitates observaveris
  Domine
	If Thou, Lord, shouldst mark
	  iniquities

Domine, quis sustinebit?	Lord, who shall stand?

<table>
<tr><td>Quia apud te propitiatio est:
Et propter legem tuam
Sustinuite, Domine.
Sustinuit anima mea in verbo
    ejus.
Speravit anima mea in Domino.</td><td>But there is forgiveness in Thee
And according to Your law
Sustain us, O Lord.
My soul doth wait in His
    word.
My soul hopes in the Lord.[12]</td></tr>
</table>

Imitation is clearly the principal technique in Josquin's motet. It may be seen with the phrases beginning "De profundis" (bars 1–13), "Domine exaudi" (14–21), "Fiant aures" (20–25), and later in the piece. Other phrases of the text are made to stand out by being set homophonically, in a declamatory fashion: "In vocem deprecationis meae" (bars 26–30) and at "Et propter legem tuam sustinuite, Domine" toward the end. The use of homophony, then, is a means of expression. The urge for expression clearly underlies the very first theme of the motet, with the characteristic descending leap of a fifth on the word "profundis" (depths) and the melisma on "clamavi" (I have cried). Another feature especially characteristic of Josquin is the use of pairs of voices: One pair imitates another (as in bars 14–21); a passage with such a voice pair is called a *bicinium*. Toward the end, the use of a rhythmic pattern along with melismatic writing on the words "in Domino" (in the Lord) provides an appropriately impressive conclusion.

Along with the motet, the Mass was important in the repertory of the Netherlands musicians of the fifteenth and sixteenth centuries. But the most celebrated composer of Masses was an Italian who adhered strictly to the Netherlands precepts: Giovanni Pierluigi da Palestrina (c. 1525–1594). The Mass as composed in the Renaissance differs from its medieval predecessor, as represented by the Mass of Machaut, in one important respect: its *cyclic* organization, its use of *cyclic form*. A composition is said to be cyclic when the same musical theme is used in two or more of its principal sections, so that its repetitions or cyclic recurrences provide a purely musical means of unifying the work. In a Renaissance Mass this results primarily from the cantus firmus; the same cantus firmus is used in all five movements of the Mass, whereas in the Mass of Machaut, for example, a Kyrie melody was used as cantus firmus in the Kyrie movement, a Gloria melody in the Gloria movement, and so on. The polyphonic Mass, then, became independent of the Gregorian melodies for the Ordinary of the Mass; actually many different melodies were used as cantus firmi for Masses, not only Gregorian chant melodies, but also secular songs, love songs, topical songs, dance melodies, and so on. Furthermore, a Mass could be based not only on a melody as cantus firmus, but on another polyphonic composition, such as a motet, with themes from the motet taken and used more extensively in the larger composition; such a work was known as a *parody Mass*.

---

[12] Modified King James Version.

The Development of Polyphony

EXAMPLE 2-16

JOSQUIN DES PREZ: *De profundis*—BEGINNING

The Historical Background

EXAMPLE 2-16 (*continued*)

The Development of Polyphony

Palestrina composed in all, apart from a number of other works, some 105 Masses, the majority of which are cyclic. As an example we may take the Mass *Assumpta est Maria*, in six parts, based on one of Palestrina's own motets, hence a parody mass. In the Kyrie we note the technique of imitation, each voice part introducing the same theme with but slight modifications. If we compare the beginnings of the Gloria and Credo movements,[13] we see the use of this same theme. Each of the movements of the Mass begins with this theme; other themes are shared by the movements.

For the rest, this Mass—in common with other Renaissance Masses—displays the technique of through-imitation, each line or phrase of the text getting its own musical theme, and each musical theme being normally treated in imitation. In this Mass, however, the six parts are frequently broken down into smaller groups of two, three, or four voices (see Example 2-17, Nos. 2 and 3), the three higher voices often used in alternation with the three lower, thus elaborating somewhat Josquin's use of voice pairs. The overall effect of the composition is also much like that of Josquin's motet: There are no sudden contrasts, the rhythms remain relatively even, there are few wide leaps in the melodic lines and no dynamic variations. This style was regarded in the eighteenth and nineteenth centuries as the most suitable for church music, and its elements are still a part of a musician's training.

Although this art of imitative polyphony was developed by musicians from the Netherlands, it quickly spread all over Europe; and although it was associated particularly with sacred music, it also made its appearance, often with modifications, in secular music. An important composer was Orlandus Lassus (1532–1594), a Netherlander who worked in both Italy and Germany.

Apart from the Netherlands a most important center of Renaissance music was Italy. Here one of the most typical forms of Renaissance secular polyphonic music originated—the *madrigal*. The original meaning of the term is not known, but it apparently has to do with a vocal composition using either a pastoral text or a text in the vernacular (*matrical*, mother tongue). In any case, the term refers generally to a polyphonic composition with a secular text in Italian (later in the sixteenth century there is a large repertory of English madrigals modelled on the Italian form). The earliest madrigals were composed by Netherlands musicians living in Italy, but Italian composers soon took up the form. An important feature of the madrigal as it was cultivated by Italian composers was the emphasis on expression, the musical interpretation or characterization of the poetical text, in pursuit of which novelties were introduced into the context of imitative counterpoint.

As a good example of this let us consider a five-voice madrigal by Don Carlo Gesualdo (c. 1560–1613), *Moro lasso*. The text deals with two violently

---

[13] The first lines of the text of each of these movements ("Gloria in excelsis Deo" and "Credo in unum Deum") are normally omitted in medieval and Renaissance settings.

EXAMPLE 2-17

PALESTRINA: *Mass Assumpta est Maria*—EXCERPTS

1. KYRIE—BEGINNING   2. GLORIA—BEGINNING   3. CREDO—BEGINNING

1.

EXAMPLE 2-17 (*continued*)

The Historical Background

opposed extremes—life and death, both of which are associated with love: "Moro lasso al mio duolo" (I die exhausted in my sorrow) and "e chi mi può dar vita" (and he who can give me life) "ahi che m'ancide, é non vuol darmi aita" (alas kills me, and does not want to give me aid). The musical setting strikingly expresses each. "Moro lasso" is quiet, with slowly moving chords comprising intensely chromatic harmonies (chromaticism in the madrigal was invariably associated with sorrow, despair, or lamenting) and without clearly articulated rhythmic shape, whereas the next phrase, "e chi mi può dar vita," is set in imitative counterpoint (some of the voices are slightly varied) using diatonic harmonies, an upbeat rhythm, with the word *vita* emphasized by a short melisma. The continuation is set in a declamatory chordal fashion, again with chromatic touches here and there. The entire first part is repeated, but in a different key and with other changes. The last part of the composition, beginning with "O dolorosa sorte" (O unhappy fate), is again primarily homophonic; but at the end particular stress is given to "ahi" (alas), which is syncopated and broken up by rests, making an appropriately dolorous conclusion.

EXAMPLE 2-18

GESUALDO: *Moro lasso*—BEGINNING

The Development of Polyphony

EXAMPLE 2-18 (*continued*)

EXAMPLE 2-18 (*continued*)

The Development of Polyphony

EXAMPLE 2-18 (*concluded*)

TEXT AND TRANSLATION:

Moro lasso al mio duolo,	I die exhausted in my sorrow,
e chi mi può dar vita,	and he who could give me life,
ahi, che m'ancide	alas, he kills me
e non vuol darmi aita.	and does not want to give me help.
O dolorosa sorte,	O unhappy fate,
chi dar vita mi può,	he who could give me life,
ahi, mi da morte.	alas, gives me death.

The difference between this piece and the motet by Josquin or the Mass by Palestrina is obvious. The compositions by Josquin and Palestrina are all

Renaissance performing group. Contemporary woodcut.

of a piece, internally consistent all the way through, the changes that are made being carefully prepared so that no obvious disruption of the essential continuity becomes evident; but in the madrigal by Gesualdo there are disruptions, sudden changes from homophony to imitative counterpoint, from chromaticism to diatonic harmony, changes in rhythm and in range, all inspired by the aim of representing, of expressing, the emotional content of the poetical text. Thus the consistency of the musical composition is abandoned in favor of another artistic end: expression.

The Renaissance also brings an extensive cultivation of instrumental music, both for solo instruments (keyboard and lute) and for small ensembles of instruments. To a large extent this instrumental music was modeled on the vocal forms of the time, in which imitative counterpoint was prominent, especially in forms such as the *canzone*, the *ricercar*, and the *fantasia*. But there are also dances, usually for the lute and the harpsichord. Furthermore, instruments often participated in the performance of polyphonic ensemble compositions, but the composers of the time did not stipulate which instruments were to be used and when; this was a matter for the performers to decide. For this reason the designation *a cappella*, meaning performance by an unaccompanied choir (that is, not accompanied by organ or other instruments), so often used in connection with the sacred music of the Renaissance, is misleading: First, because instruments were regularly used, and second, because the performance was by a very small vocal group, often an ensemble of soloists, with a small boys' choir for the soprano or discant part, and not for a large mixed chorus.

Toward the end of the sixteenth century, however, there developed in Venice a characteristic way of combining large instrumental and vocal groups in elaborate and monumental compositions. In such compositions the instrumental tone color played an important role in the artistic conception and was controlled by the composer. The art of orchestration had come into existence.

At the bottom of the Venetian style (*stile luxurians*, luxurious style, as it has come to be known) is usually said to lie an architectural feature of the cathedral of San Marco in Venice: the presence of a double choir loft, which gave rise to the possibility of having two choirs perform antiphonally, either together or in alternation. Actually this practice was by no means limited to San Marco, but it was there that composers seized on the device and developed it in a characteristic fashion. The principal composers involved are Andrea Gabrieli (c. 1510–1586) and especially his nephew Giovanni Gabrieli (1557–1613), who wrote the most elaborate works to emanate directly from this school.

The idea of having the choirs in an antiphonal relationship was productive of many things. For one thing, the choirs could be differently constituted: one in which high voices were predominant against one of largely low voices, or one of soloists against a large chorus, or one of singers against one of instruments, or both choirs could be instrumental. In practice sometimes three or four choirs were used and the same variations in their composition were possible. The dual character of the relationship between the choirs, alternatively competitive and concordant, is reflected in the term *concerto* or *concertato*, which in Latin refers to competition and in Italian to agreement. Our modern terms *concert* and *concerto* both go back to this dual conception. Two other terms used in connection with this music are polychoral (many-choired) and *cori spezzati* or *sprezzati* (split choirs).

An important work by Giovanni Gabrieli is a purely instrumental piece for two choirs of instruments, the *Sonata pian' e forte* (the loud and soft sonata), published in 1597. The term *sonata* means nothing more than a piece to be played on instruments, in contrast to *cantata*, a piece to be sung. In this work one group is composed of a trumpet and three trombones, the other of a violin and three trombones. When either choir plays by itself, the indication is *piano*, but when both play together, *forte*. This principle, that the degree of loudness is related to the number of instruments or voices that are sounding, is known as *terrace dynamics*. This work, then, displays two important features: orchestration (the composer determining which instruments are to be used) and the indication of dynamics.

Another large work by Giovanni Gabrieli is a festive motet for the dedication of a church, *In ecclesiis*, published posthumously in 1615. This work is written for four choirs: one of vocal soloists, one of brass instruments, and two choral groups, along with organ, which provides accompaniment throughout. A refrain structure, the refrain text being "Alleluia," organizes the work: Between the statements of the refrain come passages for the soloists, after which the brass choir enters; there follows a gradual culmination, still making use of the refrain principle, leading to the grandiose finale. This is perhaps the most celebrated example of the Venetian *stile luxurians*. In a way such a work may be said to parallel the lavish Venetian paintings of the time.

Toward the end of the sixteenth century there commenced another sweeping change in the art of music, much as had occurred some 150 years earlier. Once again the established values and procedures were attacked. Only now it is the Netherlands music based on imitative counterpoint that is the victim, and the attack is directed by Italian musicians. The basis for this assault is the humanistic preoccupation with music's power of expression, to make emotions manifest in music. This may be seen especially in the treatise *A Dialogue on Ancient and Modern Music*, written and published in 1581 by Vincenzo Galilei (1533–1591), the uncle of the famous astronomer. Galilei had been studying the music of ancient Greece and had been impressed with the doctrine of *ethos*. He reached the conclusion that the music of his time was denatured and deprived of its emotional power by the imitative counterpoint, which in his view prevented the proper musical expression of the emotional character of the text. Accordingly he urged a return to a monophonic kind of music similar to what was thought to have prevailed in ancient Greece. From this there developed a new kind of music, fundamental to which was an infinitely flexible melodic line intended to render the text in all clarity and to embody the expression of all its emotional connotations. This new style came to be known as *recitative*.

In Florence these ideas were taken up by several groups of scholars, musicians, and poets, one of which was known as the *camerata*. By the end of the century we find efforts to apply the new ideas to dramatic works based on Greek mythology. Thus was *opera* born. The earliest work of this kind, which is preserved only partially, is *Dafne*, performed in 1597, with music by Jacopo Peri (1561–1633); three years later, in 1600, both Peri and his colleague and rival Guilio Caccini (c. 1550–1618) produced operas based on the Orpheus and Eurydice legend. Another important composer was Emilio de' Cavalieri (c. 1550–1602). But the man who took the new form and provided it with music of genius was Claudio Monteverdi (1567–1643), and his first operatic work, symptomatically enough, was *Orfeo* (1607). It is clear that the old legend celebrating the power of music would appeal to composers engaged in demonstrating that very power. Thus was born the music of the Baroque.

Claudio Monteverdi,
Contemporary print.

Although the recitative was to be monophonic—a return to the practice of the ancient Greeks—this was modified to the extent of providing a harmonic accompaniment, which is variously known as *basso continuo* (or merely *continuo*), *figured bass*, or *thorough bass*. The continuo usually is played by two instruments: a low bowed string instrument (a viola da gamba or its modern counterpart, the violoncello) and a keyboard instrument, either harpsichord or organ, the choice depending generally upon whether the composition performed is sacred or secular. The composer simply sets down on paper the notes of the bass part, which are played by the stringed instrument and the keyboard instrument; but the player of the keyboard instrument must also play chords above these notes. Sometimes the chords to be played are left to the discretion of the player, but often the intervals to be used in making up the chords are indicated by figures written below the notes of the bass part: "5/3," a fifth and a third, thus a triad in root position; "6/3," a sixth and a third, a triad in first inversion, and so on. Thus we have the explanation of the term *figured bass*. The figures, however, are frequently abbreviated, so that, for instance, "6" means the same as "6/3," or no figure at all means a triad in root position; raising and lowering of the third of a triad may be indicated by a sharp, a flat, or a natural sign along with or instead of a figure. The keyboard player had a good deal of latitude concerning how the part was to be played: whether the chords were played as such in close position or broken into arpeggios, whether repeated, broken down rhythmically into smaller note values, whether they were played in a high range or low, ornamented or simple, and so on, which he did in accordance with convention and the character of the particular composition. This process that the keyboard player goes through is known as *realizing* the continuo. The continuo, although devised for the recitative, is used in most forms of Baroque music.[14]

As an example of the early recitative with continuo accompaniment, let us look at an excerpt from Monteverdi's *Orfeo*: "Tu se' morta," Orpheus' reaction to the death of Eurydice and his vow to venture down into the Underworld to effect her return to Earth. Orfeo is a tenor part and the continuo is to be played, according to the composer's instruction, by an organ with wooden pipes (not reed pipes) and a lute (*chitarrone*). The voice part is essentially declamatory in character, as would indeed be expected in a recitative. This aspect is clear enough from the metric freedom that prevails; there are no time signatures, and the bars vary in length, so that metric regularity is not present. Among the expressive devices used we may note dissonance, particularly the seventh against the bass (as at "Tu se' morta," bar 2, or "se da me partita," bars 6–7), chromatic changes in harmony (as from G to G sharp, in bars 2–3, 3–4, 6–7), the melodic descent at "morte" (bars 17–18) accompanying Orfeo's resolve to visit the Underworld, as well as the descent at the very end, and exclamations intensified by repetition at a higher pitch (as "mai più," bars 7–8, or "no," bar 9). Although the passage is primarily through-composed, the element of repetition is not entirely lacking: The opening passage (bars 1–5) is closely paralleled by the next passage (bars 5–7); and some rhythmic repetition goes along with Orfeo's farewell at the very end (bars 19–22). It should be noted that Monteverdi left the bass unfigured; it is assumed that the keyboard player would know which chords to use (see Example 2-19).

The new style based on solo singing was developed in Italy and subsequently was transported all over Europe, just as the Netherlands style based on imitative counterpoint back in the Renaissance. Three of the greatest practitioners in the seventeenth century of this art outside of Italy were Jean

---

[14] For illustrations of *basso continuo*, see Examples 3-1 through 3-7.

EXAMPLE 2-19

MONTEVERDI: "Tu se' morta," FROM *Orfeo*

Un organo di legno e un chitarrone

The Development of Polyphony

EXAMPLE 2-19 (*continued*)

TRANSLATION OF TEXT:

You are dead now, my life, and yet I still am breathing; you have departed from me forever, never to return, while I remain here; no! no! for if my verse has any power, I will seek out the deepest abysses and entreat the King of Darkness with my song to let me bring you to see the stars once more. But if cruel fortune denies me this, I shall remain with you in the company of death! Farewell earth. farewell skies, and sunlight, farewell.

The Historical Background

Baptiste Lully (1632–1687) in France, Heinrich Schütz (1585–1672) in Germany, and Henry Purcell (1658 or 1659–1695) in England.

Other types of music were also cultivated, some being continued from the past, others being developed along with the new. Sets of dances for harpsichord or lute, often known as suites, and contrapuntal and cantus firmus forms for organ and harpsichord are among the genres handed down from the sixteenth century that are perpetuated in the Baroque. On the other side we may mention the rise of orchestral music, which was to a considerable extent connected with the opera—the overture, introductions and conclusions to scenes, accompaniments to soloistic compositions—but orchestral music was also used in connection with dances, especially ballet, cultivated particularly in France.

One final development of the seventeenth century was the establishment of the system of keys that has characterized Western music up until the recent present: the major and minor scales which emerged from the older system of the church modes (see page 41). The use of tonality in this sense makes the music of the Baroque sound more familiar to our ears than does the music of earlier historical periods.

It thus appears that the historical periodization used for the history of music is the same as that used for art history and for the cultural history of the West in general: *Classical Antiquity* (until c. 500), *Middle Ages* (500–1450), *Renaissance* (1450–1600), *Baroque* (1600–1750); two more must be added: the *Classic and Romantic Periods* (1750–1900) and the *Contemporary or Modern Epoch* (1900 to the present). In summary (or what perhaps should be called the summary of the summary), the development of Western music up to the second half of the seventeenth century may be outlined something like this:

Classical (Greek) Antiquity
  Music and mythology.
  The development of the mathematical basis of the art (Pythagoras).
  The scale system.
  The doctrine of ethos.

The Middle Ages (500–1450): Romanesque and Gothic Periods
  The Gregorian chant repertory, going back in part to Hebrew music, with its scale system.
  Monophonic music: not only in Latin but also in the vernacular languages, particularly the troubadours and trouvères in France and the minnesinger in Germany.
  The development of polyphony: primarily in France, from the simple organum based on the perfect consonances through the more elaborate works of the Notre Dame school with the concomitant invention of rhythmic notation, the coming of the motet and the con-

The Development of Polyphony

ductus, the elaboration of isorhythm in the fourteenth century, most of the development involved with increasing elaboration of rhythm; polyphony highly linear in structure.

The Renaissance (1450–1600)

The development of the imitative contrapuntal style in the work of Netherlands composers, in connection with sacred music (Mass and motet); increased use of the secondary consonances.

The spread of the style throughout Europe, with particular developments in Italy, the madrigal and polychoral music of Venice.

The Early Baroque (1600–1685)

The Italian reaction to the Netherlands contrapuntal music, based on the ideal of expression gained from the study of Greek music.

The recitative, leading to the creation of opera.

The later development of instrumental music, particularly of orchestral music.

The establishment of the modern major-minor system of keys.

Chapter Three

Bach

Introduction

*T*he ambitious young German musician in the late Baroque was faced with two principal possibilities for pursuing a career: the way of the *Kapellmeister* (or *maestro di cappella*) or the way of the *cantor*. Generally the former would be connected with a court and would involve the aspiring musician in the composition and performance of operas, oratorios, instrumental and orchestral works, an activity more or less secular in its outlook, although religious music would by no means be excluded. The position of cantor, on the other hand, was much more restricted: Here the musician was employed by a church as music director, organist, and choirmaster, and his principal duty was to provide and perform the music for the regular services of the church as well as for special services and other observances. Apart from this he was frequently responsible for the choirboys, their schooling and their welfare in general. Such works as he might compose would for the most part remain unpublished and indeed were heard only by the local congregation. Thus, for a cantor, only a local reputation was possible, since he was not really involved with the great international musical life of the time, which centered around the Italian opera.

Such was the situation confronted around 1700 by Johann Sebastian Bach (1685–1750) as he began his life work. In his family background the tradition of being a cantor was strong, and it was a tradition the young musician felt keenly. We find him first engaged as a professional singer at St. Michael's Church in Lüneburg, in northern Germany; the celebrated organist Georg Böhm (1661–1733) lived and worked there at the time, and Bach also had the opportunity to visit the nearby large cultural and commercial center Hamburg. From 1703 to 1707 he was organist and cantor at the New Church in Arnstadt; for one year, 1707–8, he held a similar position at St. Blasius' Church in Mühlhausen. For the following ten years he was similarly engaged, but this time at a court, in Weimar, 1708–17. But then in 1717 he accepted a position as Kapellmeister at the court of Cöthen, with duties primarily involving secular and instrumental music, where he remained for six years, until

(Opposite) *Bach at age thirty.* Artist unknown. (COURTESY STAATSBIBLIOTHEK PREUSSICHER KULTURBESITZ, BERLIN [BILDARCHIV].)

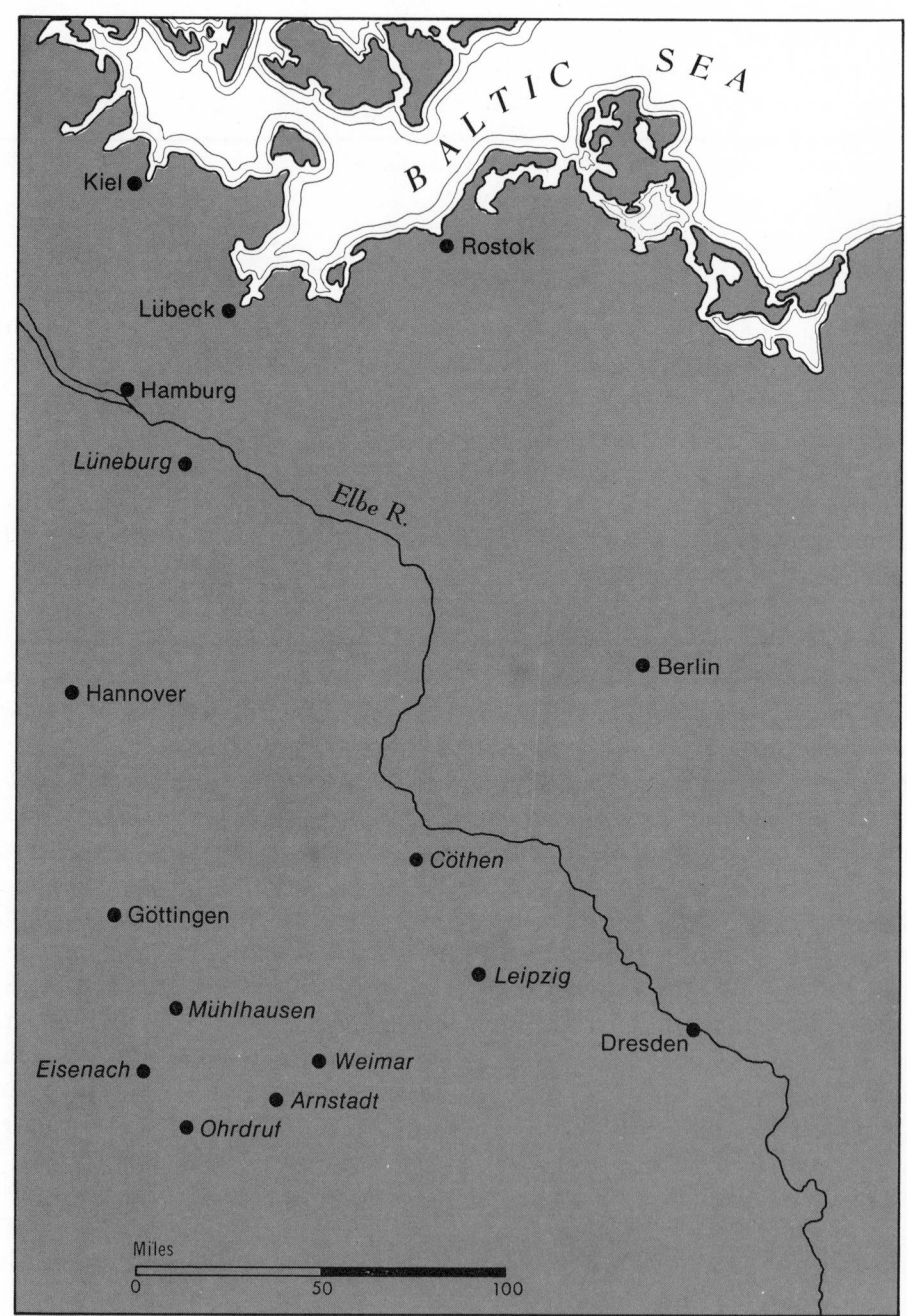

Map of part of Germany, showing (cities in italics) where Bach lived and worked.

Introduction

1723. It was then that he received a call to be cantor at the Church of St. Thomas in Leipzig, where he remained for the rest of his life.

It is clear that the way of the cantor dominated Bach's career. But Bach nonetheless had his difficulties and sometimes longed for the greater rewards, recognition, and freedom that a career as Kapellmeister had to offer. In 1705, while at Arnstadt, Bach had obtained a month's leave of absence to go to Lübeck to hear and meet the famed organist and composer Dietrich Buxtehude (1637–1707). But Bach became so interested in what he heard that he stayed four months instead of one; and upon his return his accompaniments to the hymns were so full of chromatic elaborations that the congregation and authorities protested to him, and he soon left to take up duties at Mühlhausen. In his letter of resignation the next year to the authorities at Mühlhausen, when he was about to go to Weimar, Bach stated some of his beliefs concerning church music, or as he called it, the "well-regulated" or "well-appointed" church music. In this the two principal points involved, first, the assembling of the best possible music for use in the services, and second, seeing to it that such music was given the best possible performance. At all events, the appointment at Cöthen represented a turn away from what Bach had exemplified up to that time (1717) in his career; and it is significant that most of his secular and purely instrumental compositions date from this period in his career. But the appointment at Leipzig represented his return to the way of the cantor and his renewed full-time commitment to the "well-regulated" church music.

Bach immediately set to work composing vocal compositions for use in the Leipzig services, producing the works we know as cantatas. In his first four years at Leipzig he composed around one hundred fifty of these cantatas, enough for at least three full church years, along with a number of other larger works. After 1727 his attention shifted to other types of composition; in the twenty-three years remaining to him he composed only about fifty more cantatas. Furthermore, many of the larger works, the oratorios in particular, composed after 1727, consist to a large extent of reworkings of individual compositions Bach had written much earlier. This decrease in the composition of liturgical music may in part be attributed to difficulties he had with the authorities in Leipzig. In 1730 he wrote the well-known letter to the Leipzig town council on the state of church music in Leipzig, complaining about the lack of funds for singers and players and the resultant deficiencies in the performances. A few years later he was forced to carry on a long quarrel with a newly appointed rector of the St. Thomas School, Johann August Ernesti, who usurped certain functions Bach held to be his alone. It is thus not surprising that Bach from time to time looked back on his decision to leave Cöthen with misgivings. But he also took steps to alleviate the situation, to try to get another position, to get his music published and in circulation—in short, to become better known, more in the mainstream of the musical life of the time.

To this end he began to compose and assemble a large collection of music for keyboard instruments, the *Clavierübung* (Keyboard Practice); the famous Mass in B minor is also part of Bach's endeavors in this direction. In the same spirit, he had since 1729 been director of the *collegium musicum* in Leipzig, an organization of amateur and professional musicians founded by the noted composer Georg Philipp Telemann (1681–1767) for the performance of secular and instrumental music. For this group Bach provided works for harpsichord and orchestra as well as secular cantatas. But he never left the St. Thomas School and Church, and many of his difficulties persisted until the end of his life.

St. Thomas' Church and School, Leipzig. Contemporary print.

Our survey of Bach's compositions will proceed as follows: first the liturgical compositions, vocal and instrumental; then the secular and didactic works, for keyboard, chamber music ensembles, and orchestra, in that order; and finally some remarks on the late works.

The Liturgical Vocal Compositions

Bach's liturgical music is designed for the Lutheran service—i.e., mainly the *Hauptgottesdienst*, the principal morning service, which in a general way corresponds to the mass of the Catholic Church. In this service there are three main elements: the readings from the Bible, from the Gospels and the Epistles, selected in accordance with the character of the day; the sermon, the verbal exegesis or interpretation of the text, an exhortation to the congregation; and the music. Again, in the music three aspects are to be distinguished: the chorales or hymns, in strophic form, sung by the congregation accompanied by the organ, again selected in accordance with the day; the main musical piece, known variously as *concerto* or *cantata*, which presents a musical interpretation of the character of the day and usually will involve the use of an appropriate hymn melody; and the organ music, which introduces and closes the service and which also precedes the congregational singing of the hymns.

A cantata of this kind, then, may be described as a sectional composition for voices (soloists, chorus, often both) and orchestra. Its text is usually related to the Biblical readings assigned to the day as well as to the text of a hymn also proper to the day. Most of Bach's cantata librettos (*libretto* being the term used for the text of an extensive musical composition in several parts or movements) represent a new "reform" type introduced around 1700 by Erdmann Neumeister (1671–1756), a pastor who lived and worked in Hamburg. Neumeister's new type of cantata libretto represented the systematic introduction into the liturgical cantata of the two principal elements of the Italian opera of the time, the recitative and the aria. To see the full significance of this, it is necessary to turn briefly to the development of Italian opera in the late seventeenth century.

We have already seen that the recitative was intimately bound up with the origin of Baroque music. But the recitative all through at least the first half of the seventeenth century remained an extremely flexible medium, in which the declamatory could readily give way to the lyrical-melodic as the text seemed to require. Gradually, however, in the late seventeenth century the recitative declined in importance in favor of the *aria*, the large melodic, formally organized, soloistic vocal composition, frequently virtuoso in character. With this the opera itself became a more diffuse musicodramatic form, involving a plethora of characters, with main plots and subplots, and much emphasis going to the virtuoso singers and to the production of spectacular stage effects. Then there came a "reform" of the opera, to some extent inspired by French ideals, initiated by a poet, Apostolo Zeno (1668–1750), and continued by his successor, perhaps the most celebrated operatic librettist of all time, Pietro Metastasio (1698–1782). The basis of this reform of the libretto involved the establishment of a complementary relationship between

Italian opera stage set, late seventeenth century.

the two contrasting elements, the recitative and the aria. The idea was that the recitative should present action—specific, concrete events, things taking place—whereas the aria should present emotional expression, lyrical reflection. In a normal operatic scene, then, there would be first the recitative presenting the action, followed by an aria, the emotional expression of one of the protagonists. The two elements alternate throughout the work. This structure characterized the serious Italian opera, the *opera seria*, of the Baroque.

The recitative appeared in two different forms: the *recitativo secco* and the *recitativo accompagnato* or *stromentato*. The former, which means simply "dry" recitative, was the usual type, the singers accompanied only by the continuo, the melodic line full of repeated notes and devoid of musical or melodic interest—hence "dry" not only by virtue of the accompaniment but also by virtue of the relatively limited character of the melodic line. The other kind, the accompanied recitative—and this means accompanied by the orchestra—was more elaborate and hence reserved for the big scenes, in which emotions like rage, fear, and jealousy come to expression. Here there is great variety, the melodic line as well as the accompaniment changing character rapidly to correspond to the sentiments of the text. Finally, a third style of recitative may be distinguished, *arioso*, which represents an essentially melodic, songlike passage within the context of the recitative; most often it is found in a section of *recitativo accompagnato*.

The aria, the other prime element of the Italian *opera seria*, appears in one form: the *da capo* form. This is nothing more than three-part or song form, as has already been explained, except that the repetition of the first part is not written out; instead, at the close of the middle or second part there is found the instruction "Da capo al fine" (or from the head, beginning, to the end), according to which the performers return to the beginning and continue until the end of the first part, where the word *fine* appears. A most important aspect of the Baroque da capo aria is its unity of affection, of expressive character: One emotion and only one is to be expressed in an aria. In consequence the thematic material is not changed during the course of an aria; there may be modulations through different keys, the intervals used in the melodic line may be varied somewhat, but the rhythmic patterns remain the same and the aria runs off consistently, similar throughout, all of a piece. The only contrast that might appear is in the middle section, which is usually rather short. The orchestra frequently plays an important part in establishing the character of the aria, chiefly by the instrument or instruments the composer makes predominate; such solo instrumental parts accompanying an aria are called *obbligato*. In an aria the full orchestra or one or two solo instruments will often have passages to themselves, such passages being called *ritornelli*. The scheme for a fully developed da capo aria, then, would look like this:

Ritornello—A—Ritornello—B—Ritornello—A—Ritornello

Much the same applies to ensembles (duets, trios, quartets, etc.) for soloists with orchestra, which also show the standard da capo form.

In this type of aria, then, we have a formalized way of manifesting expression in music. Here we have a close parallel between the philosophy and music of the time. In philosophy we find Descartes, who in his treatise *On the Passions of the Soul* (1649) subjected the various emotions to a rationalistic analysis and classification. In music, on the other hand, it was rather the means of expressing different passions that was rationalized in this way: That is to say, there were a number of standard, generally recognized melodic types, rhythmic patterns, keys, instrumental combinations, each of which was associated with a particular affection (or emotion). The composer had simply to devise thematic material in accordance with the affection of a particular aria's text and then to proceed with the working out of the composition.

A few illustrations may be given. For the representation of sorrow the following elements are common: a minor key (often E minor), soft dynamic level, slow tempo, triple meter, instrumentation of flute or oboe and string orchestra, and chromaticism in the harmonies. For the representation of joy, on the other hand, one might find some of the following: a major key (G major or D major), loud dynamic level, fast tempo, high and bright wind instruments (trumpet), or a virtuoso solo violin part along with the string orchestra, themes consisting largely of rapid figuration, and mainly diatonic harmonies.

But the idea of expressing an affection, as understood in the eighteenth century, included more than emotions: It also comprised purely descriptive or characteristic musical styles, such as would be used to suggest a thunderstorm, the pastoral-idyllic, or the tumult of a battle. The pastoral character, for instance, was expressed by flutes, oboes, or horns and strings, in a major key, using a dotted six-eight time (the rhythm of the siciliano dance), whereas a battle would be loud, would employ trumpets and tympani and themes in which the rhythm of driving sixteenth notes was prominent. To be sure, there were many different possibilities, but the principle of operating with stereotyped procedures for the expression of specific affections and characters, known as the theory or doctrine of the affections, is a central fact of Baroque music.

In the cantatas Bach composed to librettos that follow the precepts of Erdmann Neumeister there are found recitatives and arias that in all essentials correspond to what was current in the Italian opera of the time. But most of these cantata librettos also have sections that are based on Protestant hymn texts; in actual compositions these would be handled as cantus firmus movements,[1] the cantus firmus being the hymn melody put in one voice in long notes, while the other voices provide a contrapuntal accompaniment, which in turn could also draw on the hymn melody. Such a cantata, then, represents a combination of two elements: the new italianate recitatives and arias from the *opera seria* and the older cantus firmus procedure long associated with sacred music.

As an example we may take the cantata *Wachet auf, ruft uns die Stimme* ("Sleepers Awake! A Voice Is Calling," S. 140), composed in 1731, several years after the completion of the bulk of the cantatas, for the twenty-seventh Sunday after Trinity. The readings are II Corinthians, Chapter 5, Verses 1–10, and Matthew, Chapter 25, Verses 1–10. The latter, the parable of the wise and foolish virgins, is most important for the cantata:

> [1] Then shall the kingdom of heaven be likened unto ten virgins, which took their lamps, and went forth to meet the bridegroom. [2] And five of them were wise, and five were foolish. [3] They that were foolish took their lamps, and took no oil with them: [4] but the wise took oil in their vessels with their lamps. [5] While the bridegroom tarried, they all slumbered and slept. [6] And at midnight there was a cry made, "Behold, the bridegroom cometh: go ye out to meet him." [7] Then all the virgins arose, and trimmed their lamps. [8] And the foolish said to the wise, "Give us of your oil; for our lamps are gone out." [9] But the wise answered, saying, "Not so; lest there be not

---

[1] But at the same time, in an aria or even in a recitative, the text could be related to that of a hymn, even though the melody of the hymn would not necessarily be employed.

The Liturgical Vocal Compositions

enough for us and you; but go ye rather to them that sell, and buy for yourselves." [10] And while they went to buy, the bridegroom came; and they that were ready went in with him to the marriage: and the door was shut.

Here the marriage is an allegory in which the bridegroom represents Christ, and the virgins symbolize the church.

Among the hymns assigned to this day is Phillip Nicolai's *Wachet auf,* published first in 1599. The hymn text, in three strophes, is itself closely related to the gospel reading from St. Matthew. In the cantata, Bach uses both melody and text of all three strophes of the hymn: the first strophe in the first movement, the second in the fourth, and the third in the seventh and last movement. In between these there come recitatives and duets in the style of the Italian opera, the texts for these numbers presumably having been written by the Leipzig poet Picander (whose real name was Christian Friedrich Henrici, 1700–1764), who frequently supplied librettos for Bach. There are two pairs of these recitatives and duets. Whereas the first duet, "Wann kommst du?" for soprano and bass with violin obbligato and continuo, has an aura of inquiry and expectation (when will the bridegroom come?), the second, "Mein Freund ist mein," also for soprano and bass continuo but with oboe obbligato, is all quiet joy and confidence, celebrating the arrival of the bridegroom. Of the two recitatives, the first is an example of the *secco* type, and the second is in the *accompagnato* style.

We may take a closer look at the secco recitative for tenor and continuo, "Er kommt, er kommt," as an example of the simple recitative style. Here

EXAMPLE 3-1

BACH: "Er kommt, er kommt" (RECITATIVE), FROM *Wachet auf, ruft uns die Stimme* (S. 140)

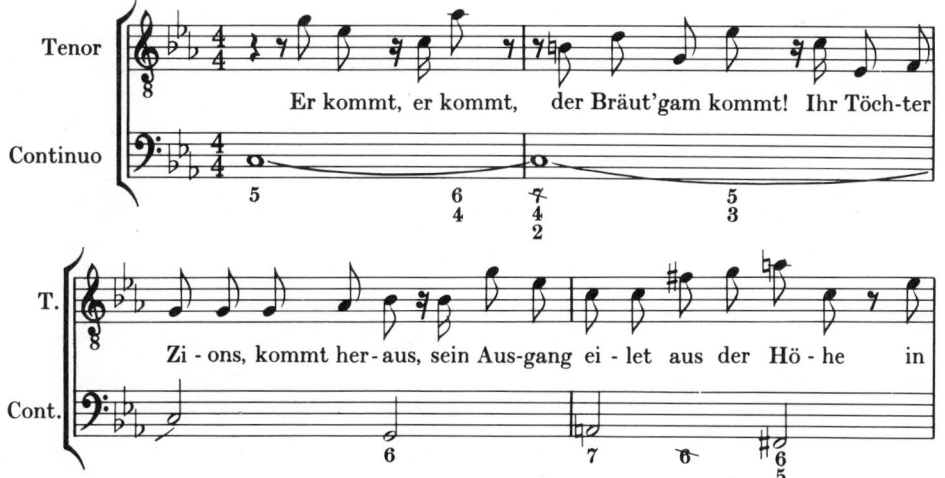

EXAMPLE 3-1 (*continued*)

the melodic style is wholly declamatory; there is no interest in making a melodic line, there are no phrases repeated, no rhythmic or melodic patterns of any kind—the melodic part is there solely to carry the text. Phrases in the text are separated by rests, and brief phrases and exclamations are set very short, as "er kommt, er kommt" (he comes, he comes), "Wacht auf" (Wake up), "dort" (there), and "sehet" (behold). When the text refers to the bridegroom hurrying from above ("sein Ausgang eilet aus der Höhe"), the musical line rises to an A and then immediately falls down a sixth.

As an example of the aria form we may take the second duet, "Mein Freund ist mein," for soprano and bass, with oboe obbligato and continuo. In

The Liturgical Vocal Compositions

expressing quiet joy, the theme presented at the beginning runs throughout the *A* part of the duet; the only element of contrast comes in the *B* part, beginning with the words "Ich will mit dir," characterized by the use of a new key (G minor; the *A* part of the duet was in B flat major), along with new melodic material for the singers and a new pattern in the accompaniment. In the *A* part of the duet, the words "scheiden" (separate) and "weiden" (graze) are heightened by the use of long running melismatic passages. There is also a ritornello for the oboe and continuo.

EXAMPLE 3-2

BACH: "Mein Freund ist mein" (DUET), FROM *Wachet auf*—BEGINNING

Bach

EXAMPLE 3-2 (continued)

EXAMPLE 3-2 (*concluded*)

The three remaining movements of the cantata employ the text and melody of the hymn *Wachet auf.* The simplest of these is the last movement, which is in what might be called "congregational style": The hymn melody, which is cast in the old *bar* form (the phrase repetitions fall into the pattern *a a b*), appears in the uppermost voice, while the three other voices form a

EXAMPLE 3-3

BACH: "Gloria sei dir gesungen," FROM *Wachet auf*—BEGINNING

The Liturgical Vocal Compositions

harmonic accompaniment. Such a homophonic setting is customary in hymns to be sung by the congregation.

Much more elaborate is the first movement. Here the notes of the cantus firmus (the hymn melody) are given in long slow notes in the soprano part, while the other voices engage in imitative passages based on phrases of the hymn melody. Throughout there is accompaniment by the orchestra in which martial dotted rhythms predominate. The instrumental part marked *taille* (an eighteenth-century term for a middle voice) is usually played by a tenor oboe.

EXAMPLE 3-4

BACH: "Wachet auf" (*Chorus*), FROM *Wachet auf*—EXCERPT

EXAMPLE 3-4 (*continued*)

The central movement of the cantata, "Zion hört die Wächter singen," which represents the awakening of the virgins, consists of three sharply divergent elements: the hymn melody and words in the tenor section of the chorus, the lyrical countermelody in the violins (which actually in this setting is more prominent than is the cantus firmus), and the continuo. This is the most well-known portion of the cantata; indeed, Bach himself published it in an arrangement for organ (see Example 3-5.)

In most striking contrast to *Wachet auf* is the cantata *Ein' feste Burg ist unser Gott* (A Mighty Fortress Is Our God, S. 80), which was composed for Reformation Sunday in September, 1724; it was repeated six years later, on the occasion of the two-hundredth anniversary of the establishment of the Lutheran Church. It is a large and elaborate composition in eight movements. Here the principal character or affection is war and battle—God at arms against sin and evil. This is evident from the hymn on which much of the cantata is based, Martin Luther's *Ein' feste Burg*. Three of the four movements

EXAMPLE 3-4 (*concluded*)

to use the hymn as cantus firmus represent the affection *battle*: the first movement, with the hymn melody both in the sopranos and in canon between the high trumpet and the bass stringed instruments, while the other parts engage in a through-imitative setting of the hymn, the emphasis going to its first phrase; the second, an aria for bass, to which comes a soprano with the cantus firmus, while rapid figuration appears as accompaniment in the violin; and the fifth movement, another large choral piece, uses a rhythmically varied version of the hymn melody (in six-eight instead of four-four time); finally, at the end, comes the usual simple four-part congregational presentation of the hymn. To these cantus firmus movements come two sets of recitatives and arias, both recitatives including passages in the lyrical arioso style.

Another cantata representing battle is *Es erhub sich ein Streit* (There Uprose a Great Strife, S. 19), for St. Michael's Day of 1726, dealing with the Archangel Michael's expulsion of Lucifer from heaven. Quite different is the cantata for Annunciation, *Wie schön leuchtet der Morgenstern* (How Brightly

Shines Yon Star of Morn, S. 1), with a pastoral quality evoked by the use of horns, oboes, solo violins, and the rhythm of the siciliano dance (a moderately moving six-eight). Exuberant joy is expressed in the virtuoso solo cantata for soprano, strings, and trumpet, *Jauchzet Gott in allen Landen* (Rejoice in God in All Nations, S. 51), of 1730, with its brilliant rapid figuration for the soprano in its highest register (known as coloratura), effectively accompanied by the

EXAMPLE 3-5

BACH: "Zion hört die Wächter singen," FROM *Wachet auf*—EXCERPT

Example 3-5 (*continued*)

trumpet. A most impressive work is a single movement for double-chorus and orchestra, probably the first movement of a large composition that was never completed, *Nun ist das Heil und die Kraft und das Reich* (Now Is Come Salvation, and Strength, and the Kingdom, S. 50), the date of which cannot be determined; the text is from Revelations, Chapter 12, Verse 10.

Most of the other choral works of Bach reveal the forms and procedures that are found in the cantatas. This is particularly true in the oratorio, represented chiefly by the passions and the Christmas Oratorio. The principal difference between an opera and an oratorio is that an oratorio is not acted out on a stage; another difference is that an oratorio, particularly in the eighteenth century, makes greater use of the chorus than does an opera. But there are secular as well as sacred oratorios. The most prominent among Bach's oratorios are the passions, musical settings of the accounts of Jesus' betrayal and crucifixion as contained in the gospels; of these Bach composed three, according to the gospels of Matthew, Mark, and John, of which the first is the best known. In a passion composition by Bach, along with the Biblical text (which is given complete), additional recitatives and arias very much like those found in the cantatas were inserted; these provided additional interpretations of, or reflections on, the action recounted in the Biblical text. Choral settings based on hymns are also included. These separate elements are distinguished by the way they are set to music. In the *St. Matthew Passion*, composed in 1728–1729, we find the following:

1. The Biblical text from St. Matthew, Chapters 26 and 27. This is set mostly in *recitativo secco* for tenor, who gives the narration, along with singers for the parts of various other characters (Jesus, Pilate, Judas, etc.); the part of Jesus, however, is accompanied by strings along with continuo; the cries of the crowd (*turbae*) are set for chorus with continuo accompaniment.

2. The added texts, mainly by Picander, which appear as *recitativi accompagnati* and large da capo arias with important solo instrumental parts (obbligato parts) in the orchestral accompaniment.
3. Hymns proper to Holy Week, inserted at intervals throughout the work.

As an example, we may look briefly at a portion of the *St. Matthew Passion*, the dramatic turning point where Jesus is betrayed by Judas and seized by the soldiers to be brought before Pilate. The passage begins with a solemn chorale (No. 31) harmonized in simple homophonic "congregational" style, "Was mein Gott will das g'scheh' allzeit" (The will of God be always done). There follows the secco recitative for the *testo* (the evangelist or narrator) with Jesus and Judas (No. 32), the text being directly from St. Matthew; the episode closes with the seizure of Jesus. There follows immediately an imitative duet for soprano and alto with sudden choral interjections (No. 33), "So ist mein Jesus nun gefangen" (So my Jesus has now been captured), with text by Picander, expressing anxiety by the restless syncopated accompaniment in the woodwinds; this moves directly to an effective representation of a cataclysmic thunderstorm by means of a fugue for double chorus with orchestral accompaniment. Here is the text of this portion of the *Passion According to St. Matthew* along with a standard English translation. The example that follows gives the music for the recitative to the narrative from St. Matthew (No. 32) and is intended to provide another illustration of the *recitativo secco*.

[No. 31: Hymn]

Was mein Gott will, das g'scheh' allzeit	What God resolves, will He achieve,
Sein Wille ist der Beste.	His will is perfect ever.
Zu helfen de'n er ist bereit,	He succors all who firm believe,
Die an ihn glauben feste.	And for the best endeavor.
Er hilft aus Not, der fromme Gott,	Our help indeed, our God indeed,
Und züchtiget mit Massen,	With gentle moderation,
Wer Gott vertraut, fest auf ihm baut,	He chastens us, if Him we trust,
Den will er nicht verlassen.	We need not fear damnation.

[No. 32: Recitative, from St. Matthew, Chapter 26, Verses 43–50]

Evangelist

Und er kam und fand sie aber schlafend, und ihre Augen waren voll Schlafs. Und er liess sie, und ging aber mals hin, und betete zum	And he came and found them asleep again, for their eyes were heavy. And he left them, and went away again, and prayed

The Liturgical Vocal Compositions

dritten Mal, und redete
dieselbigen Worte. Da kam
er zu seinen Jüngern, und
sprach zu ihnen:

the third time, saying
the same words. Then
cameth he to his disciples
and saith unto them:

Jesus

"Ach! wollt ihr nun schlafen
und ruhen: Siehe,
die Stunde ist hier, dass
des Menschen Sohn in der
Sünder Hände überantwortet
wird. Stehet auf, lasset
uns gehen: siehe, er ist da,
der mich verrät."

"Sleep on now, and take
your rest: behold, the
hour is at hand, and the
Son of Man is betrayed into
the hands of sinners.
Rise, let us be going:
behold, he is at hand
that doth betray us."

Evangelist

Und als er noch redete, siehe,
da kam Judas, der Zwölfen
einer, und mit ihm eine
grosse Schar, mit Schwertern
und mit Stangen, von den
Hohenpriestern und Aeltesten
des Volks. Und der Verräter
hatte ihnen ein Zeichen
gegeben, und gesagt: "Welchen
ich küssen werde, der ist's,
den greifet." Und alsbald
trat er zu Jesum und sprach:

And while yet he spake,
lo, Judas, one of the
twelve, came, and with him
a great multitude with
swords and staves, from the
chief priests and elders of
the people. Now he that
betrayed him gave them a
sign, saying: "Whomsoever
I shall kiss, that same is
he: hold him fast." And
forthwith he came to Jesus
and said:

Judas

"Gegrüsset seist du, Rabbi!"

"Hail, master!"

Evangelist

Und küssete ihn. Jesus aber
sprach zu ihm:

And kissed him. And Jesus
said to him:

Jesus

"Mein Freund! Warum bist du
kommen?"

"Friend, wherefore art
thou come?"

Evangelist

Da traten sie hinzu und
legten die Hände an Jesum,
und griffen ihn.

Then came they, and laid
hands on Jesus, and took
him.

[No. 33: Duet: soprano and alto with chorus. Text by Picander.]

Soprano and alto

So ist mein Jesus nun
gefangen.
Mond und Licht ist vor
Schmerzen untergangen,

Behold, my Saviour now is
taken.
Moon and stars have for
grief the night forsaken

Weil mein Jesus ist gefangen.	Since my Saviour now is taken.
Sie führen ihn, er ist gebunden!	They lead him hence, with chords they bind him!

Chorus

[Double Chorus]

Lasset ihn, haltet, bindet nicht!	Loose him! Bind him not!
Sind Blitzen, sind Donner in Wolken verschwunden?	Have lightnings and thunders their fury forgotten?
Eröffne den feurigen Abgrund, O Hölle,	Then open, O fathomless pit, all thy terrors!
Zertrümmre, verschlinge,	Destroy them, o'erwhelm them,
Verderbe, zerschelle	Devour them, consume them
Mit plötzlicher Wut	With tumult of rage
Den falschen Verräter, das mördrische Blut!	The treacherous betrayer, the merciless throng!

EXAMPLE 3-6

BACH: RECITATIVE, FROM THE *St. Matthew Passion* (PART I)

EXAMPLE 3-6 (*continued*)

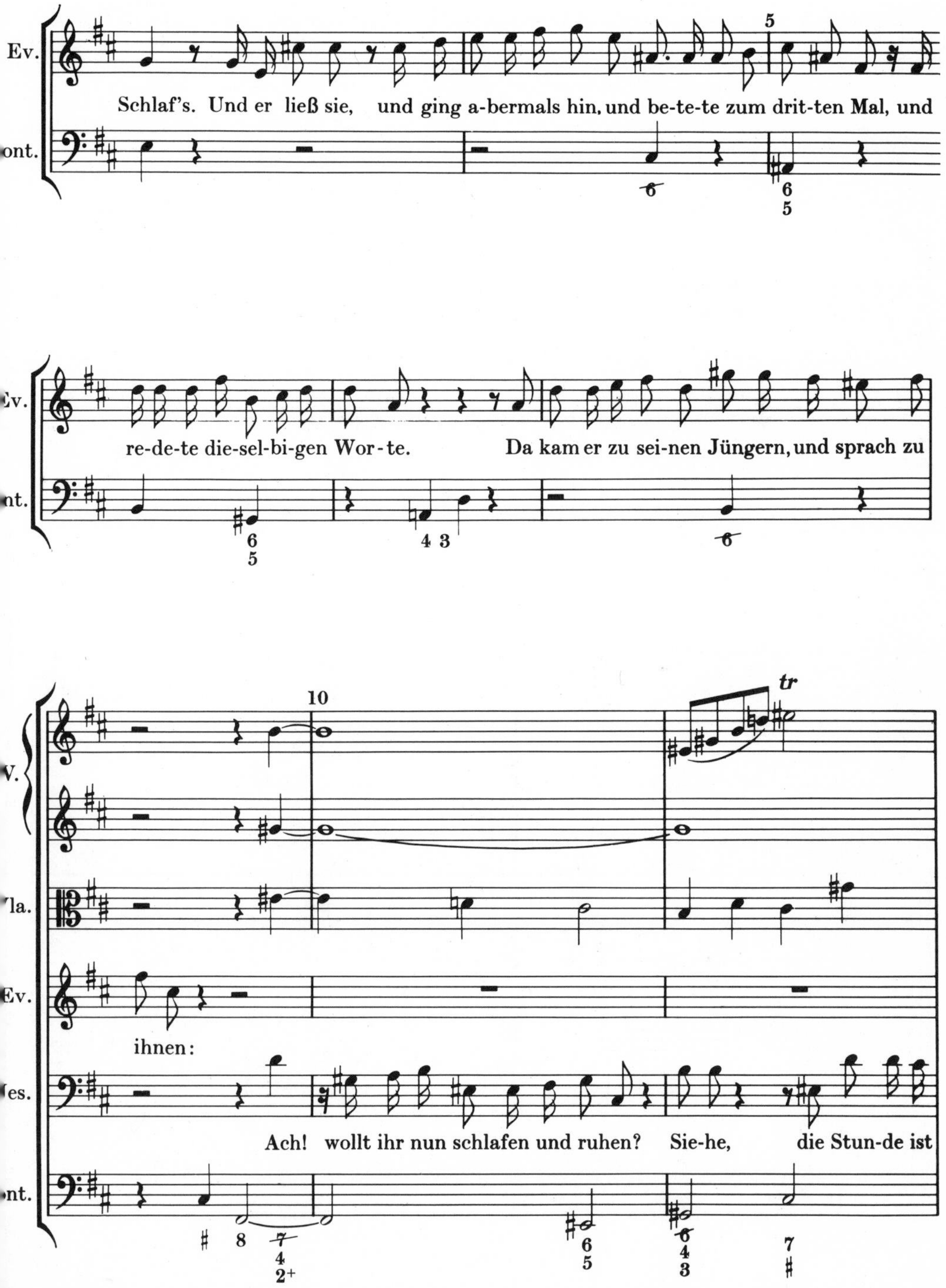

Schlaf's. Und er ließ sie, und ging a-bermals hin, und be-te-te zum drit-ten Mal, und

re-de-te die-sel-bi-gen Wor-te. Da kam er zu sei-nen Jüngern, und sprach zu

ihnen:

Ach! wollt ihr nun schlafen und ruhen? Sie-he, die Stun-de ist

EXAMPLE 3-6 (*continued*)

hier, daß des Menschen Sohn in der Sün-der Hän-de ü - ber - ant - wor-tet

wird. Ste-het auf, las-set uns gehen, sie-he, er ist da, der mich ver-rät.

The Liturgical Vocal Compositions

EXAMPLE 3-6 (*continued*)

Und als er noch re - de - te, sie - he, da kam Ju - das, der Zwöl-fen

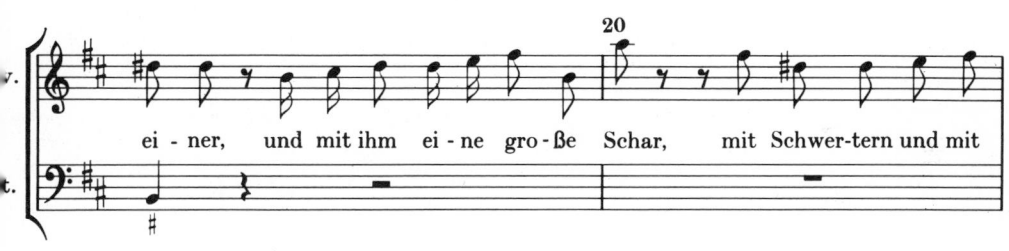

ei - ner, und mit ihm ei - ne gro - ße Schar, mit Schwer-tern und mit

Stangen, von den Hohenpriestern und Äl-te-sten des Volks. Und der Ver-rä-ter hat-te

Bach

EXAMPLE 3-6 *(continued)*

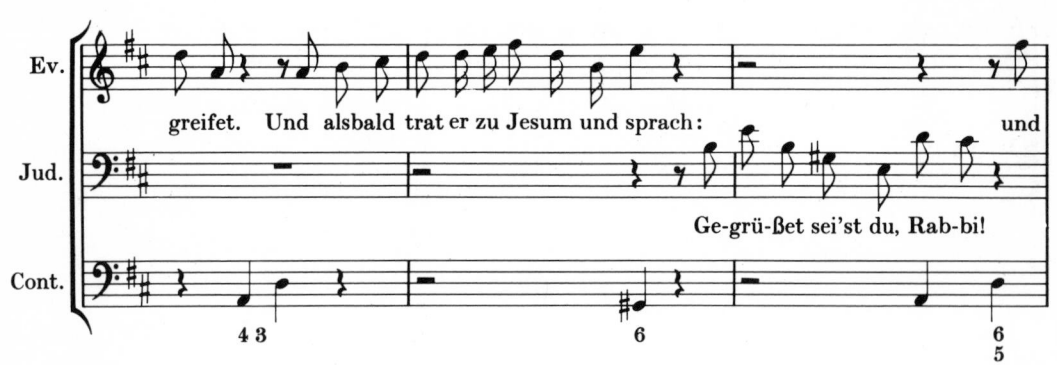

EXAMPLE 3-6 (*concluded*)

Another famous large choral work stylistically related to the cantatas is the Mass in B minor. Its first two movements, the Kyrie and the Gloria, both of which could be included in the Lutheran *Hauptgottesdienst*, were originally composed in 1733 for special commemorative services and were subsequently sent by Bach to the King-Elector of Poland-Saxony at Dresden in the hope of receiving some sort of recognition or reward. In the last years of his life Bach added the remaining movements, in the process frequently incorporating compositions previously written for cantatas, changing their texts and occasionally making other alterations.

This work represents a lengthy setting of the Ordinary of the Mass. Its length results from the fact that each section of the five main portions of the Mass is used to make a complete movement in itself, an aria, a duet, or a choral movement. This type of Mass is known as a *cantata Mass*. There are, however, neither recitatives nor chorales in the Mass. In common with the cantatas, the

Bach

EXAMPLE 3-7

BACH: CREDO, FROM MASS IN B MINOR—EXCERPTS (PIANO REDUCTION OF ORCHESTRAL ACCOMPANIMENT)

1. CRUCIFIXUS—BEGINNING
2. ET RESURREXIT—EXCERPT (FIRST EIGHT BARS OMITTED)

The Liturgical Vocal Compositions

EXAMPLE 3-7 (*continued*)

EXAMPLE 3-7 (*continued*)

emphasis in the Mass goes to the musical expression of the text, as may be strikingly demonstrated from two successive movements in the Credo, the Crucifixus and the Et resurrexit. The Crucifixus affords a good example of the operation of the theory of affections. Two characteristics associated with the musical expression of the affection lamentation or mourning in the Baroque were chromaticism and the use of a *basso ostinato*. Both are found in this movement. Briefly, a *basso ostinato* (obstinate bass) is a bass part which melodically consists of the continuous repetition of a short phrase.[2] The entire Crucifixus is characterized by incessant repetitions of a melodic phrase, four bars in length, rising an octave and then descending in stepwise chromatic motion, all notes of the same duration.[3] Above this ostinato part comes an imitative setting for the chorus, soft, accompanied by flutes and continuo, in which the "sob" or "sigh" (German, *Seufzer*) is an important feature of the melodic material: the descending interval of a second, either major or minor, with the accent on the first note, as on the syllable "fix" of "crucifixus" (see Example 3-7).

It might be mentioned that the Crucifixus movement was taken over by Bach from an earlier cantata, *Weinen, Klagen, Sorgen, Zagen* (Cantata No. 12) of 1724, where it was the first movement, the only change being made in the

EXAMPLE 3-8

GREGORIAN CHANT MELODIES IN BACH'S MASS IN B MINOR

1. CREDO IN UNUM DEUM

2. CONFITEOR UNUM BAPTISMA

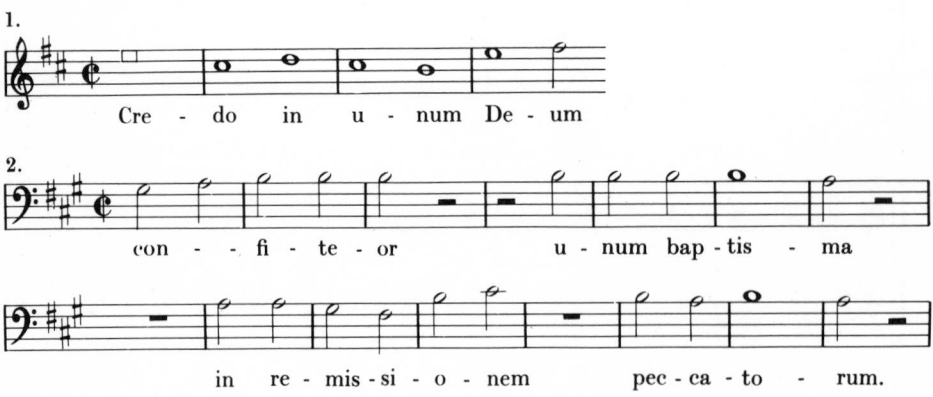

---

[2] Although the ostinato can appear in other parts (soprano, alto, or tenor), it is usually associated with the bass part.

[3] Another well-known piece of Baroque music using a chromatic *basso ostinato* to express the affection lamentation is Purcell's "Dido's Lament," from his opera *Dido and Aeneas* of 1689.

harmonies of the final cadence. This was possible because the affection, lamentation, is in both cases the same. After this somber piece, the sudden joyous onslaught of the Et resurrexit, fortissimo in D major, with trumpets and timpani, fast, with driving sixteenth-note figuration, could scarcely be more effective.

Another aspect of the Mass in B minor must also be mentioned. The first movement of the Credo part, in which Bach presents the text "Credo in unum Deum," is based on a theme in which the slow-moving, largely even rhythm of the notes suggests the old Gregorian chant; and there is in fact a Gregorian chant melody for the Credo that doubtless served as a model for Bach's theme. In another movement of the Credo portion, the Confiteor, Bach likewise introduces, with some modifications, a Gregorian chant melody, first in canon between the bass and the alto and then in the tenor in augmentation. This use of Gregorian chant melodies has been interpreted as an attempt on Bach's part to make the Mass a universal religious expression.

The Organ Music

The most strictly liturgical type in Bach's organ music is known as the *chorale prelude* or *organ chorale*. In principle this represents nothing new, since at bottom the chorale prelude is nothing more than a cantus firmus setting for organ based on a hymn melody used to introduce the singing of the hymn by the congregation (hence, a "prelude"). The largest collection of chorale preludes composed and assembled by Bach is the *Orgelbüchlein* (Little Organ Book), a project he worked on in 1713–14, when he was employed at Weimar. It contains some forty-five pieces arranged in accordance with the church year, beginning with Advent, continuing through Epiphany, Lent, Easter, Whitsunday, Trinity, and so on. Although this collection, which Bach did not complete, remained in manuscript during his life, two other smaller collections were published: the third part of the *Clavierübung*, published in 1739, and the six chorale preludes published in Jena by Schübler between 1746 and 1750. At the end of his life he planned to publish another set of eighteen.

In these works, most often the hymn melody appears in one voice, while the others form an accompaniment. This type is represented, for instance, by the chorale prelude for Good Friday, *Christ lag in Todesbanden* (Christ Lay in the Bonds of Death) in the *Orgelbüchlein*; the hymn melody is in the uppermost voice, and the chords in the accompaniment, which involves chromatic harmonies, are broken up by constant figuration. But many variations are possible. The accompaniment can become elaborate, and sometimes the various phrases of the hymn melody are treated in accordance with the procedure of through-imitation, which we have seen in the motet of the Renaissance and in some of Bach's own cantata movements. Alternatively, the hymn

EXAMPLE 3-9

BACH: "Christ lag in Todesbanden," FROM THE *Orgelbüchlein*

EXAMPLE 3-9 (*continued*)

EXAMPLE 3-10

Bach: "In dulci jubilo," from the *Orgelbüchlein*

EXAMPLE 3-10 (*continued*)

EXAMPLE 3-10 (*concluded*)

melody itself may be ornamented, or it may be treated in canon between two voices, to which the remaining voices provide the contrapuntal accompaniment.

Usually the expression of a single affection governs the entire piece. In the chorale prelude on the Christmas hymn "In dulci jubilo," the quiet happiness of the occasion is represented by the lilting triplet figuration, which accompanies the canonic presentation of the hymn melody in two voices; the two voice-parts of the accompaniment are also in canon up to bar 25.

Completely different is the striking symbolic representation of sin in the chorale prelude "Durch Adam's Fall ist ganz verderbt" (Through Adam's Fall All Was Spoiled), in which the descending diminished seventh leaps in the bass supposedly represent Adam's fall from grace, and the long winding chromatic inner parts, which some commentators regard as the musical depiction of a serpent, stand for sin. The hymn melody is in the uppermost voice.

The other principal genre in Bach's organ music, less closely linked to the liturgy, is generically known as the *toccata* or the *toccata type* (from the Italian *toccare*, to touch). This category has a long tradition in organ music, going back at least to the fifteenth century. Unlike the chorale prelude, it is a free form and it stresses the improvisational, the fantastic, the rhapsodic, and the virtuosic. It represents the oldest type of virtuoso display or "showpiece" for

EXAMPLE 3-11

BACH: "Durch Adam's Fall," FROM THE *Orgelbüchlein*

The Organ Music

EXAMPLE 3-11 (*continued*)

EXAMPLE 3-12

BACH: TOCCATA IN D MINOR—EXCERPTS

1. THE BEGINNING

2. THE MIDDLE

1.

EXAMPLE 3-12 (*continued*)

2.

EXAMPLE 3-12 (*concluded*)

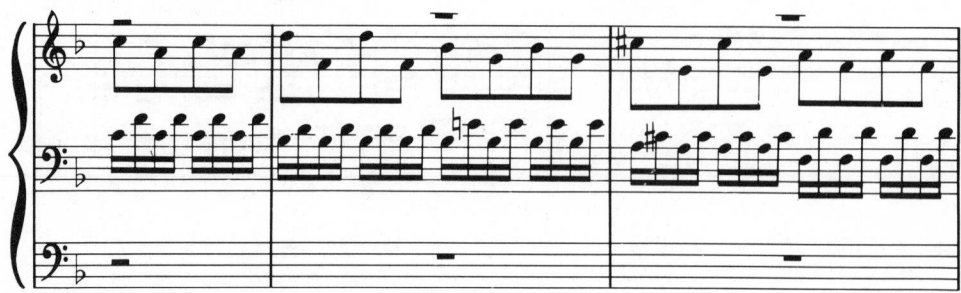

keyboard, and exploits those features most *idiomatic* (most readily playable and most effective) for the keyboard. A toccata will abound in scale passages moving up and down the full extent of the keyboard, alternating with loud and dense chords; a favorite device is to sustain a bass note by means of the pedal, while rapid scale figuration or chords are played above it, often creating striking effects, even dissonances, with the held note (such a long, sustained note in the bass is for this reason called a *pedal point* or *organ point*). This style has become known as *toccata style*. In the sixteenth century it became customary to include in such a piece passages in imitative counterpoint—i.e., fugal passages—so that two different stylistic types, the toccata style and the fugue style, appear in alternation, usually in a five-part scheme: the toccata style at the beginning, middle and end; the fugal sections in between. It seems that the toccata—in particular reference to those passages in toccata style—is the outgrowth of improvisation, in which the performer would naturally do what was idiomatic for the instrument. This circumstance helps to account for the loose organization found in some of these compositions.

As a typical example let us take Bach's well-known Toccata in D minor, composed around 1708 in Weimar or Arnstadt. Here the rhapsodic, quasi-improvisational display is seen at its most characteristic. In the fugal sections the themes are long and built out of figuration which is submitted to a rhythmic pattern featuring regularly recurring accents, so that the music seems to keep driving itself on and on. Excerpts are given in Example 3-12.

The terminology concerning the toccata is confusing, since a number of different terms are used in referring to it. Most common is *prelude and fugue*, whereby the prelude is in toccata style followed by the fugue; but this is often unsatisfactory, since the prelude may have fugal passages, whereas the fugue may have passages in toccata style. Another term meaning the same thing, so far as Baroque music is concerned, is *fantasia*, or *fantasia and fugue*. Still another is *toccata and fugue*, which is not entirely satisfactory, since there are not always two separate movements, and all one needs is simply the designation *toccata*. Where there are two separate pieces, it is assumed that the prelude (or fantasia) was employed as a prelude to the *Hauptgottesdienst* as a whole, the fugue coming as a postlude.

Somewhat different, but at least similar in function, is the Passacaglia and Fugue in C minor, composed in 1716 or 1717, either in the last year at Weimar or the first at Cöthen. Here the toccata has been replaced by an elaborate dance form, the passacaglia. Apart from its moderate triple time, the characteristic feature of the passacaglia is its *ostinato* structure: The repeating melody (Bach's is eight bars long and represents the expansion of a passacaglia theme previously used in a composition by the French organist André Raison, d. 1719) appears first by itself in the bass part, then is repeated as the upper voices bring in new thematic material, which is varied with each repetition of the ostinato melody. During the course of the work the ostinato moves to the upper voices as well, but by the end (there are in all twenty-one statements of the ostinato melody) it has returned to the bass. There follows an elaborate fugue whose principal theme is a variation of the passacaglia theme.[4]

EXAMPLE 3-13

BACH: PASSACAGLIA AND FUGUE IN C MINOR —EXCERPTS

1. PASSACAGLIA—BEGINNING

2. FUGUE—BEGINNING

[4] Another elaborate ostinato composition by Bach is the Chaconne, the last movement of the Partita in D minor for unaccompanied violin.

EXAMPLE 3-13 (*continued*)

EXAMPLE 3-13 (*continued*)

2.

Thema fugatum

EXAMPLE 3-13 (*concluded*)

The Harpsichord and Clavichord Music

First we have to deal with one of Bach's most celebrated collections, a set on which his reputation in the late eighteenth and early nineteenth centuries was based, and which today is regarded as one of his most important and characteristic works: *The Well-Tempered Clavier* (*Das wohltemperierte Clavier*), in two volumes, the first dating from around 1722, the second apparently from around 1744. The expression "well-tempered" has to do with Bach's intention that the newly devised system of *equal temperament* be used in tuning the instrument on which the pieces are performed. To explain this, a short account of temperament is necessary. If one takes mathematically correct fifths and proceeds through the whole circle of fifths (see pages 8–9), when one gets back to a C, this C will *not* be exactly in tune with the C with which one started,[5] so that for musical purposes it is necessary to adjust, to "temper," the intervals somewhat. The system in use from the Renaissance up to the early eighteenth century, the *mean-tone temperament*, employed almost, but not quite, mathematically correct fifths, and thirds that were somewhat too large; but it had the disadvantage that if the music became too chromatic, or if the key signatures got into three or four flats and sharps, then things would sound out of tune. In equal temperament the octave is simply divided into twelve equal semitones, and although the thirds and fifths are not mathematically exact, they are serviceable enough so that one can play in any key and be as chromatic as desired without sounding out of tune. This system of temperament is still in use. Each volume of *The Well-Tempered Clavier* consists of paired preludes and fugues, successively in all the major and minor keys; hence there are twenty-four preludes and fugues in each volume, forty-eight in both (or in all a total of ninety-six separate compositions). The term *clavier* was at the time a generic designation for keyboard instruments in

[5] Specifically, it will be an eighth-tone sharp.

The Harpsichord and Clavichord Music

general, so that these compositions may with equal validity be played on the organ, harpsichord, or the clavichord. By the same token, there is no inherent objection to performance on the piano, assuming the performer has some knowledge of performance practices relating to Baroque music.

In this collection a prelude, although in principle the same as a piece in toccata style, in general is a shorter piece, usually one continuous whole in which a single thematic pattern (melodic and rhythmic motive) runs all the way through. Often, as in the larger toccata, these thematic patterns are based on standard—idiomatic—types of keyboard figuration. Usually the modulations are elaborate and wide-ranging. The fugues are essentially the same as previously explained: imitative contrapuntal pieces for keyboard. In most cases they are monothematic (i.e., they employ a single theme, which in the normal terminology used for fugues is called the subject) and employ now and then the "learned" devices of counterpoint: *inversion* (turning the intervals of the theme upside down), *augmentation* (doubling the note values of the theme), *diminution* (cutting the note values of the theme in half), *retrograde motion* (the theme appears upside down and backward); the last two are relatively infrequent in Bach's *Well-Tempered Clavier*. These devices were developed by the Netherlands composers of the Renaissance and have remained a part of contrapuntal practice ever since, even though some of them are used infrequently. Another common contrapuntal device, used so much that it is not regarded as "learned," is *stretto*, a term that apart from its usual meaning of "acceleration" has a special meaning with reference to imitative counterpoint: shortening the time interval at which one voice imitates another so that an intensity of contrapuntal activity is produced. If, when the fugue begins, the second voice imitates the first after an interval of four bars, then later in a stretto passage this interval may be shortened to two bars, or one bar, or possibly less. A fugue subject is often varied in other ways: It may be varied melodically, by adding, omitting, or changing notes, or rhythmically; or it may be broken down and a motive extracted which is then used by itself. Generally in the second half of a fugue, about two thirds or three quarters of the way through, the subject in its original key will be introduced, often with stretto, and this has the effect of recalling the opening and, in a way, rounds off the composition.[6]

As an example, let us take the Prelude and Fugue in C minor from *The Well-Tempered Clavier* (Book II, No. 2). The prelude, in binary (two-part) form, displays the rhythmic consistency associated with this category of composition: figuration, both stepwise and arpeggiated (broken chords), with sixteenth notes in one part against eighth notes in the other, characterizes the principal thematic material; the first part ends in the relative major, E-flat major. In the fugue, for four voices (which will be designated soprano,

---

[6] Such a passage may also be called a *recapitulation*.

alto, tenor, and bass), we have a subject that is short, begins on an upbeat, moves in an even eighth-note rhythm except for the sixteenths toward the end, and stresses the fifth and third of the C minor triad: The melodic motion is stepwise except for the leaps of a third and of a fifth. The subject appears first in the alto and is varied when the soprano enters in the second bar. The fugue as a whole appears to fall into three clearly defined sections: The first is quite long, embracing half of the composition, cadencing in G minor (bar 14); the second part of the fugue continues until the cadence in C minor (bar 23); and the third comprises the rest of the piece. In the first section the subject first is stated in all four voices in what would be regarded as the exposition, and then is presented three more times (first in the soprano in rhythmically varied form, bars 8 and 9) against freely invented accompanying thematic material. The second part presents the subject not only in stretto but also in augmentation (alto, bars 14–15, and bass, bars 19–20) and in inversion (tenor, bar 15, and bass, bar 21). In the concluding part of the fugue, which is in the original key, C minor, the subject appears in the soprano and alto in stretto (bars 23–24), while a motive from it is used in the tenor; a toccatalike flourish brings the conclusion.

EXAMPLE 3-14

BACH: PRELUDE AND FUGUE IN C MINOR, FROM *The Well-Tempered Clavier* (BOOK II, NO. 2)

1. PRELUDE

2. FUGUE

1.

The Harpsichord and Clavichord Music

EXAMPLE 3-14 (*continued*)

Example 3-14 (*continued*)

2.

The Harpsichord and Clavichord Music

EXAMPLE 3-14 (*continued*)

EXAMPLE 3-14 (*concluded*)

Some of the compositions in *The Well-Tempered Clavier* are long, elaborate, intensely serious and demanding works. As an example, there is the
Prelude and Fugue in C-sharp minor from Book I. Here the prelude again
reveals the use of the same thematic material throughout, but its character is
lyrical. The elaborate five-voice fugue introduces during its course three
different themes which are presented simultaneously in contrapuntal combination: (1) a slow, evenly moving chromatic theme; (2) a theme based on
scale figuration (bar 36); (3) a theme characterized by the upward leap of a
fourth at its beginning (bar 49). All appear in contrapuntal combination in the
passage beginning at bar 51. The fugue, which also contains stretto, may be
called a *triple fugue.*

The other important group of Bach's harpsichord and clavichord compositions are the suites of dances, the bulk of which is formed by three sets of six:
the *English suites*, the *French suites* and the partitas; in addition there is one
more, the *Overture in the French Manner*, a suite in B minor. The "English"

EXAMPLE 3-15

BACH: FUGUE IN C-SHARP MINOR FROM *The Well-Tempered Clavier* (BOOK
I, No. 4)—BEGINNING

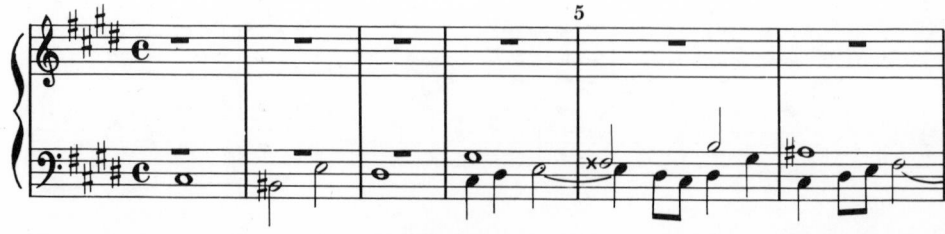

The Harpsichord and Clavichord Music

EXAMPLE 3-15 (*continued*)

EXAMPLE 3-15 (*continued*)

EXAMPLE 3-15 (*concluded*)

and "French" suites—as yet no satisfactory explanation of these designations in this context has been put forward—were composed during Bach's stay in Cöthen, but they remained in manuscript during his life, whereas the partitas and the Suite in B minor (known simply as the *French Overture*), composed in the late 1720's and early 1730's, were included in the *Clavierübung*, the composer's largest published collection of his keyboard works.

The term *suite* in the Baroque refers to a large work consisting of a number of dances in the same key; this use of the same key throughout provides the principal element of unity, although some suites are also cyclic using the same thematic material, often in varied form, in some or all of the dances. The suite, particularly associated with French harpsichord music, was cultivated in the seventeenth century by Jacques Champion de Chambonnières (c. 1602–1672), Louis Couperin (c. 1626–1661) and Jean-Henri d'Anglebert (1635–1691), as well as by the Viennese Johann Froberger (1616–1667), who spent time in France and whose work seems to have provided the model for the harpsichord suites of Bach. Among French contemporaries of Bach who worked with the suite we should mention Francois Couperin, known as *le grand* (1668–1733), and Jean-Philippe Rameau (1683–1764); the latter important in the establishment of the "tertian system" of harmony based on triads. Bach's suites, however, are far more elaborate harmonically and contrapuntally than those written by most of his predecessors and contemporaries, to say nothing of his successors.

In the posthumously published suites by Froberger, which appeared in 1697, a certain order and arrangement of dances was used, an order that remained standard for the suite. There are four basic dances, alternating slow with fast or moderately fast, as follows:

Allemande: a slow to moderate dance in duple time.
Courante: a moderately rapid dance in triple time.
Sarabande: a very slow dance in triple time, usually employing dotted rhythms.
Gigue: a very fast dance in compound triple time (six-eight), also frequently in dotted rhythm.

The courante and the gigue had Italian counterparts that were sometimes used in suites, the *corrente* and the *giga*. The courante usually was in three-two time and was rhythmically elaborate, whereas the corrente moved rather simply in three-quarter time; the gigue frequently employed imitative counterpoint, whereas the giga did not. Other dances were inserted between the sarabande and the gigue, and sometimes elsewhere as well; it is impossible here to state generally which dances or how many, but among the most common of these dances are

Minuet: a moderate dance in triple time.
Gavotte: a moderate, regular dance, in duple time.
Bourrée: a fast, regular dance, also in duple time.

Sometimes a dance in a suite will be followed by another of the same kind, which may be called a *trio*, after which the first dance is to be repeated.[7] In many suites there will be an introductory movement in the nature of an overture or prelude, which often takes a form something like that of the toccata.

In general, the individual dances of a suite display the following characteristics: The form is binary, each dance being divided more or less in the middle by a double bar, and each half is marked by repeat signs. During the first part a modulation is made to the dominant or relative major if the dance is in a minor key, and in the second part after some modulatory excursions a return is made to the tonic. Usually in thematic organization the two halves run parallel to each other, so that, if diagrammed, the binary form of the suite dance would look like this:

$$\|: \quad a \quad :\| \quad \|: \quad a' \qquad :\|$$
$$\text{Keys: I}\text{——V} \quad \text{Modulates—I}$$

Sometimes the second part will be essentially different thematically from the first, making the scheme:

$$\|: \quad a \quad :\| \quad \|: \quad b \quad :\|$$

---

[7] The term *trio* comes from orchestral music, in which such a dance was often scored for three woodwind instruments.

Finally, it will often happen that the second part either will begin with new thematic material or else will present the original thematic material in a varied form, after which, when the tonic is reestablished, the theme appears in something close to its original form: This common type is known as *rounded binary form:*

$$\text{||: a :|| ||: b \qquad a \qquad :||}$$
Keys: I—V   Modulates——I—I
(or VI)

For the rest, a suite dance is usually homophonic, a melodic line in the uppermost voice part with a harmonic accompaniment; but in the accompaniment the part-writing is usually elaborate and incorporates contrapuntal imitation. What is most characteristic is that the melodic line is ornamented or embellished with a number of common devices, trills, turns, mordents, and so on, sometimes indicated by the composer, sometimes not, but which nonetheless constitute an important part of these compositions. Some of the most common ornaments (or *agréments*) are given in Example 3–16.

EXAMPLE 3-16

COMMON ORNAMENTS

Name	Written	Performed
Appoggiatura		
French: *port de voix* or *coulé*		
German: *Vorschlag*		
*Mordent		
French: *pincé*		
Turn		
French: *double cadence* or *brisé*		
German: *Doppelschlag*		
Slide (also slur or double appoggiatura)		
French: *coulé sur un tierce*		
German: *Schliefer*		
†Trill (also shake)		
French: *cadence* or *tremblement*		
German: *Triller*		
Italian: *trillo*		

* The inverted mordent (*Schneller*) was of German origin.
   † The trill could be prefixed with an appogiatura, producing the *tremblement appuyé* or *vorbereitete Triller*, and terminated with a turnlike figure (the *Nachschlag*). The short trill consisting of but four notes (the *Pralltriller*) went out of use at the end of the eighteenth century.

As an example let us consider the Partita in E minor (No. 6) by Bach. This work, which with one exception follows the normal scheme of the suite in the arrangement of the dances, contains the following: an introductory piece called toccata, an allemande, a corrente, an air (an instrumental piece in the style of a song), a sarabande, a gavotte (as the added dance), and a concluding gigue (French form, in imitative counterpoint). The toccata begins with a passage in what we have been calling toccata style, displaying figuration, first of the broken-chord type, then scales, first separately then combined; then there commences a long four-voice fugue with extended free episodes, and at the end a recapitulation of the passage in toccata style. In the allemande a highly figured melodic line is treated contrapuntally. The corrente is an example of the Italian form, lively, in simple triple meter. The lyrical high point of the work is reached with the sarabande, with its ornate but expressive melodic line, chromatic harmonies and dotted rhythms. The gavotte is in a brisk, sturdy duple time. The concluding gigue, an elaborate example of the French type but in duple meter, displays an unusually chromatic theme with wide leaps treated in imitation; after the double bar this theme is presented in inversion.

EXAMPLE 3-17

BACH: PARTITA IN E MINOR—EXCERPTS

1. TOCCATA—BEGINNING

2. TOCCATA—FUGAL PORTION, BEGINNING

3. ALLEMANDE—BEGINNING

4. CORRENTE—BEGINNING

5. SARABANDE—BEGINNING

6. GIGUE—BEGINNING

1.

The Harpsichord and Clavichord Music

EXAMPLE 3-17 (*continued*)

Example 3-17 (*continued*)

3.

EXAMPLE 3-17 (*continued*)

Example 3-17 (*concluded*)

The Instrumental Ensemble Music

Here we have to distinguish two principal kinds, *chamber music* and *orchestral music*. Generally speaking, chamber music refers to a group of instrumental soloists (one instrument and player to a part), whereas in orchestral music there is more than one instrument and player to most of the parts, especially in the strings. In the Baroque the standard combination for chamber music was the *trio sonata*, an ensemble consisting of two melodic instruments (two violins, violin and flute, two flutes, and so on) and the continuo. But there were also sonatas for a single instrument and continuo, and sonatas for an unaccompanied melodic instrument. From the standpoint of form, two main types are to be distinguished: the *sonata da chiesa* and the *sonata da camera* (the church sonata and the chamber sonata, respectively). The former, the *sonata da chiesa*, often known simply as *sonata*, is a composition consisting of four movements in the order: slow—fast—slow—fast. These could be homophonic or fugal.[8] The *sonata da camera*, often known as *partita*, is much the

---

[8] An example of this form in the trio sonata medium is discussed below, see pp. 167-70.

The Instrumental Ensemble Music

same as a suite—i.e., a succession of dances, all in the same key. Both types of sonata were developed in the late seventeenth century by composers like Arcangelo Corelli (1653–1713) and Antonio Vivaldi (c. 1678–1741). The distinction between the two types is rigorously made in Bach's set of six sonatas and partitas for the unaccompanied violin, composed in Cöthen.

Then there is the music for orchestra, which likewise appears in two principal forms: the suite and the concerto. The suites, of which Bach composed four are as follows: No. 1 in C major, No. 2 in B minor (for solo flute with string orchestra), No. 3 in D major, and No. 4 in D major, are similar to the harpsichord suites already discussed except that both the order of the dances and the varieties of formal types are more flexible and that all four of the suites for orchestra begin with an elaborate piece of a type known as a *French overture*. This kind of overture, which goes back to Lully in seventeenth-century France, presents two different styles of music in alternation: a homophonic part, using dense and impressive chords in slow and sometimes ponderous dotted rhythms, establishing a majestic effect; there follows a fast fugal part. In some instances the slow homophonic character is brought back at the end. As example we may mention the Suite No. 3 in D major for an orchestra consisting of two oboes, three trumpets, tympani, strings, and continuo. It opens with a large French overture, after which come an air (see page 140), a pair of gavottes, a bourrée, and a concluding gigue.

The other form of orchestral music in Bach is the concerto, which in most cases appears as the *concerto grosso*, the most characteristic form of orchestral music in the Baroque. This form, which was also developed by Italian composers in the late seventeenth century, especially Antonio Vivaldi, goes back to the concertato (polychoral) principle of the Venetian School of around 1600 (see pages 74–75). Here there are two groups of instrumentalists: the group of soloists (usually two violins, but the size and composition of the group can vary) and the orchestra; the former, the soloists, was known as the *soli* or the *concertino*, the latter, the orchestra, was called the *tutti* (all), *ripieno* (full), or simply the concerto grosso. The two groups then play together and in alternation. The concerto grosso as it appeared in the work of Vivaldi—who exerted a profound influence on Bach—was a three-movement form, in the succession fast—slow—fast. It is in the fast movements that the alternation between the soloists and the tutti is the clearest. In a general way the formal plan of these fast movements owed something to the da capo aria, even though the exact repetition characteristic of that form is not present. The tutti will usually open with what is called the ritornello, generally rather extensive, after which the soli enter, often with different thematic material; the two then proceed in alternation and combination, going through different keys, with opportunity given the soli for virtuoso display, until the ritornello appears in its original form and key, after which the movement comes to an end. This procedure is called *ritornello form*:

	Tutti	Soli	Tutti	Free alternation	Tutti
	Ritornello	[New theme?]	Ritornello (short)		Ritornello
Keys:	I	V (or III)	Indefinite	Modulates	I

The section characterized by free alternation may be quite long. In the slow movements, the alternation between the tutti and soli is less pronounced, indeed is often completely absent. Sometimes a slow movement will be a kind of instrumental aria for one or more of the soli, sometimes it will be a slow fugal piece for the soli alone, without involving the orchestra. Although the concerto grosso was the standard type of concerto in the Baroque, there were also solo concertos, for one soloist instead of a group; otherwise the form remained essentially the same.

The thematic writing in these concertos is characteristic of late Baroque music: The melodic lines are long, they operate with repeating patterns which usually are short, clear, and simple, with regularly recurring accentuations used over and over again, moving through different keys. Such themes are frequently based on figuration, scales, and arpeggios of the kind that are idiomatic for the string instruments. This principle, the consistent use of a thematic motive and rhythmic pattern, often described by the German term *Fortspinnung* (spinning forth), is related to the doctrine of the affections (see pages 89–90). It produced the unity and consistency that was characteristic of Baroque compositions. This style was taken over by Bach from the concertos of Vivaldi, and is to be seen not only in his orchestral compositions but in his keyboard works as well: He made transcriptions for organ of some of Vivaldi's concertos, and passages in an orchestral style frequently appear in the larger toccatas for organ composed in Weimar and earlier; there is also a composition for harpsichord, the *Concerto in the Italian Style*, in F major (S. 971), published in the *Clavierübung*, which is also in the orchestral style.

Bach produced a number of concertos for instrumental ensemble, for one solo instrument, and for several, some original, others arrangements of concertos by other composers, notably Vivaldi. His most important group is the set of six concerti grossi known as the *Brandenburg Concertos*, composed in 1721 and dedicated to the *Markgraf* of Brandenburg. These are No. 1 in F major, for solo violin, horns, oboes, bassoon, and string orchestra; No. 2 in F major, for a solo group consisting of flute, oboe, trumpet, and violin and a string orchestra; No. 3 in G major, for strings; No. 4 in G major, for a solo group consisting of two flutes (recorders) and one violin, with an orchestra of strings; No. 5 in D major, for a solo group consisting of flute, violin and harpsichord, and an orchestra of strings; and No. 6 in B-flat major, for a string orchestra composed of violas, violoncellos, and double basses (i.e., just the lower strings). It will be noted that only three of the Brandenburg Concertos employ the opposition between a set group of soli and the orchestral tutti (Nos. 2, 4, and 5); in the others the concerto principle operates between the various sections of the orchestra. The Italian three-movement form (fast—slow—fast) is used in all but No. 1 (in four movements, some of them dances) and No. 3 (two movements). Furthermore, the Italian thematic types dominate. The instrumentation, however, particularly the choice of instruments for the solo groups, is not typically Italian; the use of the harpsichord as a member of the solo group (No. 5) is especially unusual.

As an example, let us look at the *Brandenburg Concerto No. 2* in F major, with its group of soli composed of flute, oboe, trumpet, and violin, along with

EXAMPLE 3-18

BACH: CONCERTO GROSSO IN F MAJOR (*Brandenburg Concerto No. 2*)—
  EXCERPTS

1. FIRST MOVEMENT—BEGINNING

2. ANDANTE—BEGINNING

1.

EXAMPLE 3-18 (*continued*)

EXAMPLE 3-18 (*continued*)

Example 3-18 (*continued*)

The Instrumental Ensemble Music

EXAMPLE 3-18 (*continued*)

EXAMPLE 3-18 (*continued*)

EXAMPLE 3-18 (*continued*)

EXAMPLE 3-18 (*continued*)

The Instrumental Ensemble Music

EXAMPLE 3-18 (*continued*)

EXAMPLE 3-18 (*continued*)

The Instrumental Ensemble Music

EXAMPLE 3-18 (*concluded*)

2.

a tutti of strings. The work is in the usual three movements, the outer movements fast and in the tonic, the middle movement slow and in the relative minor, D minor. The characteristic ritornello form appears in the two fast movements, while in the slow movement three of the solo instruments (the trumpet and the tutti are omitted) engage in an imitative trio to the accompaniment of the continuo (so that the slow movement may be regarded as a piece of chamber music). In the first movement, the ritornello played by the tutti makes the beginning; then each of the solo instruments is introduced in succession, their entrances being separated by the ritornello. The theme of the ritornello and the theme of the solo group are different, and this thematic contrast runs throughout the movement. The high, brilliant, piercing sound of the trumpet (brass playing has always been prominent in German musical life) with its difficult, rapid figuration endows the whole with a characteristically bright sound. Toward the end of the movement the ritornello reappears in the original key, and one has the feeling of a return to the beginning. The slow movement has already been briefly characterized. The third, and last, movement (the finale) is much like the first, except that it is shorter and monothematic; it opens with a fugal passage for the solo instruments which are then joined by the tutti, the rhythmic activity continuing unabated to the end.

The Late Works

As a cantor, Bach had always to be concerned with teaching and hence with didactic music. Perhaps the most important such work is the *Well-Tempered Clavier*; others are the *Two-* and *Three-Part Inventions*, known to keyboard students the world around. Although some of the suites for clavier seem also to have been didactic in intent, most of these didactic works are, to a greater or lesser extent, contrapuntal. It is the old art of contrapuntal imitation, developed by the Netherlands composers of the late fifteenth century and continued ever since as the proper style for serious music in general and sacred music in particular, that provides the basis for the didactic work of Bach.

Counterpoint, as has been seen, plays an important part in Bach's music generally, and in this he was somewhat out of step with the taste of his time; indeed it was this quality in his music that aroused the antagonism of the rector, Ernesti. Nonetheless, in Bach's late works preoccupation with the strictest contrapuntal forms excluded virtually everything else. It is as if all other forms of musical expression were renounced as the old master turned to the resources of the strictest and possibly purest of all musical procedures—counterpoint and canon. Among the works we can mention here are the Aria with Thirty Variations for harpsichord (*The Goldberg Variations*), which was published in 1742 as the fourth part of the *Clavierübung*; the canonic varia-

The Late Works

tions on *Vom Himmel hoch, da komm' ich her*, for organ; the *Musical Offering*; and the *Art of Fugue*. Both *The Goldberg Variations* and the canonic variations present variation form in conjunction with canon, whereas the *Art of Fugue* is a large but incomplete cycle of fugal compositions, all of which are based on the same theme, presumably intended for keyboard.

The *Musical Offering* presents the most variety among these late compositions of Bach. In a way it is the souvenir of a visit Bach made to the court of Frederick the Great at Berlin in 1747. During the visit Bach improvised a fugal composition to a theme given him by the Prussian king, who was something of an amateur musician (he played the flute). Upon his return to Leipzig, Bach set about the composition of a large group of complex works based on this theme, the group as a whole being published as a "musical offering" from the composer to the king. The full title in Latin forms an acrostic: *Regis Iussu Cantio Et Reliquae Canonica Arte Resoluta*,[9] or *ricercar*, a term which refers to a fugal form cultivated in the sixteenth and seventeenth centuries, which by the eighteenth century had acquired the connotation of a learned composition in imitative counterpoint. The two large fugal pieces in the *Musical Offering* are based on the *tema regis* (the theme given Bach by the king), one at the beginning, the other at the end, both apparently for keyboard; in the middle stands a large trio sonata of the *sonata da chiesa* type, and in between are two groups of canons, all based on the *tema regis* as well. The whole, thus, is arranged symmetrically:[10]

1. Ricercar, for three voices.
   First group of five canons.
      2. Canon perpetuus a 2.
      3. Canon a 2 violini in unisono.
      4. Canon a 2 violini per motum contrarium.
      5. Canon a 2 per augmentationem, contrario motu.
      6. Canon a 2 per tonos.

7. Sonata a 3.
   Second group of five canons: Thematiis regii elaborationes canonicae.
      8. Canon perpetuus a 2.
      9. Canon a 2.
      10. Canon a 2. Quaerendo invenietis.
      11. Canon a 4.
      12. Fuga canonica in epidiapente.

13. Ricercar, for six voices.

---

[9] The translation: At the King's command, the theme and the rest worked out in canonic form.

[10] This order is obscured both in the original edition and in that of the *Bach-Gesellschaft*.

It is assumed that the first ricercar is presented here substantially as Bach originally improvised it in the presence of the king.

The canons present characteristic examples of this strict and often abstruse musical form. They appear in two groups: The first, preceding the sonata, comprises canons accompanied by the *tema regis*, and the second, following the sonata, contains canons in which the *tema regis* itself is used as the subject. A few of these canons may be explained here in greater detail. The very first (No. 2 of the work as a whole), called *canon perpetuus* (perpetual canon), is simply a two-voice canon accompanied by a simple statement of the *tema regis*. Another canon in this group presents in one voice the *tema regis* in varied form, while the two other voices engage in a canon that involves both inversion and augmentation (No. 5). The last canon of this group (No. 6) is a "spiral" canon, since with each repetition it moves up a whole step (thus, *per tonos*), hence after six statements reaches the key in which it started, but an octave higher. In the second group are two- and four-voice canons on the *tema regis*, one of which involves retrograde motion (No. 9) and another of which, bearing the annotation "Quaerendo invenietis" ("seek and find"), may be realized in four different ways, depending upon whether the subject is presented as it is written or in inversion and upon when the following voice enters.

EXAMPLE 3-19

BACH: CANONS, FROM THE *Musical Offering*

No. 2. CANON PERPETUUS A 2

No. 5. CANON A 2 PER AUGMENTATIONEM, CONTRARIO MOTU

No. 6. CANON A 2 PER TONOS

No. 9. CANON A 2

Canon

EXAMPLE 3-19 (*continued*)

Bach

EXAMPLE 3-19 (*continued*)

Resolution

The Late Works

EXAMPLE 3-19 (*continued*)

EXAMPLE 3-19 (*continued*)

Canon

EXAMPLE 3-19 (*continued*)

Resolution

EXAMPLE 3-19 (*continued*)

The Late Works

EXAMPLE 3-19 (*concluded*)

As the large centerpiece of this work stands the *sonata da chiesa* for flute, violin, and continuo, perhaps the largest and most impressive example of the whole genre. All the movements display imitative counterpoint, and the continuo part is frequently involved in the unfolding of the thematic material of the composition. The *tema regis* appears in two movements of the work: in the second movement, in the long slow notes characteristic of the old style of setting a cantus firmus; and in the fourth, the principal thematic material of which is a variation of the theme. In the treatment of the *tema regis*, therefore, the second movement is associated with the first group of canons, and the fourth movement with the second (see Example 3-20).

As mentioned earlier, Bach's preoccupation with counterpoint characterized his work as a whole, endowing it with the "learned" quality so remarked at the time. But along with this he also shared in the commonly agreed-upon aesthetic goal of the time—that music was to express the affections, and for this, as has been indicated, there existed a number of conventions, of which Bach generally availed himself. To music, then, was imputed the power of symbolizing, of representing, the various affections. We have seen that music was regarded as symbolic by the ancient Greeks—symbolic of human emotions, indeed of all things that exist in the universe. But there is some evidence that Bach's music has symbolic aspects not involved with the affections. We know that Bach was interested in numerology and that at the time there was practiced a system of representing letters of the alphabet by numerals, thus:

A	B	C	D	E	F	G	H	I or	J	K	L	etc.
1	2	3	4	5	6	7	8	9		10	11	etc.

According to such a scheme, the name "Bach" would be $2 + 1 + 3 + 8$, or 14;

Bach

Example 3-20

Bach: Second Movement of the Trio Sonata, from the *Musical Offering*—Excerpts

1. Beginning

2. Middle (Royal Theme in continuo)

1.

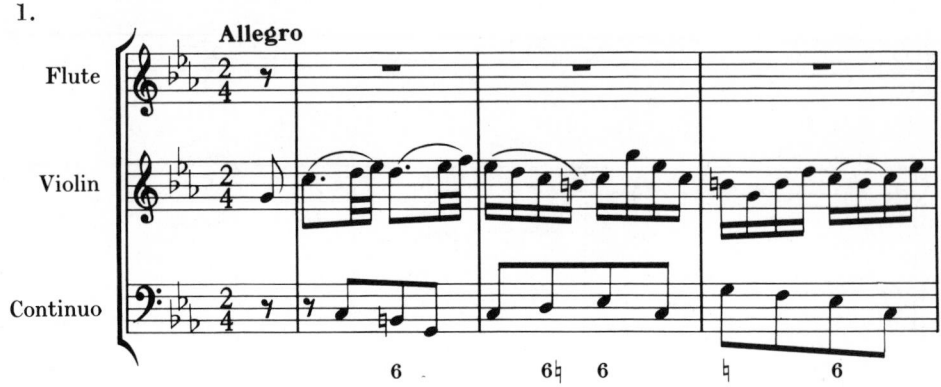

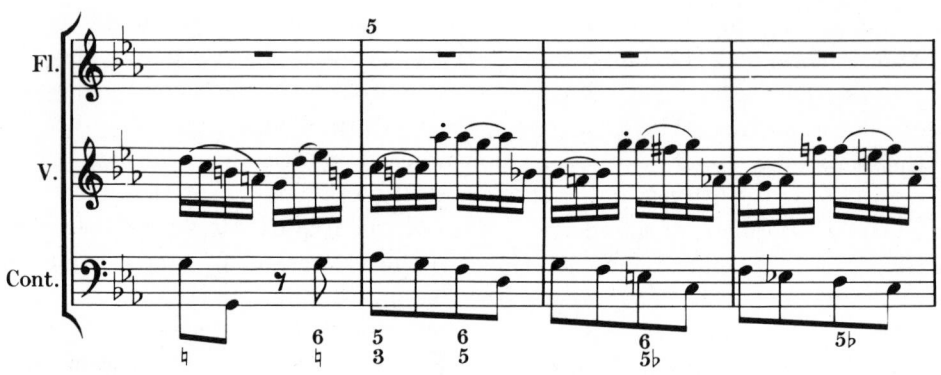

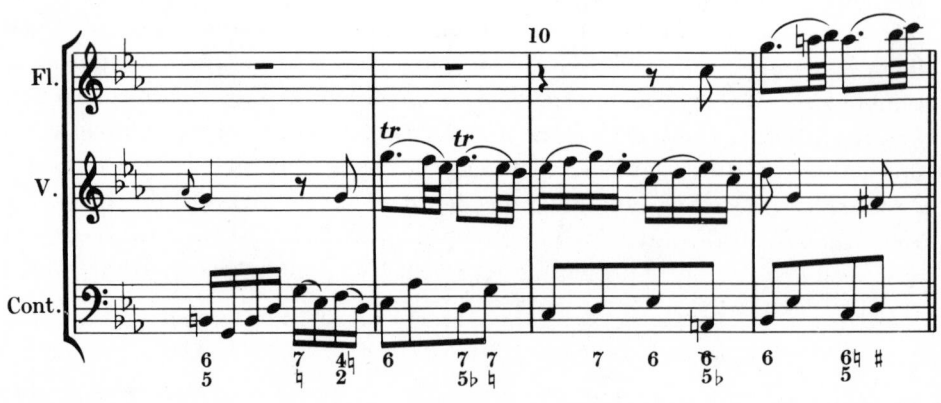

EXAMPLE 3-20 (*continued*)

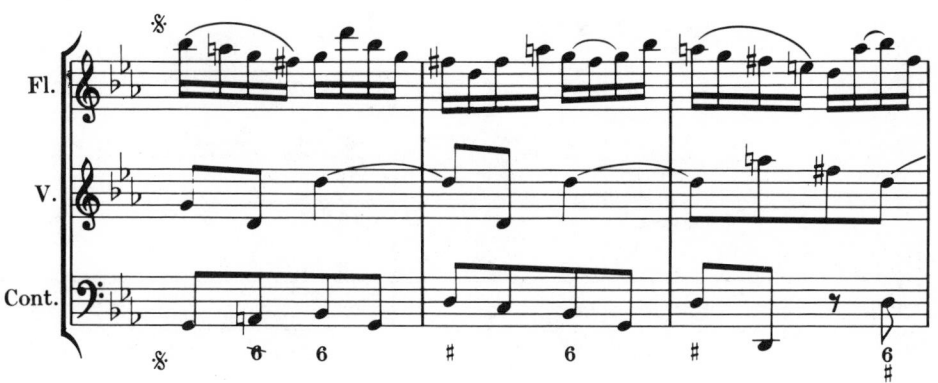

2.

EXAMPLE 3-20 (*concluded*)

and "J. S. Bach," oddly enough, would be 41, which one could interpret as the reversed (retrograde) form of 14. As it happens, in one of Bach's earliest fugal compositions there are precisely fourteen entrances of the subject; and in his last composition, the chorale prelude *Vor deinen Thron'*, the chorale melody contains in all forty-one notes, and in its first line there are fourteen. The trio sonata of the *Musical Offering* contains in all fourteen statements of the *tema regis*. But there is more. In 1747 Bach accepted membership in the Mizler Society of Leipzig, something of an honor; but he had rejected a bid extended him in 1746, which would have made him the thirteenth member, so that he could join as the fourteenth; and in the portrait painted of him for the occasion his coat and posture are carefully arranged so that precisely fourteen buttons are visible. As another example, the word "Credo" adds to forty-three, and the word appears forty-three times in the corresponding movements of the Mass in B minor. Other types of symbolism have also been found in Bach's work.

The Late Works

In contemplating the totality of Bach's achievement, one is struck by its comprehensiveness, its all-embracing quality. Bach's work has been said to represent the culmination and perfection of the great tradition of imitative polyphonic music. This procedure is surely basic to his art: in the cantatas and related pieces, in the organ works, where it is often connected with another old device of polyphonic music, cantus firmus technique. Even its most "learned," esoteric aspects are represented in a way they had not been seen since the early sixteenth century. But this tradition, which had been important in European music since the Renaissance, is by no means the only one to be seen in Bach's work. The "new music" of the Italian Baroque is also present, in the recitatives and arias of the cantatas and oratorios, in the instrumental chamber and orchestral compositions. A third tradition drawn upon by Bach goes back to France, and the cultivation of dances, for harpsichord and orchestra. All three exist in Bach's work, sometimes separately, sometimes in combination: The Italian instrumental style is applied to organ toccatas, a concerto movement serves as the basis for a movement in a cantata, themes related to French dance types appear in preludes and fugues of the *Well-Tempered Clavier*, and so forth. The author of the most comprehensive book we have on Baroque music, Manfred Bukofzer, saw in Bach "the fusion of national styles."

Chapter Four

Beethoven and the New Instrumental Music

Introduction

*t*he middle of the eighteenth century witnessed perhaps the most comprehensive change that has ever taken place in the history of Western music.

George Frederick Handel. Portrait by Denner. (COURTESY OF THE NATIONAL PORTRAIT GALLERY, LONDON)

Introduction

The change in music is naturally part of the change that took place in Western civilization generally, a change that may briefly be characterized as involving the rise of the middle class, the bourgeoisie, to political power and the concomitant decline of the aristocracy—in short, the formation of political and social life as we know it today. This change in the political, economic, and social order had a profound effect on all musical life. At bottom, it affected the economic support for the musician. Heretofore he had been under the patronage system, in the employment of and subservient to the wishes of a church or court, of a bishop, an archbishop, a rector, a prince, a duke, and so forth; but once the change had taken place, his support derived rather from the large and generally anonymous mass audience, before which he performed his works in public concerts, and which purchased the compositions he published. On the other hand, the wishes and tastes of the large audience had to be satisfied, and although the great composers' refusal to compromise brought about an improvement in the taste of this large audience, the vast majority of composers—most of them long forgotten—contented themselves with providing works that would gratify the mass taste and little more.

EXAMPLE 4-1

HANDEL: "For unto us a child is born," FROM *Messiah*—BEGINNING* (PIANO REDUCTION OF ORCHESTRA)

* Six bars of instrumental introduction are omitted.

EXAMPLE 4-1 (*continued*)

EXAMPLE 4-1 (*continued*)

EXAMPLE 4-1 (*continued*)

Introduction

Example 4-1 (continued)

EXAMPLE 4-1 (*continued*)

Introduction

EXAMPLE 4-1 (*concluded*)

Beethoven and the New Instrumental Music

A prominent composer of the late Baroque, Bach's most distinguished contemporary, George Frederick Handel (1685–1759), a German trained in the Italian manner, who in 1711 settled in London, provides in some respects an early instance of the change that was to take place. Once in London, Handel was not attached to any court or church; rather he ran his own opera companies, producing mainly his own operas, which are among the finest examples of the late *opera seria*. But opera was much criticized in England, as well as in France, and ultimately Handel, forced by economic necessity, turned to a type of composition that brought him greater success and which he made over into something entirely his own—the *oratorio*. In Handel's type of oratorio—not all of which are sacred—the text was in English (the operas had been in Italian), and although the traditional recitatives and arias continued to find their place, the chorus took on ever greater importance; in fact, it became the heart of the Handelian oratorio. Here, instead of following the Baroque dictum of the unity of affection within a musical composition, Handel juxtaposed the most astonishing and impressive contrasts to express the character of each line of his varied texts, much in the fashion of the motet and madrigal composers of the Renaissance. A particularly famous example is the chorus "For unto us a child is born," from *Messiah*, in which the imitative setting of the beginning leads to the impressive loud homophonic pronouncement at the words "And his name shall be called, Wonderful, Counsellor, the Everlasting Father, the Prince of Peace" (see Example 4-1).

Handel remained, however, an essentially Baroque composer. Even Italian composers since 1637 had been presenting operas in public opera houses, so that in this respect the connection with the public audience was not new. But toward the end of the century, there began to spring up organizations giving public performances of instrumental music, in England and on the Continent. An important institution of this kind was the *collegium musicum* of Leipzig, of which Bach served as director. Others were the *concerts spirituels* in Paris and, somewhat later, the *Gewandhaus* concerts in Leipzig; many others could be listed.

An important aspect of the sociological-political-economic change in the position of the musician and composer was a new musical style, which, although affecting all kinds of music, was most involved with instrumental music. This new kind of music may generically be called *galant*. [1] Its main features were basically homophonic texture, simple harmonies, regularly organized, well-balanced, easily grasped melodic phrases, the whole being unassuming, simple, pleasing, ingratiating, and sweet. The style as a whole was derived from the popular and unpretentious comic operas of the early and middle eighteenth century, especially those of the so-called Neapolitan School.

---

[1] As used here, the term embraces a number of different kinds of music, from French harpsichord music, through certain Italian operatic and instrumental compositions, to "expressive" works by German composers of the late eighteenth century.

Introduction

Characteristic is the name given to many of these instrumental works—
divertimento, and other names meaning the same thing are *cassation, nocturne,*
and *serenade*. Works of this type are intended as social compositions, background music, as we would say, to social gatherings of the time. As an example, we give a portion (the trio) of a minuet from a serenade by Mozart.

This galant music was regarded as corresponding to the leading aesthetic
principles of the time, which were wholly rationalistic and called for the artwork to be logically and rationally organized, clear and comprehensible to the
senses. Descartes' demand for "clear and distinct" thoughts became an
aesthetic requirement for the creative artist, a demand echoed by many

EXAMPLE 4-2

MOZART: TRIO OF MINUET, FROM SERENADE FOR STRING ORCHESTRA IN
G MAJOR (*Eine kleine Nachtmusik*, K. 525)

Beethoven and the New Instrumental Music

EXAMPLE 4-2 (*continued*)

musical theorists of the eighteenth century. At the same time, however, there ran an important countercurrent, which opposed the dominance of reason by asserting the value of imagination in an artwork. This movement came especially from England, from the writings of Anthony Ashley Cooper, the Third Earl of Shaftesbury (1671–1713) and Edward Young (1683–1765), which became known on the Continent and there exerted considerable influence, particularly in Germany. Once the works of Shakespeare in their original versions became known, they provided a strong argument against the rationalistic conception of the artwork; and again this influence was pronounced in Germany. Finally, the poems of the alleged Celtic bard Ossian—even after the deception of James Macpherson became known—had a powerful impact.

Along with this stress on the role of the imagination in an artwork goes a new interpretation of the role of the artist. This came about by virtue of the idealistic philosophy of the eighteenth-century, the revival of conceptions that

Introduction

go back to Plato. Ultimate reality was seen to lie not in the physical world, which one perceives through the senses, but in a supersensible or metaphysical realm of ideas that lies above and beyond. The objects in the physical world were regarded as poor copies of their archetypes in the supersensible realm of ideas. In this scheme the work of art had traditionally enjoyed a peculiar position: Although it necessarily belonged to the physical world, it was also held to represent or symbolize the eternal realm of ideas. The artist thus became a sort of mediator between the supersensible realm and that of ordinary physical reality, and hence, as someone in contact somehow with this higher realm, became very special indeed. Although this idea was not new in the eighteenth century, it there took on particular importance, for in connection with the new emphasis given to the role of imagination in the artwork, it had a profound effect on the idea of the artist as a creator. In Shaftesbury's phrase, the artist is a "second maker, a just Prometheus, under Jove," whose creative power is seen as analogous to that of God himself. This idea represents the beginning of the "genius theory" that became so popular in the following century; and in the understanding of the eighteenth century, the only genius was the artistic genius. As exponents of this idea in one way and another in the eighteenth century, we can refer to the dramatists connected with the *Sturm und Drang* movement in Germany, as well as the Weimar classic writers, Goethe, Schiller, and Herder, or in France, Rousseau. Toward the end of the century the German philosopher Immanuel Kant set the limits to what reason can hope to accomplish, establishing the basis for the aesthetics of the nineteenth century.

This new orientation in aesthetics had an effect on music. The musical artwork, just as in the other arts, became a vehicle for expression, no longer seen as the concrete and generalized affections of the Baroque, but rather as personal and subjective, the feelings of the artist himself. The musical artwork became the unique and individual expression of the composer. The old idea of the unity of affection prevailing throughout a composition gave way to a manifoldness, a variety of expression within a piece, which usually appears as the use of more than one musical theme, and frequently themes that contrast strongly with one another. Dynamic variations, crescendo and decrescendo, became important elements in the new music, and it is this that explains the rise of the piano in the latter half of the eighteenth century. Contrast and variety became the hallmarks of the new music.

The new expressive ideal and seriousness of purpose affected the easy, pleasant, and popular galant music of the time, which had to be adapted, changed, so that it could become a suitable vehicle for the new intent. This can be seen most particularly in instrumental music, which lay at the heart of the new music. The change was primarily made by German (or German-speaking) composers who had settled in Vienna: the Hungarian Joseph Haydn (1732–1809) and the Austrian Wolfgang Amadeus Mozart (1756–1791). It is

Joseph Haydn.
Portrait by Hardy.

they who established the new kind of instrumental music in a way that was to remain dominant for the whole of the nineteenth century and to some extent the twentieth. Thus, they paved the way for the work of Ludwig van Beethoven (1770–1827). For this reason they, along with Beethoven and possibly with the inclusion of Franz Peter Schubert (1797–1828), have come to be known as the Viennese Classical group of composers. German composers came to exercise stylistic leadership in the second half of the eighteenth century, just as had Netherlands musicians in the Renaissance and Italian musicians in the Baroque.

The Sonata Principle

The forms of the new instrumental music represent in part the drastic transformation and reinterpretation of two important genres of the instrumental music of the late Baroque, the *sonata da chiesa* (often called simply sonata) and the *sonata da camera* (or suite or partita). During the eighteenth

*Wolfgang Amadeus
Mozart. Unfinished
portrait by Lange.*

century these two gradually lost their individuality, as elements of the one made their appearance in the other. This can be observed in the suites for harpsichord by Handel, which were first published in 1720. The result was a new form, which still bore the name sonata. Added to this was the three-movement sequence of the Italian concerto grosso, which is also to be found in the overtures to the Italian *opere serie* of the late Baroque. The new form of sonata appears usually in three or four movements, in the succession fast—slow—fast, or fast—slow—minuet—fast. Generally all but one of the movements will be in the same key; it is the slow movement, usually second in position, that is in a different key, most often in subdominant relation to the main key. These new sonatas were composed for any insrument or combination of instruments—piano solo, violin and piano, violoncello and piano, and so forth; if composed for a group of four string instruments in the combination

Beethoven and the New Instrumental Music

two violins, viola, and violoncello, the work would be called a *string quartet*; if for piano, violin, and violoncello, a *piano trio*; if for piano and string quartet, a *piano quintet*; or if for piano, violin, viola, and violoncello, a *piano quartet* and so on; if composed for symphony orchestra, the work was called a *symphony*, and if composed for one or more solo instruments and orchestra, a *concerto*.[2]

One characteristic musical form or procedure was developed along with the new forms of instrumental music, a form that had nothing whatever to do with any form of vocal music, that was conceived completely in terms of instrumental music. In fact, it is not too much to say that this newly developed form or procedure made the serious instrumental form of the sonata possible. This form or procedure is generally known as *sonata principle* or *sonata form*, and these terms will be employed in the discussion to follow; other terms are also in use.[3] Sonata form or principle refers to the formal organization of a single movement, usually the first movement and the last movement, and not to the overall organization of the sonata as a whole. Although the details of the historical development of the form are by no means entirely clear, the sonata form appears to represent an expansion and intensification of the characteristic rounded binary structure so common in the dances of the Baroque suites (see pages 138–39):

$$\|: \quad a \quad :\| \quad \|: \quad \quad b \quad \quad a \quad \quad :\|$$
$$\text{Keys:} \quad \text{I—V} \quad \quad \quad \text{Modulates I—I}$$

Both parts became greatly enlarged, and a number of different musical themes were introduced into the first part, which in sonata form is known as the *exposition*. In the second part, under "b," the themes presented in the exposition undergo a development, a process of variation in which they are run through different keys, motives are extracted from them and treated separately, different themes or motives are presented contrapuntally, and so on: This part is called simply the *development*. Under the last "a," the original theme is presented in its original key and usually in something close to its original form, and then the whole first part is repeated, often with unimportant changes, but *without* making the modulation that characterizes the first part: This part is called the *recapitulation*. A movement in sonata form, then, would look something like this:[4]

$$\|: \quad \text{Exposition} \quad :\| \quad \quad \|: \quad \text{Development} \quad \text{Recapitulation} \quad :\|$$
$$\text{Keys: I——V——V} \quad \quad \quad \text{Modulates} \quad \quad \text{I——I——I}$$

Sometimes a slow introduction stands before the exposition, a practice that

---

[2] Almost all concertos were in three movements.

[3] Among them: sonata-allegro form, first movement form, development form.

[4] Repetition of the second part is optional.

goes back either to the French overture or to the *sonata da chiesa*; and some-times a coda, or concluding section, is added after the recapitulation.

Within the exposition, the various themes may be grouped by the keys in which they are presented: the *principal* theme or group of themes in the main key; the *modulatory* theme or group of themes with which the modulation to the dominant (or in the case of a work in the minor, to the relative major) is made; and the *secondary* theme or group of themes, those in the new key; often a fourth group may also be distinguished, the *closing* theme or group of themes, which brings the exposition to a conclusion. As with the term sonata form, there are a number of other names used to identify these parts of the exposition: "A" and "B" themes, "Bridge" or "Transition" themes, "codetta," and so forth.

To introduce the sonata principle we may briefly examine the first move-ment of the Serenade for Strings in G major by Mozart, a work known as *Eine kleine Nachtmusik* (A Little Piece of Night Music). Here we find on a small scale the chief elements of the sonata form. Furthermore, as a wholly galant work, the piece affords a good illustration of the form in the context in which it originally was developed. The exposition, which runs 55 bars, is followed by a short development of 20 bars, whereupon we have the recapitulation (from bar 76), a virtual restatement of the exposition, but with a short coda. In out-line, the movement is as shown in the accompanying table.

Exposition

Principal Themes

I (bars 1–5)	*Forte.* In octaves. Triadic melodic material. Phrase structure, 2 + 2, the first in G major, the second in D major.
II (bars 5–10)	*Forte.* Melodic line in violin I. Rhythmic pattern.
III (bars 11–17)	*Piano.* Phrase structure, 4 + 4.

Modulatory Passage

(bars 18–27)	A rising melodic line, with a *crescendo.* The modulation is from G major to D major and may be visually detected from the use of C sharp.

Secondary Theme

(bars 28–34)	*Piano.* The violins, in octaves, have a 4-bar phrase, modified on its repetition.

Beethoven and the New Instrumental Music

Closing

I (bars 35–39) and (bars 43–47)	*Piano.* A 2-bar phrase stated twice. Motivic figure in violins I.
II (bars 39–43) and (bars 47–51)	*Forte.* Melodic interest in violins I (later joined by violins II), with running accompaniment in violas and violoncellos.
III (bars 51–53)	*Forte.* Ascending melodic line, played in octaves.
IV (bars 54–55)	*Piano.* A 2-bar phrase.

Development

First Section

(bars 56–59)	Principal theme I in D major and B major.

Second Section

(bars 60–70)	Based on closing theme I. After a complete statement in C major, the rhythmic pattern is put through various keys: E major, A major, D major, and E-flat major.

Third Section

(bars 70–75)	The retransition to the recapitulation, by means of an ascending theme using the rhythmic pattern of closing theme I, which then rises chromatically and leads to the recapitulation.

Recapitulation

Principal Themes

(bars 76–93)

Modulatory Passage

(bars 93–100)

Secondary Theme

(bars 100–107)

The Sonata Principle

Closing

    (bars 107–128)

Coda

Extension of closing theme IV
    (bars 128–131)

Fanfare close
    (bars 132–137)

EXAMPLE 4-3

MOZART: ALLEGRO (FIRST MOVEMENT), FROM SERENADE FOR STRING ORCHESTRA IN G MAJOR—EXPOSITION AND DEVELOPMENT

Beethoven and the New Instrumental Music

EXAMPLE 4-3 (*continued*)

The Sonata Principle

EXAMPLE 4-3 (*continued*)

EXAMPLE 4-3 (*continued*)

The Sonata Principle

EXAMPLE 4-3 (*continued*)

EXAMPLE 4-3 (*continued*)

EXAMPLE 4-3 (*continued*)

Beethoven and the New Instrumental Music

EXAMPLE 4-3 (*concluded*)

In the sonata form there was, as already indicated, rarely an attempt made to maintain the same mood, character, and thematic material all the way through the movement. Rather, variety and contrast were sought. Dynamic changes, often sudden and unexpected, are not unusual, with crescendos leading up to climactic points, followed by sudden diminuendos. The texture likewise was continually varied, often homophonic but then becoming contrapuntal, or fugal, or perhaps forming a duet with harmonic accompaniment, and so forth. Much of this may be seen in the first movement of Mozart's Serenade. In the principal theme group, the octave-unison writing of the first theme gives way to homophony in the second and then to a more contrapuntal style in the third. Similarly, the first two themes of the closing group contrast with one another. In the modulatory passage, the effect of the modulation is enhanced both by the crescendo and by the rising melodic line. Generally speaking, the composer exploited what was inherent in the themes he had devised, usually concentrating on the principal theme, the character of which will often, but by no means always, determine the character of the work as a whole.

The sonata form owed its development chiefly to the work of Haydn, where it may be seen principally in the string quartets and the symphonies. Of central importance in these works was the formulation of a principal theme that would dominate the movement, out of which the composer could take motives that he could transform and present in various combinations and thus build the movement. It was here that Haydn developed mastery, and it was here that he exercised such a profound influence in the development of the new art of instrumental music.

It is the sonata form, with its emphasis on thematic development, that made possible the transformation of the typically galant genres of musical composition into something capable of intense and serious musical expression. This is what we find in the string quartets of Haydn, especially those composed after 1770, and the later symphonies and piano sonatas, as well as in the later instrumental works of his younger contemporary, Mozart. This is what provided the background and the point of departure for the work of Beethoven.

Beethoven's Life

Beethoven was born in the northern part of Germany, in Bonn on the Rhine. His father was a tenor in the service of the Elector of Cologne, who maintained his court in nearby Bonn. Beethoven's musical talent made itself evident at an early age, and a musical career was assumed for him almost as a matter of course. As he grew older and acquired more and more skill as a musician, he obtained positions at the court, becoming deputy organist at the age of twelve in 1782 and regular organist two years later. It was also arranged for him in the spring of 1787 to make a trip to Vienna, then virtually the capital of the musical world, to work with Mozart; but the illness of his mother called him back to Bonn in July. In 1790 and in 1792 he met Haydn, who passed through Bonn on his trips between Vienna and London.

In 1792, in part by virtue of a second stipend awarded him by the Elector, Beethoven set out again for Vienna to work with Haydn; and this time he remained in Vienna, never returning to his native city. Along with taking lessons from Haydn and others, Beethoven became known in aristocratic salons for the power and brilliance of his piano playing, particularly his improvisations, and he soon attracted a good deal of attention. His first public concert took place on March 29, 1795, and about this time he began publishing his own compositions and taking on pupils. In February of 1796 he made a concert tour, the only one he ever undertook, going to Dresden, Leipzig, and Berlin. In 1800 he began to receive an annual salary from Prince Lichnowsky. Thus,

at about the age of thirty, success seemed to be his; as he wrote to a friend concerning the demand for his compositions: "Everything I write now I can immediately sell five times over and get a good price for it." The publishers "no longer bargain with me—I demand, they pay. You can see it's a pleasant situation."

Then deafness struck, slowly but inexorably, plunging the young and ambitious composer into black despair, causing him to curse his fate, leaving him to struggle against implacable destiny, and finally teaching him resignation. But as the deafness was slow in coming, Beethoven was able to continue making public appearances as a pianist until 1814; he continued composing until the end of his life. In 1808 he was approached by the court at Kassel who sought him for their Kapellmeister, but after negotiating an agreement with three Viennese nobles—Prince Lichnowsky, Prince Kinsky, and the Archduke Rudolf—whereby they would pay him an annual salary under the sole condition that he continue living in Vienna, he declined the offer from Kassel.

His last years were marked by increasing withdrawal and isolation, by no means uninterrupted. The craze for the new Italian comic opera, especially as represented in the work of Rossini, swept the city, alienating the great composer. This was also a time of political reaction: The Napoleonic wars had come to an end, and Prince Metternich, who was firmly in control of the Austrian government, instituted a system of political suppression against precisely those ideals of political liberty, human freedom, and toleration that, as we will see, had long fired Beethoven's enthusiasm and imagination. By 1818 his deafness had become almost total, and the composer had to have his visitors write questions down for him either on a small blackboard in his rooms or in small notebooks which have become known as the conversation books. It was during these years that Beethoven became involved in difficulties with his nephew Karl; Beethoven became his guardian upon the death of his brother Johann, and there ensued numerous litigations against the mother, along with difficulties with the boy himself. All this came to head with the boy's attempted suicide in August, 1826. Despite it all, however, Beethoven continued to compose and produced some of his most striking works. All the same his health was gradually failing, and he died after an illness of several months, in March, 1827.

Beethoven's View of the Artwork

What sets Beethoven apart from most other composers is his deep involvement with the world of ideals; he believed in certain philosophical, ethical conceptions, according to which he strove to live and which he frequently attempted to manifest in his compositions. These ideas for the most

Opposite) *Ludwig van Beethoven. Portrait by Waldmüller.*

part were established during the years in Bonn, a city which at the time was under the influence of the French Enlightenment. Important among them were the lofty position assigned to human reason and a commitment to religious tolerance and political liberty. In the newly founded University of Bonn, established in 1786, these ideas were accorded strong expression and widespread support. Beethoven's whole being was further enriched by his contact with the exceptionally gifted and broadly educated court organist, Christian Gottlob Neefe (1748–1798), who had been his teacher. Beethoven was also accepted into the circle of the Von Breuning family, where in the evenings there were held readings and discussions of the leading intellectual topics of the time, among them Rousseau, Klopstock, Herder, Kant, Schiller and Goethe, as well as Homer and Shakespeare. The works of these writers remained guiding lights for Beethoven throughout his life.

The central conviction that developed in the young composer had to do with the moral or ethical value attributed to the artwork. Through his work the creative artist had the duty to uplift, to ennoble, those who perceived it, an idea not totally unrelated to the old Greek conception of *catharsis*. The artist, through his work, is to improve mankind, to inspire other human beings to strive for ever greater achievements. This is the corollary to the idea of the exceptional position of the creative artist that has already been discussed.

Ideas of this sort were frequently expressed by Beethoven. He felt that he belonged to an intellectual aristocracy by virtue of his intellectual powers, and this was the only kind of aristocracy that meant anything to him. Many of the anecdotes concerning his relations with members of the nobility can be understood only in this light. There is the report that when his brother, who had just bought a farm, sent him a card signed "Johann von Beethoven, Land-owner," Beethoven responded with a card signed "Ludwig van Beethoven, Brain-owner." It is man's preoccupation with and receptivity to works created by human reason, and under this works of art are included, that alone can raise him, improve him, make him more worthy. As Beethoven in 1812 wrote to a child who was studying piano with him: "Keep on going; but do not merely practice art, rather penetrate to its innermost essence. For only art and science raise man toward divinity."

Beethoven's commitment to these ideals is revealed by an amazing document, the so-called *Heiligenstadt Testament*, written in 1802 under the awareness of his impending deafness and of what it would mean to him as a musician and composer. Although ostensibly intended to be given to his brothers after his death, it is clearly addressed to a larger audience, seemingly to humanity at large, anyone that ever came to know him or his works, and it represents an effort to explain how he felt and why he did what he did. In his disillusionment and despair, everything was called into question: He was even driven to contemplate suicide. But he always stopped short: "It seemed impossible to leave the world until I produced all I felt called upon to produce." Beethoven thus felt he had been given a sort of divine mandate, a mission, to exercise the talent with which he had been endowed, no matter what obstacles an unkind and indifferent fate might put in his way. As he put it in 1821: "God, who knows my innermost being. . . knows how as a man I am everywhere fulfilling my duties, which have been laid upon me by humanity, God, and nature." He also stated that he had an "inborn need to reveal myself to the world through my works." We might say that Beethoven felt a strong ethical imperative to persist in his work as long as life remained in him.

Most of his larger works, then, are to be understood in this way. In some, however, there are concrete indications of associations with particular ideas of one kind or another, and some of the more well known of these may be indicated here. There is the ballet *The Creatures of Prometheus* (Op. 43) of 1800–1801,[5] dealing with Prometheus, the rebel god who disobeyed Zeus and brought fire to mankind, a subject that would obviously appeal to Beethoven. From 1803 there is the *Sinfonia eroica* in E-flat major (Symphony No. 3, Op. 55), originally dedicated to Napoleon, but to Napoleon as First Consul of the French Republic, the man Beethoven looked upon as having brought the ideals of the French Revolution to fulfillment. When Napoleon declared himself Emperor, Beethoven had the dedication changed. There is incidental music to Goethe's play *Egmont* (Op. 84) of 1809–10; the play concerns the Netherlands' resistance to Spanish tyranny in the early sixteenth century. Beethoven's lone opera, *Fidelio* (Op. 72), which exists in several versions composed between 1804 and 1814, deals with a man unjustly imprisoned for political reasons who is helped to escape death at the last minute by the intervention of his wife. Finally, there is the Symphony in D minor (No. 9, Op. 125) of 1824, in the last movement of which a poem by Schiller, the well-known *Ode to Joy*, is taken as text, a poem that celebrates universal human brotherhood and the power of man to advance by the exercise of his reason. The emphasis on political freedom, hatred of tyranny, and humanity all show a strong link to the ideas that lay back of the French Revolution. It will be seen that French music of the revolutionary era also exerted a strong influence on Beethoven's work as a composer. Completely apart from all this stands the Symphony in F major (No. 6, Op. 68), known as the *Pastoral Symphony*, completed in 1808, which presents a musical expression of life in the country.

It is clear from what has been said that Beethoven took his work very seriously. Perhaps he is one of the first composers who deliberately and consciously set about improving himself from year to year, from work to work, always striving for greater mastery of his art. In a letter of the year 1819 to

---

[5] The "Opus" ("Op".) numbers usually given with works of Beethoven and other composers generally represent the order in which the works were published, and not necessarily the order in which they were composed. On the other hand, the "K." numbers (for Mozart) or the "D." numbers (for Schubert) represent the attempts by Köchel and Deutsch, respectively, to arrange the works of these composers in chronological order.

the Archduke Rudolf he referred to the need for progress in art as in every-thing else. Even later he is quoted as having said to his friend Karl Holz, "art demands of us that we not stand still." This concern for progress, for never-ceasing change, development, and improvement is revealed in many of the sketchbooks; usually the great difficulty he experienced with a projected composition was the proper formulation of the principal musical theme, one from which an entire movement may be produced. As a result of this need for perfection, for continual improvement, there is a continuous change in musical style throughout Beethoven's career as a composer.

It has become customary to recognize three main periods in Beethoven's creative work: the first, running from the earliest compositions in Bonn to around 1802, when he was most closely related to the work of his great pre-decessors Haydn and Mozart; a second period, from 1802 to around 1815 or 1816, when most of the works we usually associate with him were produced; and a late period, until his death, when a number of problematic compositions came about, many of which were not understood at the time. Some justifica-tion for such a threefold division can be found in Beethoven's own statements about his life and work. Whereas in 1801 he had stated, "for only now have I learned to write quartets," in 1803 we find, "I am not satisfied with my work up to now; from now on I will try a new way." And again, in 1817, with reference to the years around 1800, he said, "in those days I did not know how to compose. Now I am writing something better." In a rough way, then, the conventional division of Beethoven's work into three periods is confirmed by the composer himself.

In the compositions of Beethoven as a whole the stress is on instrumental music. In the center stands the sonata form with its thematic development, basic to all the large forms of instrumental music: the nine symphonies, the five concertos for piano and orchestra, one concerto for violin and orchestra, thirty-two piano sonatas, sixteen string quartets, nine sonatas for violin and piano, five sonatas for violoncello and piano, a number of overtures and other works. Although vocal works surely exist among them—a number of songs, the opera *Fidelio*, two Masses, including the *Missa solemnis*, and several cantatas—it is instrumental music that clearly has the lead. In this Beethoven is heir to the tradition established principally by Haydn. But in his hands the large form became ever larger: It was expanded, the expression became more powerful, everything was intensified, so that, although the work's link to Haydn and to Mozart is clear enough, in Beethoven's hands the conception of the large forms became bigger and more important, a step that was decisive for the nineteenth century in general. In the following survey, in which some of the more repre-sentative and characteristic works will be considered, the order will be chronological, in accordance with the threefold periodization of Beethoven's work that has been presented.

The Early Works

In Beethoven's compositions up to around 1802 we can note clearly the attempt of the young composer to follow in the footsteps of Haydn and Mozart. As an example we will discuss the first Symphony in C major (Op. 21), composed in 1800, performed the following year but not published in score until 1820. As a whole, the work is much along the lines of a symphony by Haydn or Mozart. Scored for an orchestra consisting of flutes, oboes, clarinets, bassoons, horns, and trumpets, along with timpani and strings, the symphony consists of four movements, an Allegro con brio preceded by a slow introduction (Adagio molto), an Andante cantabile con moto in F major, a Minuetto (Allegro molto e vivace) and Trio, both in C major, and as finale, an Allegro molto e vivace preceded by a very short Adagio.

In the first movement we find the sonata form with an elaborate slow introduction and a coda. In the exposition, great importance attaches to the principal theme; it is *triadic*, uses mainly notes that belong to a triad, and it is

Example 4-4

Beethoven: Allegro con brio (First Movement), from Symphony in C major (Op. 21)—Exposition (Principal Theme and Modulatory Passage)*

* Oboe, clarinet, bassoon, horn, and trumpet parts have been omitted.

Beethoven and the New Instrumental Music

EXAMPLE 4-4 *(continued)*

The Early Works

EXAMPLE 4-4 (*continued*)

EXAMPLE 4-4 (*continued*)

EXAMPLE 4-4 (*continued*)

Beethoven and the New Instrumental Music

EXAMPLE 4-4 (*concluded*)

motivic, compounded of short and highly characteristic figures or motives in which rhythm, repetition, and staccato articulation play an important part (see Example 4–4). Both these qualities, the triadic and the motivic, are common in the principal themes in the instrumental music of the time. The theme is first presented softly, in C major, then in D minor, finally in the dominant of C major (G major) but fortissimo and in a varied form in which its motivic character is fully brought out. This leads directly to the modulatory passage, or bridge, in which three themes, motives, or ideas are introduced: the first (bars 21–29), fast and triadic with alternation between the violins and the woodwinds (flute, clarinet, and bassoon), then repeated in an embellished version; the second (bars 29–33), based on the principal theme and modulating to G major; and the third (bars 33–40), establishing the new key with resounding chords accompanied by a scale figure tossed between the lower strings and the woodwinds. There then follows the secondary theme or theme group which likewise consists of three elements and a closing theme. Toward the end the principal theme is heard again, thus rounding off the exposition.

In the development Beethoven works primarily with the principal theme and a portion of the secondary theme. At the outset the two are heard in alternation. There then ensues a passage dominated by a triadic figure that is related to the principal theme, which also moves through various keys. This is followed by a passage based on part of the bridge theme. The principal theme—or, rather, its characteristic motive in dotted rhythm—then reappears and dominates the remainder of the development, eventually reaching a fortissimo climax in E minor that moves to the recapitulation. This, unlike the exposition, begins loud. The thematic material of the exposition is restated with some modification in the recapitulation, and there is a brief coda.

The movement serves as a good example of the sonata form as it had developed by the end of the eighteenth century. Variety and contrast are present in abundance. Yet the principal theme, as the theme in the main or principal key, is also the dominant theme: Its central motive produces most of the movement, and against it the other themes make a contrast. At the same time, there is no one central character that is maintained, nor even any particular emotional quality or affection that one could say is expressed, unless one wishes to employ epithets like "strong," "forthright," "jovial," "direct," and so on.

In the second movement, Andante, in F major (subdominant relation to C major) we find another example of the sonata form. The principal theme begins fugally, but the contrapuntal imitation is dropped and the texture becomes homophonic once all the voice parts have entered. The modulatory passage is a continuation of the principal theme; there are two secondary themes and a closing theme, the latter characterized by a dotted-rhythm pattern in the accompaniment. The development works only with the upbeat pattern from the principal theme and the first part of the secondary theme, to the accompaniment of the dotted rhythm from the closing section. The keys involved are the flat keys: C minor, D-flat major, B-flat major, and then to C major, which leads to the recapitulation. This is regular, except that the fugal presentation of the principal theme is accompanied by sixteenth-note scale

EXAMPLE 4-5

BEETHOVEN: MINUET, FROM SYMPHONY IN C MAJOR (OP. 21)—FIRST PART

figuration. The coda is based on the principal theme, but introduces toward the end the dotted rhythm characteristic of the closing theme.

The third movement in this symphony, as in most symphonies of the time, consists of a minuet followed by a second minuet, called the trio, after which the first minuet is repeated, thus making a da capo structure. Sometimes, as in this symphony, both minuet and trio are in the same key; more often they are in different, but related keys. Both minuet and trio are in the rounded binary form characteristic of the dance of the eighteenth century, and hence they represent the most obvious remnant of the old Baroque suite in the new instrumental music. But here the basic rounded binary scheme is varied by greatly extending the recapitulation of the first part so that the form as employed here must be thought of as

$$\|: \quad a \quad :\| \quad \|: \quad b \quad a' \quad :\|.$$

The minuet proper is characterized by an upward-driving stepwise line, staccato, thrust forward by an upbeat, with chromatic elements and driving rhythms. The passage embodies an intensification; the strings carry the melodic drive, which rises and in so doing makes a crescendo, whose top is reinforced by the woodwinds, brass, and percussion. In the second part of the minuet a descending motive of three notes is important, as are dynamic contrasts. Here the modulations pass through the "flat" keys to D-flat major; a crescendo moving through chromatic harmonies and powered by incessant rhythms leads to the repeat of the first part, which is enlarged. In the trio two principal elements appear: the repeated chords in the woodwinds and horn and the rapid scale passages in the violins. Thematically, then, the trio embodies a strong contrast to the minuet proper.

As finale there is a piece in sonata form preceded by a short introduction. This introduction is a sort of musical joke of the type associated with Haydn, since melodically it involves successive attempts to ascend the scale, beginning with G, each time adding more notes until finally the scale is complete, whereupon it suddenly is played fast and immediately goes off into the principal theme of the movement. This principal theme differs markedly from that of the first movement: It is not so pronouncedly motivic, and its phrase structure displays a repetitive organization—a first part (bars 6–14) consisting of a four-bar period played twice and a second part (bars 14–30) consisting of a eight-bar period played twice, first by the violins and then by the bassoons. In the first part the harmonic progression is characteristic: The tonic triad is used exclusively until the last two bars, when there occurs a cadence on the dominant (bars 13–14). The second part of the theme features a descending series of staccato repeated notes accompanied by ascending scale segments. For the thematic development to follow, the most important elements are the upbeat ascending scale passage of the first part and the repeated-note motive in the second part. The modulatory passage is also in two parts. A sudden

Beethoven and the New Instrumental Music

diminuendo leads to the first part of the secondary theme, where the melodic interest—a short-breathed melodic line with many rests—is in the violins. The closing theme is loud and features first rapid alternation between the strings and the wind instruments and then recalls the rapid ascending scale figure of the principal theme. In the development, as already indicated, it is the principal theme that is exploited the most, particularly this ascending scale figure, which appears in combination with the repeated-note figure of the second half of the principal theme; it also appears both in its regular form and in inversion and then accompanied by the closing theme. A statement of

EXAMPLE 4-6

BEETHOVEN: FOURTH MOVEMENT, FROM SYMPHONY IN C MAJOR (OP. 21)
—INTRODUCTION AND PRINCIPAL THEME*

* Only the string parts are given.

The Early Works

EXAMPLE 4-6 (*continued*)

the modulatory theme is followed by another of the scale figure from the principal theme which brings the recapitulation. A coda based on both parts of the principal theme forms the conclusion.

There is, then, no overall consistency of character in this symphony. Its overall form depends on the contrast among the various movements, and out of this carefully arranged interplay of contrasting characters emerges the balanced unity of the work as a whole. This can be regarded as the typical "Classic" aesthetic—the "harmony" of the work as a whole—i.e., its unity is the result of the reconciliation of opposites or of opposing characters. The most weighty movement is the first, and it is here that the sonata form with its thematic development is displayed most impressively. Then comes the lyrical slow movement, followed by the dance, a minuet, with a brilliant light finale to bring the piece to an end. Generally speaking, this represents the symphony as it stood at the end of the eighteenth century. This provided Beethoven's point of departure. Among other early works that display essentially the same features we may mention the three piano trios (Op. 1), the piano sonatas (Op. 2, Op. 7, and Op. 10), the sonatas for violin and piano (Op. 12), for violoncello and piano (Op. 5), the six string quartets (Op. 18), and the septet in E-flat major (Op. 20).

The Middle Period

Beethoven, as has been indicated, did not long remain with this type of composition. It served as his starting point, but he soon expanded it in all directions: His compositions became longer, the accents stronger and more intense, greater dynamic contrasts were exploited, the use of crescendo and decrescendo became more pronounced, the thematic development more concentrated, and the rhythmic element more forceful. Furthermore, many of the new compositions were more clearly associated with Beethoven's ethical ideas concerning the proper role of the artist and of the artwork. Often the composition as a whole was organized, not as a harmony of contrasts as was the Symphony in C major (Op. 21), but as a powerful surging onward from the beginning to the climax in the last movement.

Much of this was manifested at one stroke in what may well be one of the most important musical compositions ever written: the Symphony in E-flat major (No. 3, Op. 55) of 1803–4, first performed in 1805, to which Beethoven himself gave the name *Sinfonia eroica* ("Heroic Symphony"). The story of the intended dedication to Napoleon has already been related; in its place Beethoven substituted "to celebrate the memory of a great man." According to a note in the first violin part, Beethoven wished the symphony, because of its great length, to be played toward the beginning of the program rather than toward the end.

The Middle Period

Even without the dedication to Napoleon, the association of the work with heroism, with France and the ideals of the French Revolution, which had fired Beethoven's imagination since the early days in Bonn, is clear enough. In connection with the celebration of "the memory of a great man," the second movement is significant: It is a funeral march for a hero. It had never been usual to include funeral marches in symphonies and similar works, although Beethoven himself already had employed the form in his Sonata for Piano in A-flat major (Op. 26). It seems that Beethoven was deliberately drawing upon a French custom from the days of the revolution, of mounting large outdoor public funerals for dead military leaders and heroes of the revolution, in which massed brass bands and gigantic choral groups participated. In the finale of the Symphony in E-flat major Beethoven brought in another concrete association, this time from Greek mythology: Prometheus, the benefactor of mankind, whom Beethoven had already celebrated in a ballet—and a theme from the ballet is employed in the finale of the symphony.[6]

The *Sinfonia eroica*, scored for an orchestra of flutes, oboes, clarinets, bassoons in pairs, three horns, two trumpets, tympani, and strings (an orchestra not much larger than that used in the Symphony in C major [Op. 21]) is in four movements, all of which are about double the length they would have had in an eighteenth-century symphony: an opening Allegro in sonata form, the "Marcia funèbre" (Adagio in C minor), the scherzo[7] and trio in E-flat major, and the finale, an Allegro, based on the theme from Prometheus.

In the first movement, the heroic character that dominates the work as a whole is immediately established by the two loud E-flat major chords which precede the principal theme. This principal theme shows the same features that we noted in the opening movement of the Symphony in C major (Op. 21); it is triadic and motivic. But the earlier symphony does not prepare one for what happens here: the immediate motivic breaking down of the theme, the sharp accentuations on weak beats, and the dramatic crescendo leading to the fortissimo restatement of the principal theme that ushers in the modulatory passage. A number of new themes appear here, but particular attention must be directed to the first, a terse motive in dotted rhythm, which passes from instrument to instrument and plays an important role as the movement unfolds. A second crescendo leads to the secondary theme, in B-flat major, first

---

[6] There is some evidence that Beethoven was influenced by Parisian orchestral and operatic music of the 1780's and 1790's by composers like Cherubini, Méhul, Kreutzer, and Grétry, as may be seen in certain of his works as far back as the Symphony in C major (Op. 21), where the principal theme of the first movement has been connected with that of Kreutzer's *Overture for the Day Marathon*.

[7] The term *scherzo* refers simply to a compositon much like a minuet, except that it is faster and its themes are more motivic. Beethoven should, however, not be regarded as an innovator in having the scherzo replace the minuet, since there is abundant precedent for this in the work of Haydn.

EXAMPLE 4-7

BEETHOVEN: ALLEGRO, FROM SYMPHONY IN E-FLAT MAJOR (OP. 55, *Eroica*)—BEGINNING

The Middle Period

EXAMPLE 4-7 (*continued*)

EXAMPLE 4-7 (*continued*)

The Middle Period

EXAMPLE 4-7 (*continued*)

EXAMPLE 4-7 (*continued*)

The Middle Period

EXAMPLE 4-7 (*continued*)

EXAMPLE 4-7 (*continued*)

The Middle Period

EXAMPLE 4-7 (*concluded*)

in the winds and then in the strings. Still another crescendo brings the concluding group, which once more features syncopations and, near the end, fortissimo dissonant diminished seventh chords, followed by a brief recalling of the principal theme of the movement.

All the themes appear in the development, the length of which greatly exceeds that of the exposition (248 to 151 bars). Predominant is the principal theme which appears both by itself and in combination with themes from the modulatory section. Unusual is the introduction of a new theme, in E minor, one not heard before but which has been regarded as being related to the secondary theme. Finally, some comment has been occasioned by the passage near the end of the development, the so-called retransition to the recapitulation: In a diminuendo, as the strings sound a B-flat harmony, the horn enters softly with the principal theme in E-flat, the tonic, thus making a dissonance. After the recapitulation, which is quite regular, comes a coda, but its length is so great that it has been regarded as a "second development." It, too, uses the new theme that had been introduced in the development. At the very end the principal theme is stated four times, each time using more instruments and louder, making a crescendo in stages: first in the horn, then the first violins, then the lower strings; then finally as the trumpets and timpani begin with a "military" triplet figure in the accompaniment, it appears fortissimo in the brass instruments, after which the movement rapidly comes to a close.

Although it is unusual to have a funeral march in a symphony, there is ample precedent in the galant instrumental music of the late eighteenth century for the presence of a march. Since a funeral march is indeed a kind of march, it might be expected to show to some extent at least the same formal organization characteristic of a march. In the suites and divertimentos of the time, a march was organized much like a minuet: there would be the march

EXAMPLE 4-8

BEETHOVEN: "Marcia funèbre," FROM SYMPHONY IN E-FLAT MAJOR (OP. 55, *Eroica*)—MAIN THEME

1. *a* PHRASE—BEGINNING

2. *b* PHRASE—BEGINNING

The Middle Period

proper, then another march called the trio, after which the march proper is repeated; both march and trio would be disposed according to rounded binary form. Beethoven's funeral march in the *Sinfonia eroica* plainly has this standard march form in its background, although some important changes have been introduced. The opening portion of the movement, the march proper, displays the rounded binary form that would be expected except that double bars are not used, all repetitions being written out in full since the instrumentation is varied. The trio, in C major, uses triadic and scale figuration as its thematic materials; in the crescendos, martial triplet patterns in the trumpets and timpani are important. Here the rounded binary form is reduced to a simple ternary scheme with the third part varied (*a b a'*). Now come the departures. After the "bright" trio it seems as if the funeral march is going to be repeated, but after a few bars there is a sudden interruption and a powerful fugue on a variant of the funeral march theme in F minor is presented. After the fugue comes to its dramatic end with loud repeated diminished-seventh chords, the funeral march is again introduced but in G minor, not C minor, only to be rudely broken off again by a strident fanfare passage employing dotted rhythms in the brass instruments and furious triplets in the strings. As this subsides, the funeral march is reintroduced, but with the triplet patterns from the fanfare passage retained in the accompaniment, and this time it continues all the way through. At the very end the march theme is heard with simple accompaniment, but broken up with short rests and anxious syncopations which are related to the conventional "sob" figuration pattern of the time (see page 114) and which here have a particularly poignant effect.

The scherzo, again in the main key of the work, E-flat major, presents something rather different from the usual minuet: driving rhythms, great crescendos, effective syncopations, and so on. In the trio the use of the three horns as solo instruments with the typical "hunting call" type of thematic material is to be noted.

In the finale, which is based, as we have seen, on a theme from *The Creatures of Prometheus*, we find an unusual type of theme and variations form, one that has some aspects in common with the ostinato form of the Baroque. In the usual theme and variations form, as represented for example by Mozart's variations for piano on "Ah! vous dirai-je Maman" (a tune we know as "Twinkle, Twinkle, Little Star"), first the theme, a melody with simple accompaniment, is stated, after which it is repeated over and over again with changes or variations (see Example 4-9).

In the case of the finale of the *Sinfonia eroica*, after an introductory flourish, the bass part of the theme is presented by itself, pizzicato by the lower strings, and then follow two variations built on this bass part, which appears first in the violoncellos and then in the first violins; with the third variation the melody proper makes its appearance, first in the oboe, then taken up by the full orchestra. During the movement the variations, many of which are fugal,

EXAMPLE 4-9

MOZART: VARIATIONS FOR PIANO, "Ah! vous dirai-je Maman"—THEME
AND VARIATIONS I–III

EXAMPLE 4-9 (*continued*)

VAR. II

EXAMPLE 4-9 (*continued*)

The Middle Period

Example 4-9 (*concluded*)

Example 4-10

Beethoven: Finale, from Symphony in E-flat major (Op. 55, *Eroica*)—Principal Theme and its Bass

draw on either the melody or its bass, or both. Most important are variations IV (a fugue on the bass part) and VII (a fugue on the inversion of the bass part). Toward the end the themes appear in a slow tempo, making a majestic effect. After the last variation there is a coda, in which after a soft passage in the minor characterized by a rapid triplet rhythm in the viola, a sudden rush of E-flat major figuration fortissimo in the full orchestra brings the conclusion.

Here, then, we have a large and ambitious work which manifests the affection *heroism*. The heady crescendos, coupled with sudden unexpected accentuations and exciting rhythmically driven figuration, are elements of what the French composers of the time called the *élan terrible*, which Beethoven used here to express the herioc character. In its very length it dwarfs any symphony previously composed, and the daring and magnificence of its grandiose conception have given pause to Beethoven's successors. Even late in his life when asked which of the symphonies he liked the best, Beethoven unhesitatingly named the *Sinfonia eroica*. In short, we have here all at once a sudden manifestation of Beethoven's power as a composer, a work that in some ways he was never to surpass.

Similar features are present in the more popular Symphony in C minor (No. 5, Op. 67), composed between 1804 and 1808 and first performed in 1808. This piece may be regarded as the "ideal symphony." Its characteristic progression from stormy strife in the minor, through the repose interrupted by episodic military outbursts that constitutes the slow movement, then through the mysterious sounds toward the close of the march in the third movement to the triumphant affirmation in bright C major of the finale. The whole, then —moving as it were from darkness to light—has been associated with Beethoven's own struggle against destiny. He has unreliably been reported as having described the famous principal theme of the first movement as "thus Fate knocks on the door," and he is reliably reported to have said that in life one must seize Fate by the throat. In any case, the symphony has become the model for many others composed in the nineteenth and twentieth centuries.

The principal theme of the first movement may be taken as the archetype of such themes. Again it should be noted that it displays the two characteristic features already mentioned: triadic and motivic. The entire first movement is dominated by this terse powerful theme, and although the descending leap of the third is varied, the rhythm remains the same. This theme precedes and accompanies the contrasting secondary theme in E-flat major. At the same time, this theme and the way it is handled appear to owe much to a composition by an Italian composer who worked in Paris and whom Beethoven greatly admired, the *Hymn of Pantheon* by Luigi Cherubini (1760–1842). In Cherubini's piece this theme goes with a text: "We all swear, with steel in hand, to die for the republic." The conventional association of the movement with battle, then, seems to be concrete, and the music represents the *élan terrible*. As a whole, this movement is perhaps the most impressive

EXAMPLE 4-11

BEETHOVEN: ALLEGRO CON BRIO, FROM SYMPHONY IN C MINOR (OP. 67)—
   BEGINNING

EXAMPLE 4-11 (*continued*)

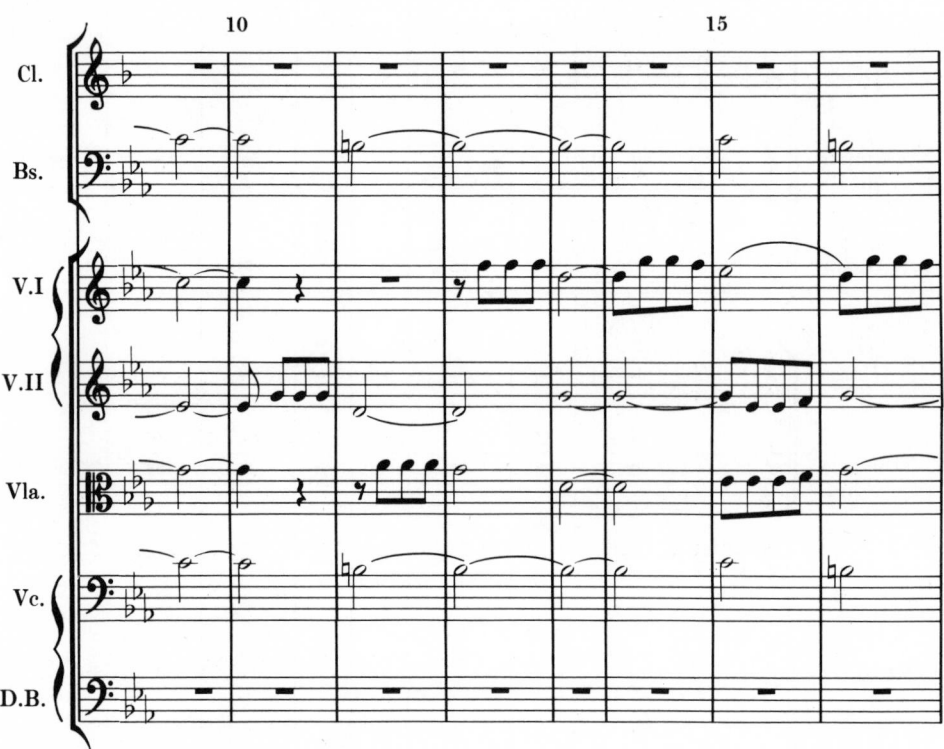

EXAMPLE 4-11 (*continued*)

Beethoven and the New Instrumental Music

EXAMPLE 4-11 (*concluded*)

example of thematic economy and concentration, of constructing a large and elaborate symphonic movement out of a short but highly characteristic thematic fragment.

The Andante, in A-flat major, presents a theme in two distinct parts, the first lyrical, a long chromatic line featuring dotted rhythms; the second military, fanfarelike. These are presented in alternation, but the first, on its various repetitions, is subjected to variations; and between the second and third variation there is a short development, and at the end comes a coda.

The Allegro, which serves as scherzo with trio (although not expressly so designated by Beethoven), after its mysterious introduction presents a strong martial theme, first in the horns; the rhythm and the use of repeated notes in this theme show similarities with the principal theme of the first movement. Most remarkable, however, is the transitional passage that connects the third movement with the finale. During the repetition of the Allegro after the "trio," the dynamic level gets softer and softer, with the winds and strings playing pizzicato, until the end is reached and the harmony suddenly shifts to an A-flat major triad which is sustained by the strings, and the only motion is the soft beating of the timpani; then a motivic figure based on the scherzo theme appears in the first violins, is repeated over and over, but moves higher as the harmonies begin to change; finally, the other instruments enter, a crescendo develops, and in a blaze of glory the triumphant C-major principal theme of the finale appears. The finale is in sonata form with a large coda. Just before the recapitulation the transition passage from the scherzo is heard once more in an abbreviated form. This movement has all the earmarks of a "symphony of victory," or what the French called *éclat triomphale*; and it is similar to other works by Beethoven of this type, such as the music for the last scene of Goethe's *Egmont* or the first three overtures to *Leonore-Fidelio*. Once more, then, the conventional interpretation of this movement has something concrete to support it. Excerpts appear in Example 4-12.

The Middle Period

Many compositions that Beethoven wrote in these years reveal similar features. It is impossible to take them up here, but a few of the more important works or groups of works may at least be mentioned: the Symphony in A major (No. 7, Op. 92), the three sonatas for violin and piano (Op. 30), the famous *Kreutzer* sonata in A major, also for violin and piano (Op. 47), the Sonata for Violoncello and Piano in A major (Op. 69), a number of piano

EXAMPLE 4-12

BEETHOVEN: ALLEGRO AND FINALE, FROM SYMPHONY IN C MINOR (OP. 67)—EXCERPTS

1. SCHERZO—THEME*

2. TRANSITION AND BEGINNING OF FINALE

1.

* Woodwind, trumpet, and timpani parts are eliminated.

Beethoven and the New Instrumental Music

EXAMPLE 4-12 (continued)

The Middle Period

EXAMPLE 4-12 (*continued*)

2.

EXAMPLE 4-12 (*continued*)

The Middle Period

EXAMPLE 4-12 (*continued*)

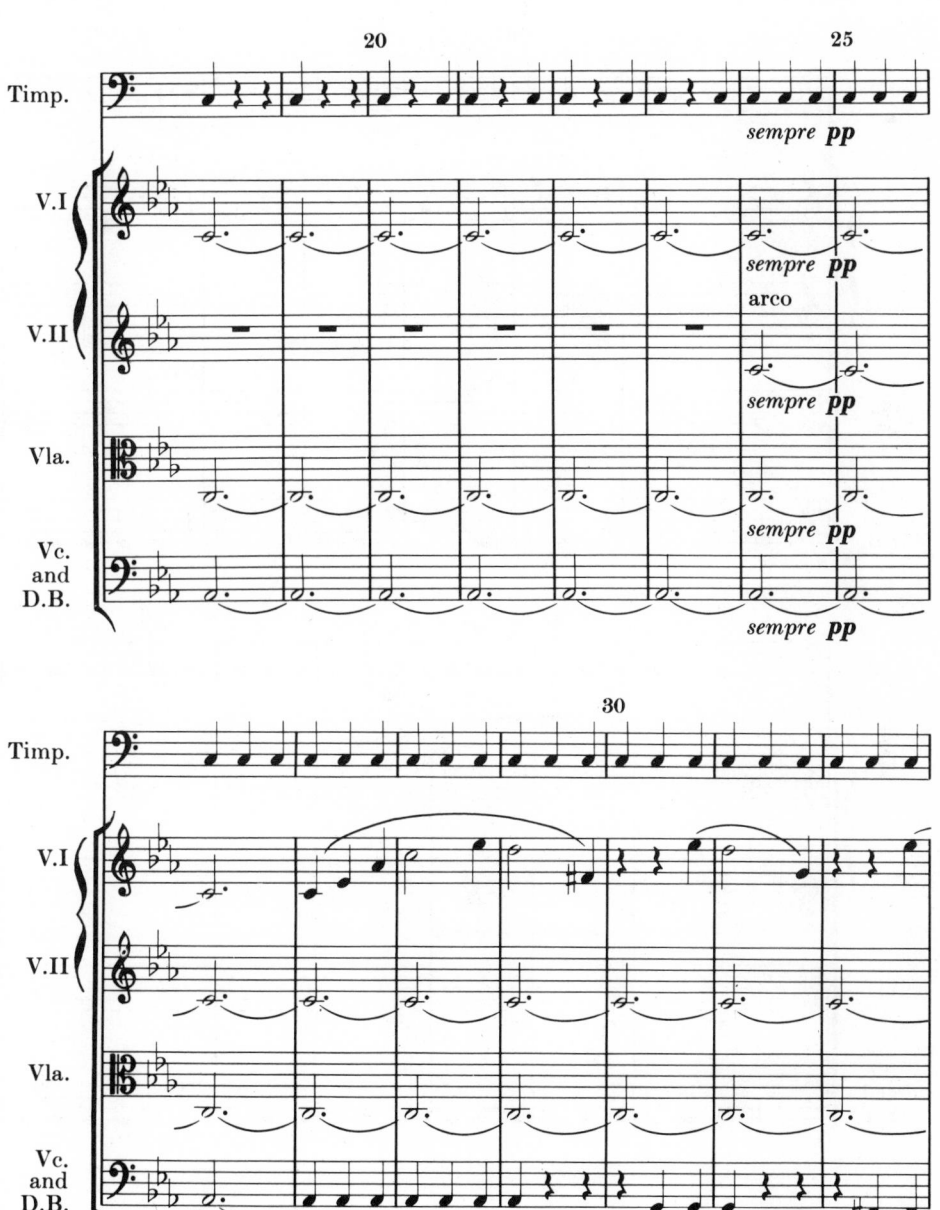

EXAMPLE 4-12 (*continued*)

EXAMPLE 4-12 (*continued*)

EXAMPLE 4-12 (*continued*)

EXAMPLE 4-12 (*concluded*)

Beethoven and the New Instrumental Music

sonatas, but especially those in C major (Op. 53) and F minor (Op. 57), known respectively as the *Waldstein* and the *Appassionata*, the Trio for Piano and Strings in B flat (Op. 97), called the *Archduke*, and the three *Razumovsky* string quartets (Op. 59).

One symphonic composition of the time stands somewhat apart: the Symphony in F major (No. 6, Op. 68), to which Beethoven gave the descriptive title *Pastoral*. Whereas in the earlier *Sinfonia eroica* Beethoven set about composing a heroic work, so here the aim was to express the pastoral character. The intention, as we have it from the sketches he made for the work, was not exclusively to engage in tone painting, to imitate in music specific pastoral sounds, but rather to present an expression of feeling. There are in all five movements, the last three of which are to be played without pause; each movement has a title: "Happy Feelings upon Arrival in the Country," "Scene by the Brook,"

EXAMPLE 4-13

BEETHOVEN: SYMPHONY IN F MAJOR (OP. 68, *Pastoral*)—EXCERPTS

1. FINALE: TRANSITION AND PRINCIPAL THEME*

2. ALLEGRO (FIRST MOVEMENT)—PRINCIPAL THEME

1.

* Flute and oboe parts eliminated.

The Middle Period

EXAMPLE 4-13 *(continued)*

EXAMPLE 4-13 (*continued*)

2.

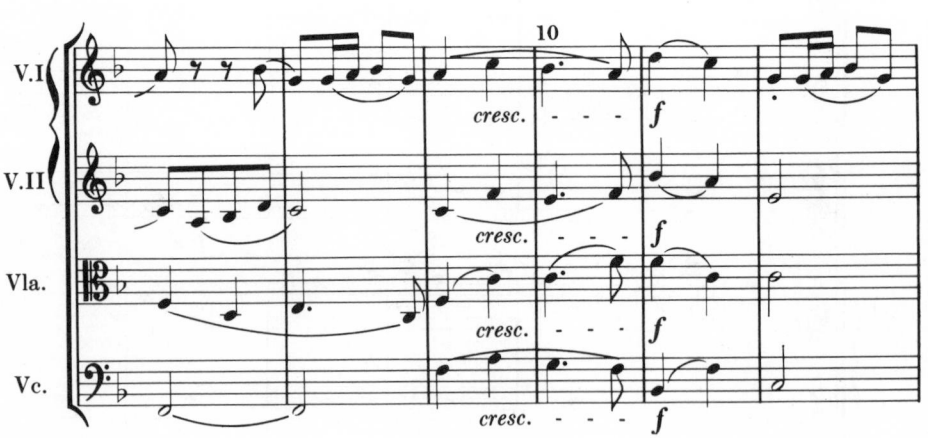

The Middle Period

EXAMPLE 4-13 (concluded)

"Happy Gathering of the Peasants," "The Storm," and "The Hymn of Thanksgiving." This particular arrangement has ample precedence in pastoral compositions of the eighteenth century and does not represent an innovation on the part of Beethoven. Despite Beethoven's disclaimer, there are in the composition undeniable examples of tone painting: the bird calls at the end of the second movement, the peasant dance in the third movement, and the storm in the fourth. For the most part, although Beethoven avoided such explicit tone painting, he nonetheless employed in great elaboration a style of composition long associated with the expression of the pastoral character: the use of triadic, in some cases "yodeling," themes, with short regular phrases that are constantly repeated over a static, drone, or slow-moving bass, a type of music related to the sound of bagpipes. This is adumbrated right at the very beginning of the work, in the principal theme of the first movement, but the use of such thematic material dominates the symphony as a whole. At its simplest it appears as the horn-call which ushers in the song of thanksgiving. A piece of music that draws on specific style-types with explicit connotations of one sort or another—as here the pastoral—is said to be *characteristic*. The work as a whole must be regarded as within the traditions of the eighteenth century.

A type of composition with which Beethoven was particularly involved during the earlier years in Vienna was the concerto. It was chiefly by means of this genre of composition that a composer made contact with the audience of concertgoers. This had been true since the days of Mozart in Vienna in the 1780's, and it was Mozart's example that Beethoven followed. Although he composed a Concerto in D major (op. 61) for Violin and Orchestra and a

Beethoven and the New Instrumental Music

"Triple" Concerto in C major (op. 56) for Piano, Violin, Violoncello and Orchestra, the five piano concertos make up his main contribution to the genre. The production of piano concertos ceased when Beethoven's deafness reached the point where he could no longer appear in public as a pianist—that is, around 1808—although some sketches he made for such a piece in 1815 are extant.

Of all the large instrumental forms dealt with by Beethoven, the concerto had the longest tradition, one that extended back through the concerto forms of the Baroque to the polychoral music of late-Renaissance Venice. It was the Baroque type of instrumental concerto as modified in the late eighteenth century, particularly by Mozart, that provided the basis for Beethoven's work with the genre. The three-movement plan of the Baroque concerto continued to exist, so that the structural changes effected by Mozart and taken up by Beethoven had to do primarily with the first movement: the rapprochement between the old ritornello form with its alternation between the soli and tutti, characteristic of the Baroque concerto, and the sonata form which had become basic in the new instrumental music. In the new procedure this tutti-solo alternation was applied to the exposition part of the sonata form, which appeared twice, first scored for the tutti, then repeated by the soloist with additions to the accompaniment of the tutti, after which came a second tutti, the length and importance of which varied considerably from concerto to concerto. This then led to the development and to the recapitulation, in which both solo and tutti participated.

Toward the end, in a tutti passage, a great climax was worked up, ending on a sustained six-four chord marked by a fermata: At this point the soloist commenced an extensive passage known as the *cadenza* during which he was not accompanied by the orchestra. Here the main themes of the movement were subjected to further development. In Beethoven's time the cadenza was improvised by the soloist, who in most cases was also the composer of the concerto; as the nineteenth century came on, cadenzas began to be composed either by the pianists or by the composers themselves. A concerto was rather different from a symphony in that the emphasis went to virtuoso display of the soloist and of his powers as a performer: there was a profusion of themes, much greater than would be found in a symphony, sonata, or piece of chamber music, a good deal of virtuoso figuration, scale passages, arpeggios, rapid chords, trills, and so forth, in the solo part. Particular attention was given to the first appearance of the soloist, which usually but not always was at the end of the tutti part of the exposition, after which the soloist entered, either with striking figuration or with a completely new theme that had not been presented before; in a few cases the soloist was introduced immediately at the very beginning and then was silent while the tutti exposition ran its course. Schematically the first movement of a concerto of this period would look something like this:

The Middle Period

Exposition

Tutti
>   Principal theme
>   Modulatory passage
>   Secondary theme
>   Closing theme (ends in tonic)

Solo
>   New theme for entrance of soloist
>   Repeat of tutti exposition with new themes added
>   Tutti passage

Development

Solo and tutti in development of themes

Recapitulation

Tutti and Solo
>   Principal theme
>   Modulatory passage
>   Secondary theme
>   Closing theme
>   Cadenza
>   Closing theme or coda

Beethoven's Concerto for Piano and Orchestra in G major (No. 4, Op. 58), composed in 1805–6 and given its first performance by Beethoven himself in March, 1807, in three movements (Allegro, Andante con moto in E minor, and Vivace in G major), is on the whole typical of the concerto form that has just been described. The work begins, however, with a departure from the usual: The soloist enters immediately, before the orchestra, with the principal theme; this theme is chordal, stresses repeated notes, and displays the use of a rhythmic pattern. To this the orchestra responds in B major, then works back to G major and continues quite traditionally with the tutti part of the exposition; the secondary theme, lyric, is in A minor and there are two closing themes. The solo exposition, marked as would be expected by the reentrance of the soloist, then parallels the tutti exposition except for the addition of a new secondary theme. The development is dominated by the principal theme, and the recapitulation, with the cadenza, runs as already explained.

In the slow movement the connotation of opposition inherent in the term *concerto* is of basic importance: the abrupt, staccato, unison-octave theme, fortissimo, in the strings on the one hand, the subdued chordal response from the soloist on the other. The two opposing elements continue to alternate, but as the movement progresses the orchestra gradually gets softer and the soloist becomes dominant; eventually the orchestra is silent as the soloist goes into a cadenzalike passage that culminates in trills and chromatic scale runs; toward the end the tutti very softly recalls its once proud theme (see Example 4-14).

Without a pause comes the finale which, like most concerto finales, is an example of *rondo* form. Here there is a fully developed principal theme, the rondo proper, which is stated usually four times; in between its statements there appear two episodes, in different keys, which bring in new thematic material; the first episode normally appears twice, the second once. Schematically, this type of rondo may be represented thus:

Rondo—Episode—Rondo—Episode—Rondo—Episode—Rondo
         I   II   I

The form, however, rarely appears in this simplicity and completeness. Usually it runs true to course up to the entrance of Episode II, but thereafter changes in the plan are not uncommon. Often the statement of the rondo after Episode II is cut out. Another possibility, quite common in the work of Haydn, is for Episode II to take on the character of a development, in which case the form becomes known as the *sonata-rondo* form. In the finale of the concerto under

EXAMPLE 4-14

BEETHOVEN: ANDANTE CON MOTO, FROM CONCERTO FOR PIANO AND
ORCHESTRA IN G MAJOR (OP. 58)—BEGINNING

The Middle Period

EXAMPLE 4-14 (*continued*)

consideration, both of these variations occur. At the end of the last statement of Episode II there is a climax which ends on a sustained six-four chord, whereupon there is a cadenza for the soloist. In the movement as a whole the soloist and tutti are continually both involved in the presentation of the thematic material. The rondo theme itself is characterized by rapidly repeated notes in an upbeat rhythmic pattern, whereas Episode I consists of a lyric theme, presented first in the solo part and then in the tutti, where it is treated in imitation.

An important work which caused Beethoven much trouble was his single opera *Fidelio* (Op. 72), or as he preferred to call it, *Leonore*. Composed between 1803 and 1805, it was not well received when given for the first time on November 20, 1805, and an immediate revision, cutting the three acts down to two, which was given on March 29, 1806, was likewise unfavorably received. Beethoven then let the work lie for about eight years, when a thorough revision and reworking, involving the libretto as well as the music, was undertaken. This version, performed first on May 23, 1814, at last met with success, and it is in this form that the opera is performed today. There also exist four different overtures to the opera.

Beethoven and the New Instrumental Music

As already pointed out, *Fidelio* is another of those works in which Beethoven was involved with ethical—here specifically also political—ideals. Like the *Sinfonia eroica*, *Fidelio* is connected with revolutionary France. The revolutionary period had been a time of political turmoil, with leaders rising and falling as different factions vied with each other to seize and hold power; people were frequently thrown into prison and many were executed because of their political beliefs and their opposition to the faction that held power. It was a time of uncertainty, but also a time of individual heroism and of high idealism. This found artistic expression in a kind of opera popular in Paris during the 1790's, the plot of which involved a man being imprisoned for political reasons and about to be executed, who is saved at the last minute: This type of opera has been named the *rescue opera*. There are innumerable examples of rescue operas, one of the most important being Luigi Cherubini's *Les deux journées* (*The Two Days*) of 1800, which was translated into German as *Der Wasserträger* (*The Water-Carrier*), in which form it was given in Vienna in 1803, where it made a profound impression on Beethoven.

Fidelio is also a rescue opera. Its libretto goes back to a French opera, *Leonore*, composed by Pierre Gaveaux in 1798. The protagonist (the scene is Spain) Don Florestan, unjustly imprisoned by his rival Don Pizarro, is set free by the heroic efforts of his wife Leonore who, disguised as a boy under the name Fidelio, has won the confidence of the jailkeeper Rocco (and thus has even become engaged to Rocco's daughter Marcelline—such things are possible, even common, in opera). She succeeds in delaying the intended execution until help from outside arrives, heralded by the famous offstage trumpet signals. The idea of the heroic wife who sets her unjustly imprisoned husband free is coupled with the lofty ideals of revolutionary France: political liberty, equality, and human brotherhood. It was this combination that meant so much to Beethoven.

Before we can look at *Fidelio* itself, it is necessary to review the principal changes that had taken place in the history of opera since the grandiose *opera seria* of the late Baroque. In consequence of the new taste that developed in in the first half of the eighteenth century, there developed a new type of opera, the *opera buffa*, or comic opera. The earliest of these were simple works, the two acts of which were sandwiched in between the three acts of an opera seria. Unlike the opera seria, the characters in an opera buffa were drawn from the contemporary middle class (and not from classical antiquity, early history, or the Bible) and frequently represented stock character-types from the popular theater, or *commedia dell'arte* of the time: the jealous and miserly old man, the shrewd and pert servant girl, the brave young lover, the comic doctor, and so on. The opera buffa grew into an independent genre of opera in its own right and indeed soon usurped the position in the repertory that had been occupied by the opera seria. This may be seen from the work of Mozart, who moved away from the opera seria to the opera buffa and whose

The Middle Period

most well-known works are of this type: *Don Giovanni* and *The Marriage of Figaro*. An attempt to salvage the opera seria by reforming it in the sense of the French rationalistic aesthetics of the eighteenth century was made by Christoph Willibald Gluck (1714–1787) in Vienna and Paris.

While the two main musical styles—the recitative in its two forms and the aria—were maintained, some changes are to be noted. The da capo aria lost its importance and other aria types came in to replace it: the short aria or *cavatina*, the small strophic forms, the rondo aria in a form approaching the instrumental rondo, and the large two-part aria, first slow and then fast. Perhaps more important was the overcoming of the polarity between recitative (action) and aria (expression) that had been characteristic of the Baroque opera. This was done by means of a new kind of ensemble in which dramatic action and musical expression were brought together: The various characters in the scene were assigned different musical themes, and they proceeded in combination in a fashion not unrelated to the technique used in the development section of an instrumental composition; the character of the music changed in accordance with the needs of the dramatic situation. Frequently at the end of an act was a long, continuously composed ensemble in a number of contrasting sections, known as a finale. In the development of this new kind of ensemble and finale, Mozart was of great importance.

Another development in the eighteenth century had to do with the establishment of particular types of opera in the various countries of Europe. The only serious rival to the Italian opera up to the end of the Baroque had been the French. But this form, known as *tragédie lyrique*, had even taken its point of departure from the Italian opera of around the middle of the seventeenth century. It differed from the Italian opera seria in its emphasis on the recitative, choral writing and ballet, and in the relative lack of importance assigned to the arias. In the eighteenth century, however, it was the comic opera that came to the fore all over Europe: in France, the *opéra comique* and *vaudeville*; in Germany, the *Singspiel*; in Spain, the *zarzuela*; and in England, the *ballad opera*. All of these differed in one important respect from the Italian opera buffa: In place of the recitativo secco, they had spoken dialogue. Otherwise they consisted of arias, favoring the smaller kinds, often using strophic forms, and ensembles, along with choral and instrumental pieces, many of them dances. In Vienna the singspiel was cultivated extensively and Mozart left behind two important compositions, *The Abduction from the Seraglio* and *The Magic Flute*, the latter a long and elaborate work involving serious elements along with the comedy. Generally speaking, the German opera of the nineteenth century took its point of departure from the singspiel.

Beethoven's *Fidelio* may be classified as a singspiel, since it has spoken dialogue between most of the musical numbers. This comic aspect of the work is especially clear in the first scenes, before the real thrust of the opera is revealed, when the love situation between the jailkeeper's daughter and her lover Jacquino and the disguised Leonore is presented: Once the governor of the prison, Don Pizarro, enters and makes the decision to do away with the long-imprisoned Florestan, the opera takes on a completely different character, while still remaining, from the standpoint of genre, a singspiel. The simpler arias and ensembles (some of which are comic), among them the famous canonic quartet "Mir ist so wunderbar," all appear toward the beginning. But the big arias are serious compositions: Pizarro's aria of revenge, with chorus, "Ha! welch ein Augenblick!" and two larger arias, each preceded by an elaborate recitativo accompagnato, Leonore's "Komm' Hoffnung" and Florestan's "In des Lebens Frühlingstagen." Ensembles of the Mozartian type exist in abundance, particularly in the first scene of the dramatic second act, at the end of which Florestan's rapid and unexpected release is effected. The chorus is also employed effectively, the famous and poignant "Prisoner's Chorus" toward the end of the first act and the jubilant choruses of the final scene deserving special mention here. It is in these scenes particularly that Beethoven's involvement with the ideals represented by the work becomes most apparent.

As examples from *Fidelio* let us first take Leonore's big scene in the first act, the recitativo accompagnato "Abscheulicher! Wo eilst du hin?" and the connected aria "Komm' Hoffnung" (No. 9). Leonore has just overheard Pizarro's plan to do away with the prisoner he has kept so long in solitary confinement and, suspecting this prisoner to be her husband, expresses her agitation in a strong recitative. This is a fine example of the fully developed recitativo accompagnato, full of sudden changes, chords, and tremolos in the orchestra, the phrases often fragmentary. The recitative comes to a close and leads into the large aria, which is in two parts, the first in slow tempo, the invoking of the power of hope, and the second fast, the expression of Leonore's will to do what must be done. Prominent in the accompaniment are three horns.

EXAMPLE 4-15

BEETHOVEN: "Abscheulicher! Wo eilst du hin?" (RECITATIVE) AND "Komm' Hoffnung" (ARIA), FROM *Fidelio*—RECITATIVE AND BEGINNING OF ARIA (PIANO REDUCTION OF ORCHESTRA)

The Middle Period

EXAMPLE 4-15 (*continued*)

EXAMPLE 4-15 *(continued)*

The Middle Period

EXAMPLE 4-15 (continued)

EXAMPLE 4-15 (*continued*)

fern, ___ die Lie - be, sie wird's er - reichen, ja, ja, sie wird's er-

rei - - - - - - - - - - - - - - chen,

sie wird's er-rei - - - - - - - - - - chen.

TRANSLATION OF TEXT:

RECITATIVE O hateful one! Where are you rushing off to?
To what act is your wild anger driving you?
The call of pity—the voice of humanity—
Can nothing stir your tigerish feelings?
Yet, though anger heaves in your soul like ocean waves,
I perceive softly glowing a rainbow
Which lies bright above dark clouds.
It seems so still and peaceful,
It recalls old times once more,
And my blood flows quietly again.

The Middle Period

EXAMPLE 4-15 (*concluded*)

ARIA Come, Hope, do not let the last star
Grow pale before her who is tired.
O come, light me to my goal, no matter how far it is,
With love I will reach it.
I follow my inner drive,
I will not falter,
I am strengthened by the duty
Of the true love of my husband.
O you, for whom I have suffered everything,
If only I could get to you,
Where Evil has imprisoned you in chains
And bring sweet comfort to you.

As a second example we have the famous quartet in the second act (No. 14). The disguised Leonore and the jailkeeper Rocco have descended to the dungeon, have dug the grave for Florestan, and have given the condemned man, whom Leonore has recognized as her husband, some wine and bread. Before the number gets under way, Pizarro has just entered; he quickly reveals himself to Florestan. But just as he is about to dispatch Florestan, Leonore throws herself between them and, finally, after astonishment has been adequately registered and when Pizarro threatens her as well, brandishes a pistol; at this point the offstage trumpet sounds, signaling that help is at hand. This quartet will serve as an example of the operatic ensemble as it had been developed by Mozart: first, Pizarro's threats and the revelation of his identity, set to wide leaps, chromatic modulations, with a strong motivic figure in the orchestral accompaniment; then Florestan's rejoinder in martial D major accompanied by trumpets, horns, and timpani; and finally Leonore's sudden entrance into the fray, the reaction of the other three, and the gradual culmination up to the sounding of the offstage trumpet. Here is the text of the quartet with an English translation (lines bracketed together are sung simultaneously):

Pizarro

Er sterbe!—Doch er soll erst wissen,
Wer ihm sein stolzes Herz zerfleischt.
Der Rache Dunkel sei zerrissen,

He shall die! But first he must find out
Who it is that crushes his proud heart.
Let the darkness of revenge be dispelled,

Sieh' her! du hast dich nicht getäuscht.
  (He opens his cloak.)
Pizarro, den du fürchten solltest,
Pizarro, den du stürzen wolltest,

Look! you have not been deceived.

Pizarro, whom you should fear,
Pizarro, whom you tried to overthrow,

Steht nun als Rächer hier.

Is here now for revenge.

Florestan (coolly)
Ein Mörder, ein Mörder steht
vor mir.

Pizarro
Noch einmal ruf' ich dir, was
du getan, zurück,
Nur noch ein Augenblick, und
dieser Dolch—

Leonore (throws herself forward)
Zurück!—Durchbohren musst
du erst diese Brust,
Der Tod sei dir geschworen für
deine Mörderlust.

Florestan
O Gott!

Rocco
Was soll?
Halt ein! halt ein!

Pizarro (pushes her aside)
Wahnsinniger! Er soll bestrafet
sein.

Leonore
Töt' erst sein Weib'!

Pizarro and Rocco
Sein Weib?

Florestan
Mein Weib?

Leonore
Ja, hier siehe Leonore.

Florestan
Leonore?

Leonore
Ich bin sein Weib, geschworen
habe ich ihm Trost,
Verderben dir!
Ich trotze seiner Wuth!

Pizarro
Welch' unerhörter Mut!

Florestan (to Leonore)
Vor Freude starrt mein Blut!

Rocco
Mir starrt von Angst mein Blut.

A murderer, a murderer stands
before me.

Once more I remind you of
what you did to me,
Just one minute more, and
this dagger—

Stand back!—First you
must stab this breast,
I hereby condemn you to death
for your murderous instincts.

O God!

What's this?
Stop! Stop!

You are crazy! He shall be
punished.

Then first kill his wife!

His wife?

My wife?

Yes, I am Leonore.

Leonore?

I am his wife, to him I have
sworn comfort,
To you death!
I shall defy his anger!

What unheard-of courage!

I can hardly breathe for joy.

I can hardly breathe for fear.

Pizarro
Ha! Soll ich vor einem Weibe beben?
So opfr' ich beide meinem Grimm;

Geteilt has du mit ihm das Leben,
So teile nun den Tod mit ihm!
(He starts after her.)

Ha! Am I afraid of a woman?
I shall sacrifice both to appease my anger;
You shared his life,
Now share his death!

Leonore
Der Tod sei dir geschworen!
Durchbohren musst du erst diese Brust.

I have vowed to kill you!
First you must stab this breast.

(She quickly draws a pistol and points it at Pizarro.)

Noch einen Laut, und du bist tot.

One more sound and you are dead.

(The trumpet on the tower is heard.)

Ach! Du bist gerettet! Grosser Gott!

Ah! You are safe now! Thank God!

Florestan
Ach! Ich bin gerettet! Grosser Gott!

Ah! I am safe now. Thank God!

Pizarro (stunned)
Ha! Der Minister! Höll' und Tod!

Ha! The minister! Death and damnation!

Rocco (stunned)
O! Was ist das? Gerechter Gott!

O! What is this? Almighty God!

(The trumpet sounds louder. Pause. Jacquino, two officers and soldiers with torches appear at the top of the stairs.)

Jacquino
Vater Rocco, der Herr Minister kommt an. Sein Gefolge ist schon vor dem Schlosstor.

Rocco, the minister has arrived. His followers are already before the castle's gate.

Rocco (aside)
Gelobt sei Gott!
(to Jacquino, very loud)
Wir kommen, ja wir kommen augenblicklich, und diese Leute mit Fackeln sollen heruntersteigen und den Herrn Gouverneur hinaufbegleiten.

God be praised!

We are coming, we are coming immediately. You men with torches should come down and accompany the governor back up.

(The soldiers with torches descend and come forward.)

Leonore	
Es schlägt der Rache Stunde.	The hour of revenge has struck.
Du sollst gerettet sein!	You shall be saved!
Die Liebe wird im Bunde	Love joined with courage
Mit Mut dich befrei'n.	Shall set you free.
Florestan	
Es schlägt der Rache Stunde.	The hour of revenge has struck.
Ich soll gerettet sein.	I shall be saved.
Die Liebe wird im Bunde	Love joined with courage
Mit Mut mich befrei'n.	Will set me free.
Pizarro	
Verflucht sei diese Stunde!	Cursed be this hour!
Die Heuchler spotten mein.	The hypocrites make fun of me.
Verzweiflung wird im Bunde	My revenge has turned
Mit meiner Rache sein.	To despair.
Rocco	
O fürchterliche Stunde!	O fearful hour!
O Gott! Was wartet mein?	O God! What awaits me?
Ich will nicht mehr im	No longer will I
Bunde	serve
Mit dieser Wütrich sein.	This angry tyrant.

The Late Period

In 1814–15 Beethoven was at the height of his fame. But in the ensuing years, as a result of the political climate after the Napoleonic wars, his increased deafness, and the Viennese craze for the most popular kind of opera buffa as represented by the work of Gioacchino Rossini (1792–1868), as well as the difficulties with his nephew Karl, whose guardianship he had assumed, Beethoven began to live more and more in isolation. His productivity as a composer had declined, and very little was written in 1815. Then, beginning slowly in 1816, there commenced a remarkable succession of works—in number relatively small compared to what he had composed from 1800 to 1814—which make up what we know as his "late works": the last five piano sonatas, the last two sonatas for violoncello and piano, the "Diabelli" variations for piano, the last five string quartets, and the two largest works he completed—others were planned—for soloists, chorus, and orchestra: the Ninth Symphony and the *Missa solemnis*.

These late works have stimulated much discussion and criticism and, with the exception of the Ninth Symphony, found but little understanding and acclaim among his contemporaries. Generally speaking, the large-scale form, with the emphasis on thematic development and powerful expression, gave way to music that stressed the more learned types of writing: the variation form and the fugue, of which the latter appeared both as an entire movement and as forming a development of a movement in sonata form. These works also

The Late Period

Street scene in Vienna, early nineteenth century. By Jacob Alt. (BY PERMISSION OF THE HISTORICAL MUSEUM OF THE CITY OF VIENNA.)

display Beethoven's continuing use of movements manifesting specific characters, as the passionate recitative style, the *pathétique* aria style from the opera, the religious style of church music (see later), the military march, and so on. The themes used in these late works tended to become more lyrical and melodic while losing none of their motivic character. But frequently in these works continuity is disrupted: Melodies are begun and suddenly broken off right in the middle, or without any transition slow and soft chords may be heard after furious figuration. The harmonic progressions are often most unusual. The overall large form, the conception of individual movements forming the whole, was maintained by Beethoven in these works, except that it became more common for themes or passages from earlier movements to appear in subsequent movements, thus bringing in the element of cyclic form.

As an example we may consider the Sonata for Piano in A-flat major (Op. 110) composed in 1822, which shows many of the features just mentioned. The work is in four movements. The opening one, Moderato cantabile, molto expressivo, presents an intense lyric theme based on a short rhythmic motive, with simple accompaniment; the secondary theme brings little contrast, and in the development the lyrical principal theme is brought to a climax. There then comes an Allegro molto—which stands for the scherzo—with a brusque chordal theme featuring irregular accentuations, along with a trio consisting mainly of figuration. From this point on, the organization of the work becomes less traditional. First there is one of those deeply felt slow movements so characteristic of Beethoven's late works, with a hint of opera in the background: a recitative and an *arioso dolente* (melancholy arioso); this is followed

EXAMPLE 4-16

BEETHOVEN: SONATA FOR PIANO IN A-FLAT MAJOR (OP. 110)—EXCERPTS

1. MODERATO CANTABILE, MOLTO ESPRESSIVO—BEGINNING

2. ADAGIO MA NON TROPPO—BEGINNING

3. FUGA—BEGINNING

The Late Period

EXAMPLE 4-16 (continued)

3.

EXAMPLE 4-16 (*concluded*)

by a fugue, after which the arioso is heard again, but with its expression heightened by the use of "sob" figures; a passage of repeated A-flat major chords in a great crescendo ushers in a repetition of the fugue, this time with the subject inverted.

A particularly remarkable instance of Beethoven's use of a characteristic musical style may be seen in the long slow movement, Adagio, of the Quartet in A minor (Op. 132), composed in 1825. The movement has a descriptive title: "Holy Song of Thanksgiving of a Convalescent to God Upon His Recovery, in the Lydian Mode." Here Beethoven deliberately works in an archaic style, recalling the sound and character of the Netherlands music of the Renaissance, a style long regarded as the most proper for religious music. The impression is fostered by the use of the old Lydian mode, the major scale on F but with B natural instead of B flat (see page 41), and the chord progressions thus produced. Furthermore, the use of slow and largely even rhythmic values likewise contributes to the archaic impression of the piece, recalling at least the aura of the plainsong. The movement as a whole is in five-part form (*A B A B A*), in which the *A* passage displays the "religious style," and the *B* bears the explanation, "Feeling new strength" (see Example 4-17).

Beethoven's late period is also characterized by works on a very large scale. One of these is the *Missa solemnis* in D major (Op. 123), composed in 1819–23, parts of it being first performed in 1824, an extended setting of the Ordinary of the Mass. Here Beethoven's deep seriousness of purpose and his belief in humanity are plainly evident. The work is prefaced by a motto: "Von Herzen—Möge es wieder zu Herzen gehn" (From [my] heart—may it go on [again] to [others'] hearts). Furthermore, both the Kyrie and Sanctus

The Late Period

movements are marked to be performed *Mit Andacht* (with devotion). Beethoven's belief in humanity led him to give extraordinary emphasis to the word "homo" in the "Et incarnatus est" section of the Credo. Finally, in the Agnus movement, the section with the words "Dona nobis pacem" (Give us peace) is given a supplementary title, "Bitte um innern und äussern Frieden" (Plea for Inner and Outer Peace) (it should be recalled that the work was composed a few years after the Napoleonic wars); in this section there is suddenly injected a short but impassioned recitative accompanied by military fanfares in the trumpets and timpani, thus making Beethoven's meaning unequivocal.

EXAMPLE 4-17

BEETHOVEN: ADAGIO, FROM STRING QUARTET IN A MINOR (OP. 132)—
BEGINNING

EXAMPLE 4-17 (*continued*)

The Late Period

In this Mass each line of the text gets its own musical interpretation, some treated fugally, others homophonically, the musical style and character depending on the nature of the text. Thus the fundamental procedure is the same as that employed in the Renaissance Mass; the difference lies in the vastly greater length of the working-out in Beethoven's composition. Unlike the string quartet movement in religious style just discussed, Beethoven here uses the most modern harmonic procedures, at the same time retaining the principle of line-by-line setting of the text of the Mass, occasionally employing contrapuntal imitation. Long fugal passages appear at the end of both the Gloria and Credo movements: at "in gloria dei patris. Amen" of the former and at "et vitam venturi saeculi. Amen" of the latter. An element of unity or rounding off is introduced at the end of both these movements: the "Gloria in excelsis Deo" theme appears at the very end of the Gloria movement and the "Credo in unum Deum" theme is employed in the "Quoniam" section in connection with the words "in spiritum sanctam." The main point, however, has to do with expression: The "Gloria in excelsis Deo" is set to a joyously explosive rising figure; the "Crucifixus," in the Credo, is characterized by the descending leap of a tritone and a conventional "sob" figure accompanied by minor and diminished triads; the immediately following "Et resurrexit" is bright and uses a rapidly rising theme.[8] Particular attention must be drawn to the Benedictus portion of the Sanctus: It opens with a solemn instrumental "Praeludium" scored for the lower strings with flute and bassoon; in the Benedictus itself the chorus, hushed, using melodic materials that frequently suggest plainsong recitation, is accompanied by solo violin and woodwinds, both in their uppermost register, in harmonies that can only be described as ethereal.

By all odds the most celebrated, influential, and popular of the late works is the Symphony in D minor (No. 9, Op. 125) with the concluding choral movement that includes a setting of Schiller's *Ode to Joy*. Composed in 1822–24, the symphony had its first performance on May 7, 1824, but the idea of composing music for Schiller's popular poem had been in Beethoven's mind as far back as 1792, and he had even revived it around 1812. At all events, the decision to incorporate such a setting into a symphony was made relatively late during the work on the Symphony in D minor. As we will see, this decision had an enormous impact on the nineteenth century.

The first three movements, although large and complex, represent the tradition of the purely instrumental symphony as it had been manifested in the earlier work of Beethoven. The first movement is an Allegro in sonata form, but already in the presentation of the principal theme one senses something completely different: The ambiguous fifths (A–E) in the accompaniment, all pianissimo, are taken up in the theme itself; and as the rhythmic motion

---

[8] A similar contrast between a Crucifixus and an Et resurrexit has been pointed out in Bach's Mass in B minor.

EXAMPLE 4-18

BEETHOVEN: ALLEGRO (FIRST MOVEMENT), FROM SYMPHONY IN D MINOR (OP. 125)—BEGINNING

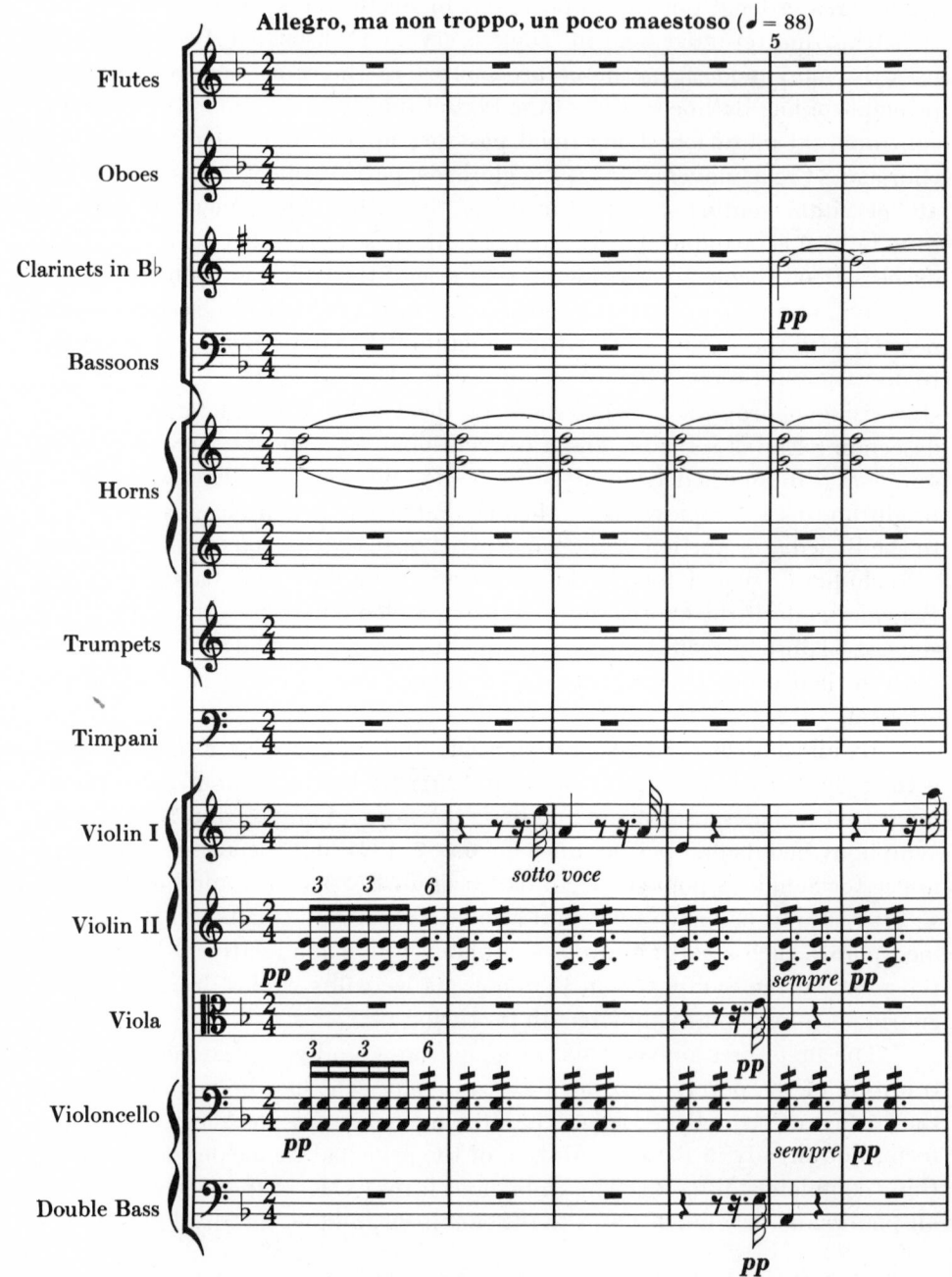

EXAMPLE 4-18 (*continued*)

Example 4-18 (*continued*)

and the crescendo intensify, suddenly when the ambiguous harmony has been clarified and becomes recognizable as the dominant, the full theme is given forth, fortissimo and in octaves, by the whole orchestra in D minor. This organic, as it were primordial, unfolding of the theme had considerable influence on symphonies to come. For the rest, the movement proceeds in accordance with the rather free attributes of the form. But the development is long; in the recapitulation the principal theme is presented fortissimo over a pedal point in the timpani, and there is an elaborate coda.

The scherzo is notable for its octave leaps, timpani solos, driving rhythms, and fugal writing; in contrast the trio is dominated by essentially the same brief passage presented with some variations over and over again. The Adagio molto, in B-flat major, is a theme and variations structure, in form—if not in spirit—similar to the slow movement of the Symphony in C minor (Op. 67): Two themes, presented in succession, are then submitted to variation; but toward the end there are episodic fanfares, passages of military character.

The finale has aroused the most attention. This grandiose movement centers around Schiller's poem, the *Ode to Joy* (*An die Freude*). The poem, written in 1785, portrays joy and human brotherhood as the driving forces of humanity, raising man toward divinity; this idea, as we have seen, lay very close to Beethoven. Moreover, the poem, in strophic form, was originally specifically intended by Schiller to be set to music (indications of what was to be sung by the soloist and what by a chorus appear in the printed text) as a social song, to be sung in gatherings where good fellowship prevailed. The poem was extremely popular at the time and had often been set to music. All this was exploited by Beethoven in the conception of this movement. From his sketches it is clear that he was greatly concerned with the problem of how to introduce the vocal element into a symphonic composition. This was finally done by means of an extensive instrumental introduction: At the beginning, the dissonant chord and the fanfare passage in the brasses and woodwinds with percussion, followed by the recitative for the violoncellos and double basses; then during the course of what seems to be a search for the proper musical theme, the principal themes of the three previous movements are successively stated in fragmentary form and rejected in turn by the recitative. After this the "joy theme" begins to take shape in the woodwinds and is greeted enthusiastically by the recitative. And after a climactic cadence, the theme is stated in its entirety four times, each time somewhat louder: first in the lower strings, then in the strings with bassoon, then the full string orchestra, and finally by the full orchestra led by the brass choir.

When this is brought to an end there occurs one of those disruptions of continuity so characteristic of Beethoven's late work: Suddenly the raucous introductory fanfare is heard again, followed by the entrance of the baritone with a short recitative, "O friends! Not these tones, but let us sing something

The Late Period

EXAMPLE 4-19

BEETHOVEN: FINALE, FROM SYMPHONY IN D MINOR (OP. 125)—EXCERPTS

1. ALLEGRO ASSAI, D MAJOR: VOCAL PRESENTATION OF STROPHE I

2. ANDANTE MAESTOSO—BEGINNING

3. ALLEGRO ENERGICO, SEMPRE MARCATO—BEGINNING

1.

EXAMPLE 4-19 (*continued*)

The Late Period

EXAMPLE 4-19 (*continued*)

EXAMPLE 4-19 (*continued*)

The Late Period

EXAMPLE 4-19 (*continued*)

Beethoven and the New Instrumental Music

E<small>XAMPLE</small> 4-19 *(concluded)*

2.

3.*

more pleasant, more joyful." The vocal presentation of the first three strophes of the *Ode to Joy* follows for the soloists with choral refrain. After a massive climax comes the tenor solo with the fourth strophe, accompanied by male chorus and woodwind-brass ensemble with Turkish music (percussion, tambourines, and cymbals), comparing man's accomplishments to the victories of a hero. This runs immediately into a fugal section for the orchestra alone, full of driving rhythms, after which comes a second statement of the first strophe of the *Ode to Joy.*

We now have a sudden change of key and character as religious ideas are brought in: "Be embraced, O ye millions; rise up now and seek your creator." The chorus sings first in octaves, then in simple four-part homophony, accompanied by solemn intonations of the trombones. In its atmosphere, produced in part by unusual and archaic-sounding harmonic progressions, this section

* Instrumental parts omitted.

resembles the sacred contrapuntal music of the sixteenth century and is thus related to the "Holy Song of Thanksgiving" of the Quartet in A minor. In the next section this "religious theme" is combined with the "joy theme" in an elaborate double fugue, after which a coda, built on the same two themes, brings the work to its magnificent conclusion.

In this monumental conception many things are brought together: the strophic form of the German popular social song, the operatic recitative, the military wind-band with Turkish music, the soft serene religious music, and the driving rhythms characteristic of a Baroque fugue. All are united by the single central conception: joy and human brotherhood. This ethical idea dominates Beethoven's artistic achievement.

Chapter Five

Wagner and
the Romantic Age

*i*n the aesthetics of the late eighteenth century, which governed the work of Beethoven, the artwork was viewed as an independent totality or entity in which a number of parts or elements were subordinated to make up a whole in accordance with the dictates of reason. The element of detail, of color, was thought of as being supplied by the imagination. The idea of the artwork as a whole organized rationally is eminently classical, and in this sense the music of this time may be regarded as classical. This music is classical also in the sense that it provided the model, the norm, for much of the musical composition that was to follow.

But in the early nineteenth century, with the increased emphasis on personal and subjective expression, an emphasis by no means entirely lacking in eighteenth-century music, this lofty conception of the large musical artwork began to change as imaginative elements that had been regarded as details made themselves more and more prominent. The overall unity of the large form either began to break down or else was sought by entirely different means. The large forms of instrumental music, although they continued to be cultivated throughout the nineteenth century, nonetheless lost ground and were replaced, quantitatively at all events, by smaller and simpler forms.

Of great importance here was the power of expression that was imputed to music: music came—because of its lack of the denotative power to express concrete meanings—to be looked upon as the most essentially Romantic of all the arts, as the art in which it is possible to express "the Unspeakable." Music thus came to occupy a central position in the aesthetics of the time, as can be confirmed by the work of the philosophers Hegel and Schopenhauer, to mention only two. In consequence there arose genres in which music was associated with something nonmusical which it somehow was to express or make manifest: a novel, drama, poem, or painting. Purely instrumental music of this type, related to a work of literature or a painting, has come generally to be known as *program music*.

A final aspect of general significance for nineteenth-century music was the outgrowth of the increase in public concerts since the eighteenth century: the rise of the virtuoso, the skilled player of his instrument who performs to the amazement and acclaim of the audience. In this we may see a special application of the idea of the artistic genius, to which reference has already been made (see pages 182–83). The model here was provided by the Italian violinist Nicolò Paganini (1782–1840), who made a tremendous impression on audiences all over Europe. But it was not only his extraordinary skill in playing the instrument, it was also the aura with which he deliberately invested his public performances: In appearance he was thin, gaunt, almost emaciated, with a pale face, long thin black hair, and a piercing glance; he would step before an audience in black formal evening dress on a dimly lit stage, there to perform his dazzling, seemingly supernaturally or demonically inspired feats of musical legerdemain. The aim of establishing the idea of a link with the supernatural is clear enough. Somewhat later in the nineteenth century this idea was taken over by a man who became the foremost virtuoso pianist of the time, Franz Liszt (1811–1886), who established the solo recital for piano in its modern form.

New Forms of Romantic Music

The change that came with the rise of Romanticism, then, had a good deal to do with repertory, the musical forms and genres that got the most attention, and those that were neglected. Generally speaking, there was a shift away from the large forms of instrumental music—the symphony, the piano sonata, the many types of chamber music (even though there are many celebrated examples by nineteenth-century composers which testify that these forms by no means died out)—in favor of a number of smaller forms which were more in accordance with the conceptions of the age, particularly the leading ideas concerning the expressive power of music and the close link that was felt to exist between music and literature. There are three principal categories of musical composition that call for particular comment here: the *art song* or *lied*, the *character piece* for piano, and the *symphonic poem* for orchestra.

The art song or *lied* (this German word is used in English) is the most obviously related to literature, since it involves a poetical text being set to music, usually for a solo voice with piano accompaniment. Songs with keyboard accompaniment had been popular throughout the Baroque, especially in late eighteenth-century Germany. But these late eighteenth-century German songs generally were, from the musical standpoint, modest compositions. Since composers aimed at a popular, almost folklike quality, the songs were usually very simple, using regular, balanced melodic phrases, simple harmonies, simple homophonic accompaniments, and were cast in strict strophic form, all strophes of the poem being set to the same music. With the coming of the nineteenth century, in the work of the Viennese composer Franz Peter Schubert (1797–1828), this old type of song was transformed into a genre capable of elaborate and serious artistic expression.

Franz Peter Schubert.
Portrait by Rieder.

The transformation wrought by Schubert around 1815 has two principal aspects, both involved with the idea of making possible an adequate musical representation or expression of the text: first, the overcoming of the strophic form, to permit the composer to invent a melodic line in accordance with his interpretation of the poem and to change the melodic line in accordance with changes in the character of the poem; and second, the elaboration of the piano accompaniment so that it could express the character of mood of the piece. Actually, though, in Schubert's work all the different types are to be found: the old strophic form, as in his setting of Goethe's popular poem "Heiden-röslein" ("Heather Rose"); the modified strophic form, in which either whole or part of one of the strophes is changed, the rest remaining the same, as in "Die Forelle ("The Trout")—many songs of this type take the familiar three-part form (*A B A*), so common that it is often known simply as *song form*, as may be seen in "Geheimes" ("Secret"); finally, the through-composed form, in which there is no regular repetition at all.

As an example of the last, let us look at Schubert's setting of a ballad by Goethe, "Der Erlkönig" ("The Erl King"). As a literary genre, the ballad represents an old type of narrative poetry, usually in strophic form, which recounts a grim story generally ending in a violent death and involving the

New Forms of Romantic Music

supernatural. The oldest ballads are anonymous, but the genre was revived by poets of the late eighteenth and early nineteenth century and experienced great popularity. Goethe's gripping poem tells in dialogue form of the ride of a father and his boy on horseback through a storm at night and the boy's fears of the evil Erl King, a demon he sees and hears, while his father, who sees and hears nothing, offers natural explanations for what the boy says he sees and hears. After trying to lure the boy in several tantalizing ways, the Erl King finally loses patience and uses force, and when the father has reached home he finds the boy in his arms dead. In setting this poem, Schubert exploits the piano accompaniment to establish the atmosphere: the minor key, the fast, almost hammering sixteenth-note triplets in octaves, and the rising scale figure in the bass. After the opening strophe, which establishes the emotional aura, the three characters are set off from one another musically: the anxious comforting father, the frightened child, and the lyrically seductive Erl King for whom the accompaniment goes over to the major and becomes liltingly dancelike in character. Toward the end, after the narrative character of the very first strophe has been resumed, the turbulent accompaniment gradually comes to a stop, and the last line is set effectively in recitative style. Here is the text of Goethe's poem, along with an English version by Sir Walter Scott:

ERLKÖNIG

Wer reitet so spät durch
Nacht und Wind?
Es ist der Vater mit seinem
Kind;
Er hat den Knaben wohl in dem
Arm,
Er fasst ihn sicher, er hält
ihn warm.

"Mein Sohn, was birgst du so
bang dein Gesicht?"
"Siehst, Vater, du den Erlkönig
nicht!"
"Den Erlenkönig mit Kron' und
Schweif."
"Mein Sohn, es ist ein
Nebelstreif."

"Du liebes Kind, komm, geh' mit
mir!
Gar schöne Spiele spiel' ich
mit dir;
Manch' bunte Blumen sind an
dem Strand,
Meine Mutter hat manch' gülden
Gewand."

THE ERL KING

O who rides by night thro' the
woodland so wild?
It is the fond father embracing
his child;
And close the boy nestles within
his loved arm,
To hold himself fast, and to
keep himself warm.

"My boy, upon what dost thou
fearfully gaze?"
"O father, see yonder! see
yonder!" he says;
"O, 'tis the Erl King with his
crown and his shroud."
"No, my son, it is but a dark
wreath of the cloud."

(*The Erl King speaks*)
"O come and go with me, thou
loveliest child;
By many a gay sport shall thy
time be beguiled;
My mother keeps for thee many
a fair toy,
And many a fine flower shall she
pluck for my boy."

"Mein Vater, mein Vater, und
hörest du nicht
Was Erlenkönig mir leise
verspricht?"
"Sei ruhig, bleibe ruhig,
mein Kind!
In dürren Blattern säuselt
der Wind."

"Willst, feiner Knabe, du mit
mir gehn?
Meine Töchter sollen dich
warten schön;
Meine Töchter führen den
nächtlichen Reihn,
Und wiegen und tanzen und
singen dich ein."

"Mein Vater, mein Vater, und
siehst du nicht dort
Erlkönigs Töchter am düstern
Ort?"
"Mein Sohn, mein Sohn, ich seh'
es genau;
Es scheinen die alten Weiden
so grau."

"Ich liebe dich, mich reizt
deine schöne Gestalt,
Und bist du nicht willig, so
brauch' ich Gewalt."
"Mein Vater, mein Vater, jetzt
fasst er mich an,
Erlkonig hat mich ein Leids
getan!"

Dem Vater grauset's, er reitet
geschwind,
Er hält in Armen das ächzende
Kind,
Erreicht den Hof mit Mühe und
Not;
In seinen Armen das Kind war
tot.

"O father, o father, and did
you not hear
The Erl King whisper so low in
my ear?"
"Be still, my heart's darling
—my child, be at ease;
It was but the wild blast as it
sung thro' the trees."

Erl King
"O wilt thou go with me, thou
loveliest boy?
My daughter shall tend thee with
care and with joy;
She shall bear thee so lightly
thro' wet and thro' wild,
And press thee, and kiss thee,
and sing to my child."

"O father, o father, and saw you
not plain
The Erl King's pale daughter glide
past through the rain?"
"O yes, my loved treasure, I
knew it full soon;
It was the gray willow that
danced to the moon."

Erl King
"O come and go with me, no longer
delay,
Or else, silly child, I will
drag you away."
"O father, O father, now, now,
keep your hold,
The Erl King has seized me—
his grasp is so cold!"

Sore trembled the father; he
spurr'd thro' the wild,
Clasping close to his bosom his
shuddering child;
He reaches his dwelling in doubt
and in dread,
But, clasp'd to his bosom, the
infant was dead.

New Forms of Romantic Music

EXAMPLE 5-1

SCHUBERT: "Der Erlkönig" ("The Erl King")—EXCERPTS

1. FIRST STROPHE

2. THIRD STROPHE—BEGINNING

1.

EXAMPLE 5-1 (*continued*)

Not unrelated to the song is the character piece for piano, which also figured prominently in the work of Schubert. Symbolic of the character piece in general is the title used for a large set of such compositions by Felix Mendelssohn-Bartholdy (1809–1847): *Songs without Words*. This is precisely what many of these pieces are: lyrical compositions in which a melodic line is given a characteristic accompaniment, usually cast in three-part form. A number of titles or names are used for such pieces: impromptu, intermezzo, fantasia, album leaf, musical moment (Schubert), nocturne; more specifically suggestive titles are also used: "The Happy Farmer" (Schumann), "The Fountains in the Este Gardens" (Liszt), and "Wild Hunt" (Liszt). It is not uncommon for dances to be treated as character pieces, waltzes, polonaises, and so on. Even study pieces, known as *études*, may appear as character pieces, as in the work of Liszt and Chopin. In many cases, then, the character piece is closely related to the romantic belief in the expressive power of music.

New Forms of Romantic Music

Frederic Chopin.
Portrait by Delacroix.
(COURTESY MUSÉE DU
LOUVRE, PARIS.)

We can take an example from the work of Frederic Chopin (1810–1849), the Polish composer whose work was to a large extent given over to piano music, most of which is in some form of character piece. Typical are the nineteen nocturnes (or night pieces), a lyrical type extensively cultivated prior to Chopin by the Irish pianist and composer John Field (1782–1837). The main features of a nocturne include the simple three-part formal plan and the lyrical melodic line often embellished with rapid filigree figuration (called *fioriture*), over a harmonic accompaniment consisting of simple broken chords. Usually the middle section brings contrast; it will be louder, move faster, use a new theme, and often work up to a climax, which then subsides and leads to the restatement, frequently in somewhat varied form, of the beginning. Furthermore, a nocturne was to be performed in *tempo rubato* (*rubato* meaning "robbed," i.e., some notes are shortened, robbed, of part of their value and the other notes correspondingly lengthened); thus the written rhythmic values are not to be interpreted strictly, but with a certain freedom. As an example, we may take the Larghetto in F-sharp major (Op. 15ii), composed around 1833. This nocturne commences with the typical lyrical melody over a regular accompaniment, the melody eight bars in length and consisting of two parallel

EXAMPLE 5-2

CHOPIN: NOCTURNE IN F-SHARP MAJOR (Op. 15ii)—FIRST SECTION

EXAMPLE 5-2 (*continued*)

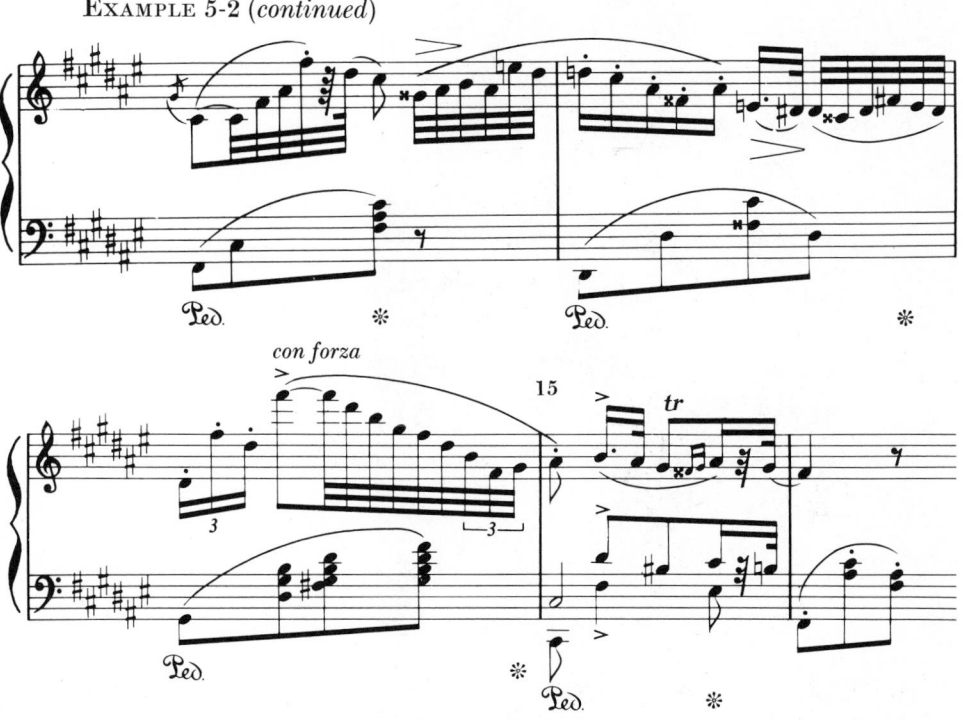

phrases, each being stated twice in its entirety, but greatly embellished the second time; the middle section is twice as fast, features figuration, begins softly, gradually attains a climax, then falls off, followed by a single embellished statement of the original theme and a short coda.

Larger than either of these is what has come to be known as the symphonic poem: an extended composition for orchestra based usually on a literary work. Historically, apart from pictorial compositions representing battles or pastoral scenes, an important predecessor of the symphonic poem was the overture of the late eighteenth and early nineteenth century, such as those by Mozart to his operas *Don Giovanni* and *The Magic Flute*, or by Beethoven to *Fidelio* or to Goethe's *Egmont* and Collin's *Coriolan*. In each of these the overture was closely connected to the opera or play for which it was written: it established the atmosphere or mood of the piece, and in some cases, as the two overtures by Mozart just mentioned or Beethoven's overture to *Fidelio*, even employed themes subsequently used in the opera itself. It is this last aspect of the overture that came to have decisive importance: The overture thus became a purely instrumental summation of the opera by virtue of its use of the themes of the principal arias and scenes of the opera. As the nineteenth century wore on, this was carried out on a more comprehensive basis, so that most of the main themes used in an opera would occur in the overture.

Hector Berlioz.
Portrait by Courbet.
(COURTESY MUSÉE DU LOUVRE, PARIS.)

Along somewhat different lines ran the work of the French composer Hector Berlioz (1803–1869), who composed symphonic compositions, in many ways corresponding to the German symphonic tradition, but based on literary texts or programs. Perhaps his most well-known work was the celebrated *Symphonie fantastique* in C major (Op. 14), composed in 1830. Here the literary program on which the work is based was conceived by Berlioz himself and can be related to events in his life, the courting of the actress Harriet Smithson. This program is highly Romantic. Bearing the subtitle "Episode in the Life of an Artist," it recounts how an artist, depressed because his beloved has rejected him, seeks refuge in opium and has visions: First he is at a ball where he sees his beloved; then in the country where her presence makes itself felt everywhere; then he is seized, marched to a scaffold, and executed; finally, his spirit participates in a witches' sabbath, which culminates in a bacchanalian dance. The work is unified by the use of a single theme in all the movements, so that it is yet another manifestation of cyclic form. The difference is that this theme is expressly associated with the literary program: It stands for the artist's *idée fixe* (fixed idea), his beloved; and as his beloved haunts him throughout, so does this musical theme appear in every movement of the work.

In the first movement it serves as the principal theme (after the slow introduction) in a sonata form; in the second movement it appears in alternation and in combination with a waltz; in the third movement as the secondary theme; in the third movement, just as the hero is about to be executed, it appears, abruptly broken off with the blow that dispatches him; and in the elaborate finale it appears in burlesqued form. An important symbolic touch is Berlioz' suggestion of death by the use, in the finale, of the Gregorian chant melody *Dies irae*, a part of the Requiem Mass. Apart from all this, the *Symphonie fantastique* abounds in novel, brilliant, and highly effective ways of employing the instrumental resources of the symphony orchestra. Other compositions by Berlioz in a similar vein are *Harold en Italie* (Op. 16) composed in 1834, based on Byron, and the large *Roméo et Juliette* (Op. 17) of 1839 for soloists, chorus, and orchestra, based on Shakespeare. In each case, the use of the literary program goes along with some semblance of the forms and procedures of the symphony, so that these works are frequently called *program symphonies*.

This is changed in the work of Franz Liszt, who after having become known as the preeminent virtuoso of the piano, in 1849 suddenly abandoned this spectacularly successful career and settled down as conductor at the court of Weimar, where he also devoted himself to composition. It was in the years at Weimar (1848–59) that Liszt developed the form and the name *symphonic poem*: an orchestral work related to an extramusical, usually literary source

EXAMPLE 5-3

TRANSFORMATIONS OF THE IDÉE FIXE IN BERLIOZ' *Symphonie fantastique*

Original form (First Movement)

In waltz time (Second Movement)

As shepherd's piping (Third Movement)

At moment of execution (Fourth Movement)

Burlesque version (Fifth Movement)

in which the composer's interpretation of the model determined the form as well as the thematic content. Here again, as with Berlioz' works, it is cyclic form—the presentation and variation of one or more themes which are expressly related to particular aspects of the program in all parts of the composition—that is decisive. In *The Battle of the Huns*, apart from the obvious battle music, the Gregorian chant hymn *Crux fidelis* represents the Christians; in *Tasso*, a Venetian gondola song is used to suggest the famous sixteenth-century Italian poet. Easily the most popular of Liszt's symphonic poems is *Les Préludes*, based on Lamartine.

Wagner's Life

The notion that music can express something that is not musical reached its culmination in the work of Richard Wagner (1813–1883). Born in Leipzig, Wagner's musical talent manifested itself early, coupled with an interest in the theater, the latter having been spurred on by the striking performances of the great singing actress Wilhelmine Schröder-Devrient. By 1833 he had composed his first theatrical work, a magic opera, *Die Feen* (*The Fairies*). His professional career in music first involved conducting at opera houses in three of the smaller cities in Prussia: Magdeburg (1834–36), Königsberg (1836) and Riga (1837–39). During this time he pursued a stormy courtship with an actress, Minna Planer, whom he finally married in 1836. Only one opera was composed during these years, *Das Liebesverbot* (1835), based on Shakespeare's *Love's Labor Lost*. Wagner's taste for luxurious living, however, tended to exceed what he was able to earn, so that he was constantly borrowing money and being badgered by creditors whose efforts to seek repayment were regarded as a meddlesome distraction by the great artist. In any case, things eventually came to a head, and in 1839 the young couple was forced to make a hasty departure from Riga by sea at night. They went first to London and then to Paris.

In Paris, Wagner was caught up in the intellectual and cultural activities for which that city was the center of Europe. He was in contact with many leading figures: Liszt, Berlioz, the German poet Heinrich Heine, Chopin, Delacroix, and many others. He managed to support himself somehow by journalistic activity and by writing critical essays. A profound experience was the performance of Beethoven's symphonies under the famous conductor Françoise Antoine Habeneck, an experience that had important consequences for his own career as a composer. While in Riga he had commenced work on a large-scale historical opera of the type known as *grand opera* (see later):

(Opposite) *Richard Wagner. Contemporary photograph.* (COURTESY GERMAN INFORMATION CENTER, NEW YORK)

Festival House, Bayreuth.

Rienzi. This he brought to completion and in Paris began something new, a work that incorporated for the first time those features we generally associate with a typical Wagnerian opera: *The Flying Dutchman.*

It was the more conventional opera, *Rienzi*, however, that secured what appeared to be his big break: an engagement in 1842 as conductor in Dresden, where the opera was to be performed. Soon afterward, *The Flying Dutchman* was completed and performed at Dresden in 1843. This work was not received with unqualified acclaim. Undaunted, Wagner commenced work on *Tannhäuser*, which was given its first performance in 1845, and then began *Lohengrin.*

Apart from musical composition Wagner was active politically. He associated with radical socialistic elements who were violently opposed to the monarchy and to the big industrialists. In common with Marx, Wagner had the idea of the decadent old world crumbling. But as things turned out in 1849, it was the revolution that crumbled, and Wagner, who had been perhaps too prominently associated with it, again had to make a rapid and unplanned exit, this time into exile.

The exile lasted some fifteen years and was spent mainly in Zurich, but also partly in Paris, London, Brussels, Vienna, and St. Petersburg. During its early years, especially in 1850–51, Wagner abandoned composition and gave himself over to making critical observations on his work, on the course of opera, Romanticism and music in general, as well as on the proper relation that should exist between the musician and society. This reflection produced three important literary works which are essential to any understanding of Wagner's intentions and methods: *Art and Revolution, The Art-Work of the Future*, and *Opera and Drama*, of which the last is the largest and most comprehensive— and doubtless the most important—treatise on opera written in the nineteenth century. Wagner then returned to composition and worked out the idea for his most grandiose work, *The Ring of the Nibelung*, which ultimately consisted of four related operas. At the same time he also began work on *Tristan und Isolde* and *Die Meistersinger von Nürnberg*.

In 1864 came the miracle. There ascended to the throne of Bavaria, which at the time was a sovereign state, a youth of eighteen, Ludwig II, who for some time had been an ardent admirer of Wagner's work. The young king immediately sent for Wagner to come to Munich, offered him a position, and provided support for the realization of Wagner's artistic aims. This included the completion in 1873 of a theater especially designed for the performance of Wagner's works in Bayreuth; annual festival performances were instituted, a tradition still maintained by Wagner's descendents. After the death of his wife Minna, Wagner attracted Cosima, Liszt's daughter, from her marriage with the famous pianist and conductor Hans von Bülow (1830–1894). During this period he completed his artistic work: the concluding parts of *The Ring of the Nibelung* and the last opera, *Parsifal* (1882).

The Early Operas

An important influence on Wagner was exercised by a type of opera called *grand opera* that was current in Paris from the late 1820's on and which subsequently spread all over Europe. Grand opera was characterized by magnificence. Dealing with the subjects from mythology or history and frequently involving the supernatural, it projected them on a vast scale. In grand opera, arias were present in great profusion and variety, ranging from elaborate virtuoso showpieces to simple songs with catchy popular tunes. The ensemble was transformed into a large showy piece for soloists, often with choral accompaniment. Crowd scenes with chorus, representing processions, ceremonies, and the like, often with ballet, were given a prominent position. Novel orchestral effects were exploited. But just as important was the emphasis on spectacular visual effects, as in Auber's *La Muette de Portici* (1828), which closes with the eruption of Vesuvius.

Wagner's first large-scale opera, *Rienzi*, was of this kind. Set in fourteenth-century Italy, it recounts the story of a revolt against the nobility which after a period of seeming success is put down. At the end, Rienzi, the leader of the revolt, is publicly stoned to death before his burning house, which collapses as the curtain falls. Although Wagner later turned away from grand opera, deriding it as "effects without causes," it nonetheless continued to exercise an influence on his compositions.

His first really characteristic opera was *The Flying Dutchman* (1843). The subject matter of this work was taken from mythology, the story of the accursed ghost sea captain, doomed to sail the seas for all eternity but permitted to land every seven years to seek the love of a mortal woman, which alone can bring him redemption; Wagner took the story over specifically from the version by Heine. Although the splendor of grand opera is not present here, spectacular effects are not entirely lacking: In Act I the Dutchman's ship sails up out of the dark, stormy sea, with wind furiously blowing through its sails and rigging; in Act III there is the terrifying chorus of the Dutchman's specter crew; and then at the very end, when the Dutchman has departed and Senta, the woman whose love he has won, hurls herself from a cliff into the sea, we see the Dutchman and Senta together rise slowly toward heaven. In place of the variety of grand opera, Wagner has colored the entire work with the mood of the story: the tragic figure of the Dutchman and his search for love and salvation, engulfed in the dark atmosphere of the northern sea coast. In this he was doubtless influenced by the opera *Der Freischütz*, composed in 1820 by the early Romantic composer Karl Maria von Weber (1786–1828), which is permeated by the atmosphere of the Bohemian forests and involves the supernatural as well. According to Wagner himself, *The Flying Dutchman* as a whole was generated from one central number, the ballad that Senta sings foretelling the arrival of the doomed captain. Equally unlike grand opera is the message that *The Flying Dutchman* brings: redemption through unselfish love which finds fulfillment in death. This idea recurs again and again in the works of Wagner.

On a larger and more elaborate scale is *Tannhäuser*, composed between 1842 and 1845 and first performed in Dresden on October 19, 1845. In 1861 it was revised for performance in Paris, the main change being the addition of the large Bacchanale in the first act. Both versions are still in use. In *Tannhäuser*, which has the subtitle "The Singers' War on the Wartburg," two Medieval stories were combined by Wagner. The first is the legend of the minnesinger Tannhäuser, who had ventured onto the Venusberg (Mount of Venus) and been enchained by the pagan goddess of sensual love; he then managed to free himself, pledging from that moment on to follow Mary, or pure and spiritual love, and undertook a pilgrimage to Rome to obtain indulgence from the Pope for the sins incurred on the Venusberg; but the pardon was refused and Tannhäuser sadly returned home. But one hope was held out by the Pope: Should Tannhäuser's walking stick ever put forth flowers, that would be a sign that his pardon had been granted. Different versions of the story have different outcomes, some having him return to the Venusberg, others having him reprieved by the eventual blooming of the walking stick. In Wagner's version, Tannhäuser is saved by Elizabeth, who offers her life to him in love, and by dying redeems him; thus the walking stick blooms at the end. We have already noted the use of this theme of redemption in love through death in *The Flying Dutchman*. The second legend drawn upon by Wagner was the story of the singers' contest on the Wartburg, which was won by Heinrich von Ofterdingen. Wagner has identified Heinrich with Tannhäuser, an association that has no foundation in either of the two legends. But two characters in the opera represent minnesingers who really lived: Wolfram von Eschenbach (c. 1170– c. 1220), best known for his epic *Parsifal*, which itself was subsequently also used by Wagner, and Walter von der Vogelweide (c. 1170–c. 1230).

Many of the traditional elements of opera are represented in *Tannhäuser*. There are arias, ensembles, choral scenes, and impressive finales. Noteworthy is a tendency on Wagner's part to break down the distinction between the recitative and the aria: to introduce more and more melodic elements into the recitative, so that the need for separate compositions serving as arias decreased. Of particular significance in the construction of the opera is the use of recurrent musical themes associated with important aspects of the drama. Our discussion can conveniently center around these. Preponderant is the religious-Christian element, by which Tannhäuser during the opera is rejected but which in the end accepts him. This element is represented primarily by the familiar melody of the "Pilgrims' Chorus," appearing in Act III, as the pilgrims return from Rome: It is a broad melody accompanied in solemn measured chords, organized in three-part form, with an effective crescendo between the middle section and the repetition of the beginning, and then diminuendo at the end. In the scene it is sung by the choir with interjections from Elizabeth and Wolfram, who are awaiting the return of Tannhäuser. Then there is the primarily instrumental music associated with the pagan sensual world of the Venusberg: In rapid tempo, it features a dotted figure, chromatic accompaniment, and brilliant orchestration, including cymbals and the triangle; this theme demonstrates the intoxicating quality often found in Wagner's music, the constant rising and ebbing, the piling of one climax on top of another, the endless repetition of short motives, and the continual modulating. Two other themes, both used in arias, are also connected with the Venusberg: the first is Tannhäuser's hymn to Venus, a strophic composition appearing in Act I and again in Act II, at the singing contest, when Tannhäuser, once more momentarily under the spell of Venus, explains only too clearly his conception of love and its source, thus bringing about his expulsion from the group. Finally, there is Venus' song of seduction, sung when she tries to dissuade him from leaving the Venusberg. These themes are presented in the overture to the work as a whole, which thus becomes a succinct statement of the principal thematic elements in the opera.

Wagner and the Romantic Age

EXAMPLE 5-4

WAGNER: *Tannhäuser*—EXCERPTS

1. PILGRIMS' CHORUS (ACT III)—BEGINNING (PIANO REDUCTION OF ORCHESTRA)

2. VENUSBERG THEME (OVERTURE)—BEGINNING

3. TANNHÄUSER'S HYMN TO VENUS (ACT I)—BEGINNING (PIANO REDUCTION OF ORCHESTRA PART)

1.

The Early Operas

EXAMPLE 5-4 (*continued*)

EXAMPLE 5-4 (*continued*)

Wür - - - de es er - fül-le!

Herz für die Ent-schei - dung ih-res Le-bens!

Durch Sühn' und— Buss' hab' ich ver-

söhnt den— Her - ren,— dem— mein Her - ze— fröhnt, der—

mei - ne Reu'— mit Se - gen krönt, den— Her - ren,—

EXAMPLE 5-4 (*continued*)

Wagner and the Romantic Age

EXAMPLE 5-4 (*continued*)

EXAMPLE 5-4 (*continued*)

Wagner and the Romantic Age

EXAMPLE 5-4 (*continued*)

The Early Operas

EXAMPLE 5-4 (*continued*)

EXAMPLE 5-4 (*continued*)

The Early Operas

EXAMPLE 5-4 (*continued*)

EXAMPLE 5-4 (*continued*)

3.

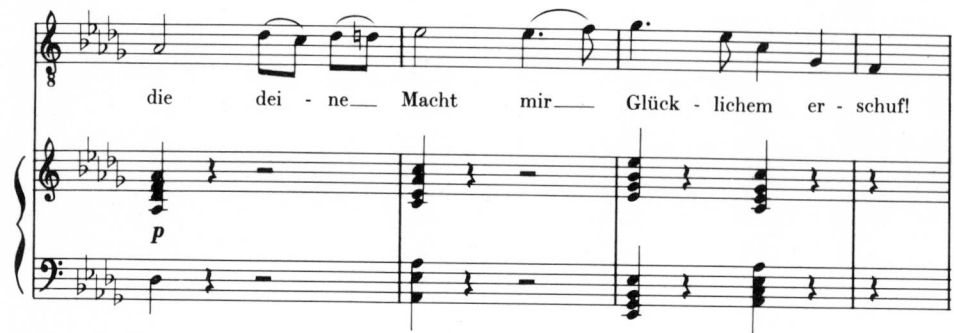

1. TEXT AND TRANSLATION

Pilgrims

Beglückt darf nun dich, O Heimat, ich schauen
und grüssen froh deine lieblichen Auen;
nun lass' ich ruh'n den Wanderstab,
weil Gott getreu ich gepilgert hab'.

By good fortune I may look upon you, O homeland,
and joyfully greet your lovely fields;
now I put my walking stick to rest,
because I have made my pilgrimage in obedience to God.

Elisabeth

Dies ist ihr Sang—

That is their song—

Wolfram

Die Pilger sind's—

It is the pilgrims.

Elisabeth

Sie sind's.

Here they are.

EXAMPLE 5-4 (*continued*)

Wolfram

Es ist die fromme Weise,	It is the pious song,
die der empfangnen Gnade Heil	which proclaims praise for favors
verkündet.	that have been received.

Elisabeth

Sie kehren heim!	They are returning home!
Ihr Heil'gen, zeigt mir jetzt	You saints, show me now my duty,
mein Amt,	
dass ich mit Würde es erfülle!	that I may fulfill it with dignity.

Wolfram

O Himmel, stärke jetzt ihr Herz	O heavens, strengthen her heart now
für die Entscheidung ihres	for the great decision of her
Lebens!	life!

Pilgrims

Durch Sühn' und Buss' hab' ich	By atonement and penance I have
versöhnt	expiated
den Herren, dem mein Herze	the Lord, to whom my heart is
frönt,	a slave,
der meine Reu' met Segen krönt,	who crowns my pain with blessing,
den Herren, dem mein Lied	the Lord, for whom my song
ertönt.	resounds.
Der Gnade Heil ist dem Büsser	The grace of salvation is given
beschieden,	to the penitent,
er geht einst ein in der Seligen	he may one day enter into the
Frieden!	peace of the blessed!
Vor Höll' und Tod ist ihm nicht	He is not afraid of Hell and
bang,	death,
drum preis' ich Gott mein	therefore I shall praise God the
Lebenlang.	rest of my life.
Halleluja! Halleluja in	Hallelujah! Hallelujah forever!
Ewigkeit. In Ewigkeit!	Forever!

3. TEXT AND TRANSLATION (STROPHE I):

Dir töne Lob! Die Wunder sei'n	Let praise resound to you. Let
gepriesen,	the miracles be praised,
die deine Macht mir Glücklichem	which your power created for
erschuf!	happy me!
Die Wonnen süss, die deiner Huld	The sweet joys, stimulated by
entspriessen,	your favors,
erheb' mein Lied in lautem	shall uplift my song in a loud
Jubelruf!	cry of jubilation!
Nach Freude, ach! nach	Joy, O! splendid pleasures
herrlichen Geniessen	
verlangt' mein Herz, es	are demanded by my heart, are
dürstete mein Sinn:	thirsted for by my senses:

EXAMPLE 5-4 (*concluded*)

da, was nur Göttern einstens du erwiesen,	since what once you granted only to gods
gab deine Gunst mir Sterblichen dahin.	your favor has bestowed on a mortal, me.

Apart from this, *Tannhäuser* abounds in scenes characteristic of the grand opera. The famous "Pilgrims' Chorus" has already been mentioned. Especially impressive is the procession of nobles and guests into the Wartburg prior to the singers' contest, with a large crowd, much ceremony, and the effective use of an onstage ensemble of trumpets. Finally, there is the Venusberg scene at the beginning (greatly enlarged in the Paris version of 1861) representing the Bacchanalian revels associated with the pagan goddess. *Tannhäuser* contains one popular aria, "O du mein holder Abendstern" (O thou my holy evening star) for Wolfram (baritone), which is a piece in a closed musical form, so that it can be, and is, often excerpted and performed by itself.

The principles evidenced in *Tannhäuser* were also maintained in *Lohengrin*, composed between 1846 and 1848 and performed for the first time in 1850. Like *Tannhäuser* and *The Flying Dutchman*, it is based on Germanic legend: the mysterious but virtuous white knight brought by the swan to rescue Elsa of Brabant from the charges of murder raised against her; but in exchange she must respect one condition, that she not ask who he is and where he comes from; the sorceress Ortrud, however, undermines Elsa's faith in Lohengrin, and she ultimately is led to ask the forbidden question, so that he is required to depart. In Wagner's view, Lohengrin stands for divine love, which requires unconditional human love in return, a demand that Elsa, representing humanity, is unable to fulfill. The work as a whole reveals even greater continuity—achieved by increased use of a melodious type of recitative and the elimination of arias as separate compositions—than was found in *Tannhäuser*. As Wagner wrote to Liszt of this work: "Nowhere in the score . . . have I written the word 'recitative.' Singers should know that there are no recitatives in it. Quite the contrary, I have tried to work out the speech rhythm so exactly and precisely that the singers have only to sing the notes in accordance with their rhythmic values and the rhythm will be correct." There are, however, a number of ensembles and choral pieces of the type found in the conventional opera of the time.

The Theories of 1850–51

Although many characteristic elements of Wagner's mature work appear in the earlier compositions such as *Tannhäuser* and *Lohengrin*, he took a decisive step in formulating a theory of opera in the three principal literary works of 1850–51: *Art and Revolution, The Art-Work of the Future*, and *Opera and Drama*. Here his artistic intentions find their fullest and most systematic explanation. In common with much German Romantic literary theory, Wagner seemed to feel a yearning for the lost unity of the artwork found in the golden age of Classical Antiquity. It was here that he saw the perfection of theatrical art: Greek tragedy and *mousiké*, hand in hand, the arts of poetry and music participating equally in the dramatic work. Furthermore, the Greek drama had immediate contact with the populace because of its roots in Greek mythology. Both aspects are important for Wagner's own work. Since Classical Antiquity there has, in Wagner's view, been nothing but decline, the spoken drama and the opera going separate ways; and in opera particularly interest had shifted from a musicodramatic work to a work in which music held the greatest interest, a shift plainly symbolized in the split between the recitative and the aria that had been dominant in opera since around 1680. Ideally, according to Wagner, drama should be the object of the expression, music the means. Wagner felt that the only hope was to restore the lost unity that had been possessed by Greek drama.

Here there arose the conception of *The Art-Work of the Future*, a form of dramatic work in which poetry, music, and stagecraft all were to play an equal role: what resulted was the *Gesamtkunstwerk*, the collective or universal artwork, the product of the union of all the different arts. As with Greek drama, the artwork of the future was to be based on mythology, which would insure its close relation to the people (or *Volk*, folk, as Wagner put it), but Germanic mythology instead of Greek mythology. And indeed, from *The Flying Dutchman* on, all of Wagner's music dramas—with the exception of *Die Meistersinger von Nürnberg*—drew on Germanic legends. Wagner then modeled himself on the old Greek *rhapsode* (the rhapsodist), the bard or singer-poet: He not only composed the music but also wrote the librettos. In many of the librettos he employed *Stabreim*, an old German verse form based on alliteration or assonance—precisely that form of verse found in the Medieval German epics.

But something more was injected, a philosophical-ethical lesson, which Wagner may have learned in part from the German Romantic philosopher Arthur Schopenhauer (1788–1860), whose most important book, *Die Welt als Wille und Vorstellung* (*The World as Will and Representation*), was first published in 1819 but came to enjoy great popularity around 1850. The lesson was that life and human activity are inherently evil and destructive so that true peace and the perfection of being are to be found only in withdrawal, inactivity, contemplation, and ultimately death. In Schopenhauer this is connected with the Hindu idea of *nirvana*. Wagner, for his part, gave this idea a characteristic twist: Earthly love is evil and its taint can be overcome only by a renunciation of sensual love and indeed of life itself, which will then lead to redemption, to a pure disembodied spiritual love. The idea was suggested in *The Flying Dutchman*, and all of Wagner's later operas, with the possible exception of *Die Meistersinger von Nürnberg*, are based in one way or other upon it.

It is important to realize that Wagner's announced aims went far beyond the opera and music: rather, his universal artwork was to represent the highest fulfillment of all of mankind's artistic aspirations, the final goal toward which all the arts had gradually been progressing. His universal artwork, as he put it, "is to include all phases of art and, in so doing, to consume, to destroy each one, so to speak, in favor of the combined purpose of them all." And although later he came to assign to music a superior position in the hierarchy of the arts, he continued to maintain that all the arts found their fulfillment, or as he preferred it, their redemption, in his universal artwork. Hence he regarded himself not as a composer and poet but as *the* great artist of his age.

The Wagnerian gesamtkunstwerk rests on the idea of the expressive power of music: the idea that music can speak the unspeakable. Accordingly, Wagner distinguished in an opera two kinds or levels of action, which he called the outer action and the inner action. The former has to do with external events, happenings, in the plot, the stages in the actions, the things that take place; this is to be expressed by means of words. The inner action, on the other hand, is psychological and emotional, involving what goes on in the characters' minds and hearts; this finds its proper expression in the music. Since psychological-emotional action is continuous, so too should the music be continuous, without interruption; this is an important quality in Wagner's operas. The constant stop-and-go between recitatives and arias, or between separate musical numbers (arias, ensembles, choruses), as we have seen it in, for example, Beethoven's *Fidelio*,[1] is done away with, and the music proceeds continuously. Music, as he put it, is "the art of transition."

In Wagner's account of the musicodramatic form since classical antiquity, stress is laid on the decline brought about by the ever increasing importance given to the aria and the consequent neglect of the recitative. In his work Wagner proposed to overcome both the decline of the recitative and the separation between recitative and aria through the use of an infinitely flexible melodic style, which would at times lean toward the declamatory-recitative quality and at other times toward the melodic-aria quality. This melodic style he called *Sprechgesang* ("tone speech"), which because of its continuity has become known as "endless melody." This he had already used in *Lohengrin*. The style has some precedence in the recitative of the seventeenth-century Italian opera.

In order to correlate specifically and concretely the poetry and the music, Wagner resorted to a device similar to what we have already seen in the operatic overture and in the work of Berlioz and Liszt: musical themes that are expressly associated with characters, events, or situations in the opera. In

---

[1] For this reason, an opera of this kind is known as a *number opera*.

Wagner such a theme is called a *leitmotiv* (leading motive). The difference between these leitmotivs as used by Wagner and the recurring themes used by his predecessors is essentially one of degree: Wagner employed a large number of these themes in a work, at least one for every character, and a good many more besides, and these provide the thematic raw material of the composition; they are constantly drawn on, varied, used in different combinations, so that they permeate the entire composition. It is almost as if Wagner's operas were long continuous development sections (as the term is used in reference to sonata form).

We see, then, that instrumental music, particularly the technique of composition that had been developed for instrumental music, was of decisive importance for the Wagnerian music drama. Along with this went a considerable expansion and elaboration of the role of the orchestra, so that frequently the singer was treated almost as one of the instruments in the orchestra, a circumstance that often makes it difficult in performance for the singer to be heard over the sound made by the orchestra. It also makes possible the performance of many sections taken from Wagner's operas in concert halls with the singers' parts omitted altogether.

Symbolic of Wagner's system is the interpretation he gave of Beethoven's work and the influence it exercised on his own music dramas. In the *Art-Work of the Future*, during the course of a review of the development of music in the recent past, Wagner referred to the symphonies of Haydn and Mozart and then went on to single Beethoven out as *the* great innovator, calling him a musical Columbus who set sail across desolate and vast seas to make epochal discoveries. The key composition turns out to be, as one might suspect, the Ninth Symphony, with its last movement a vocal composition using Schiller's poem. According to Wagner, Beethoven, having exhausted the capabilities of pure instrumental music, was forced to turn to the word, to a poem with its explicit meaning, to pursue his ideal form of expression in music. In this work he found the way and took the critical, epoch-making step, opening thereby the door to nineteenth-century music in general and to Wagner in particular.

"This last symphony of Beethoven's," says Wagner, "is the redemption of music out of its own element as a universal art. It is the human gospel of the art of the future. Beyond it there can be no progress, for there can follow on it immediately only the completed artwork of the future, the universal drama, to which Beethoven has forged for us the artistic key." Furthermore, Beethoven's technique of thematic development was of critical importance to Wagner's conception of music in his universal drama.

Wagner's comprehensive reinterpretations of Greek drama as manifested in his music dramas attracted the attention of Friedrich Nietzsche (1844–1900), the German philosopher who began his career as a classical philologist and whose first important book, *The Birth of Tragedy from the Spirit of Music* (1872), is closely related to Wagner's own work. The two men met in 1868 when Nietzsche received a professorship at the University of Basel and Wagner was living in nearby Triebschen; they became friends, but in the later 1870's they had a gradual falling-out which led to a final break. An important aspect of Nietzsche's *Birth of Tragedy* involves two polar types of drama, the Apollonian and the Dionysian, which, as we have seen, correspond to the logical-rational and the emotional-orgiastic, respectively. According to Nietzsche, early Greek drama had stressed the Dionysian element (and he indeed demonstrated that, as a form, tragedy emerged from the choral dances of the Dionysian rites), but in its subsequent development the Apollonian had more and more become dominant; and finally coming to his own time, Nietzsche saw Wagner as the man who, through the emotional power of his music, would be able to reassert the Dionysian element which he felt was the heart of tragedy.

The Ring of the Nibelung

Wagner's longest and most grandiose work was *The Ring of the Nibelung*, a group of four music dramas which Wagner—pressing the analogy with Greek tragedy—insisted be regarded as a trilogy with a prologue. The four works, the librettos for which were written between 1848 and 1852, are *Das Rheingold* (composed in 1853—54, first performed in 1869), *Die Walküre* (*The Valkyrie*, composed in 1854–56, first performed in 1870), *Siegfried* (composed between 1856 and 1871 and first performed in 1876), and *Götterdämmerung* (*The Twilight of the Gods*, composed between 1869 and 1874 and performed in 1876). A number of medieval epics were drawn upon by Wagner in the librettos of this large work, the most important being the German *Nibelungenlied* (*Song of the Nibelungs*) and the Icelandic *Edda* legends; but Wagner made many changes in accordance with his artistic intentions.

It is difficult to summarize this large and complex work in a few pages. Its scenes of activity include heaven, hell, and earth: heaven represented by the gods, chiefly Wotan, Erda, and Fricka; hell by the evil dwarfs who work underground, the Nibelungs, among them Alberich, Mime, and Hagen; and men represented by the Wälsungs, Siegmund, Sieglinde, and Siegfried, by Hunding, and by the Burgundians, Gunther and Gutrune. The crucial figure, however, is Brünnhilde, daughter of Wotan, and thus a goddess, who during the course of the work becomes human. At the center is the gold stolen from the depths of the Rhine by Alberich: a ring made from this gold confers omnipotence on him who renounces love, which Alberich does. The gods, headed by Wotan, fear such power and, assisted by Loge (the Germanic equivalent of Hermes), obtain the ring from Alberich by deception; and in his enraged frustration Alberich curses the ring. The gods, however, have just had their palatial dwelling Walhal built by two giants, and in payment for this

Wotan is forced to give up the ring. All this takes place in the prologue to the trilogy, *Das Rheingold.*

In the first opera proper of the trilogy, *Die Walküre*, attention shifts from the cursed ring to Wotan's efforts to secure his position against the accumulation of opposing and threatening forces which he sees: the guilt incurred by the trickery with which he stole the ring from Alberich, and fear of the power of the ring now in the possession of the giant Fafner. To this end he has begotten two races, the Valkyries, warrior maidens who ride through the night skies over battlefields and transport dead heroes to Walhal, and the two Wälsungs, begotten in union with a mortal woman: Siegmund and Sieglinde. This latter race, free of any lust for power, is to retrieve the ring and return it to the Rhine. The two Wälsungs meet, and in violation of Sieglinde's marriage (she is married to Hunding) Siegfried is conceived. This puts Wotan in a bad position, since he must choose between upholding the sanctity of marriage (as urged by the goddess Fricka) and protecting Siegmund from the vengeful Hunding. But when Siegmund and Hunding fight the duel—which Wotan has been forced to allow Hunding to win—Brünnhilde the Valkyrie intervenes, defies Wotan, slays Hunding, and leads Sieglinde to safety. As punishment for her disobedience, Wotan orders that Brünnhilde be put to sleep behind a curtain of fire, to be awakened only by a hero brave enough to penetrate the flames; but she will have become a mortal woman.

In the second opera of the trilogy, *Siegfried*, we meet the youthful and exuberant Siegfried, the son of Siegmund and Sieglinde, who forges his sword, goes forth, and slays the dragon (actually the giant Fafner who has possession of Alberich's cursed ring), whose spilled blood makes Siegfried invulnerable except where a leaf that stuck to his body prevents the blood from making contact. After obtaining the ring, Siegfried, led on by the song of a forest bird, goes to the mountain where Brünnhilde is asleep, walks through the wall of fire, and after awakening her claims her as his bride.

The catastrophe is presented in the final opera, *Götterdämmerung*, in the prologue of which the thread of destiny, spun by three ancient crones, the Norns, suddenly breaks, thus heralding the end of the reign of Wotan. Siegfried takes leave of Brünnhilde and travels down the Rhine Valley to the Kingdom of Burgundy, ruled by Gunther, among whose courtiers is Hagen, the evil son of Alberich. By means of a potion Siegfried is made to forget Brünnhilde and to fall in love with Gutrune; to gain her hand he uses a magic cape, which makes him invisible, to subdue Brünnhilde, who is to become Gunther's bride. Eventually Hagen, having discovered that Siegfried is vulnerable from the rear, is able to slay him, but is prevented from taking the ring. Brünnhilde, realizing what has happened, hurls herself upon Siegfried's funeral pyre, throwing the cursed ring back into the Rhine from where it had originally come. Since Brünnhilde, having rebelled against Wotan and as punishment for this having been changed into a mortal woman, may act freely—i.e., no

Stage set for Die Walküre, *Act III.*

longer subject to the control of Wotan—her free act of self-sacrifice brings
redemption, precipitating the cataclysm and the doom of Walhal, which is
seen aflame in the distance.

In this mammoth work all facets of Wagner's art are to be seen. The
comprehensive reworking of Germanic mythology is combined with Wagner's
own conceptions concerning the decadence of society and the necessity for a
violent overthrow of values (beliefs that in 1849 had led to his period of exile)
as well as redemption through death in love, as exemplified by Brünnhilde's
self-immolation at the very end. In the music there is the extensive employment of a large number of leitmotivs and the sprechgesang, or endless melody.
Out of many possible scenes we may take one which shows the procedure
reasonably well: an excerpt from "Wotan's Farewell" to Brünnhilde as she is
put to sleep behind the wall of fire at the end of *Die Walküre*. The scene as a
whole is a large monologue in three parts with instrumental interludes, the
first two parts featuring Wotan, the last, known as the "Magic Fire Music,"
principally for the orchestra; but since thematically the last two parts closely
parallel one another, the overall form of the scene may be represented as
a b b'.

We will discuss the second part of Wotan's monologue here. This is preceded by an orchestral interlude built on the leitmotiv of Brünnhilde's plead-

The Ring of the Nibelung

ing, which is stated several times, progressively getting louder until a great climax is reached with the slumber theme being heard fortissimo. This then subsides and the slumber theme dominates the orchestral accompaniment for Wotan, who in a lyrical arioso melodic line bids farewell to Brünnhilde, his favorite child. Wotan's continuously spun-out melodic line provides an excellent illustration of the Wagnerian endless melody, the sprechgesang, or tone speech. At the end, as Wotan resigns himself to his fate, foreseeing the decline of the gods and the rise of man, there are heard in succession the theme of Fate (Example 5-6, bars 29–34) in the trombones and tuba, and the disconsolate theme of the renunciation of love in the English horn. A characteristic instance of Wagner's urge for continuity is found at the end of the passage, when the resolution of the dominant chord (G major) does not go to C, as would be expected, but to an A-flat major chord, thus leading in to what follows.

Mention may be made of other noteworthy portions of this gigantic work: In *Das Rheingold*, the prelude, at the very outset, presents a graphic representation of the river Rhine by a triadic theme in E-flat major rising out of the depths of the orchestra; later the realistic representation of Alberich and the Nibelungs, complete with the ringing of anvils; and at the end the splendid pomp and majesty as the gods enter their new home, Walhal. In *Die Walküre* there is Siegmund's lyrical narrative to Sieglinde and Hunding, followed by the love scene with Sieglinde, and the whole of Act III, beginning with the famous "Ride of the Valkyries" and culminating in the long scene between Wotan and

EXAMPLE 5-5

WAGNER: LEITMOTIVS IN "Wotan's Farewell," FROM *Die Walküre* (ACT III)

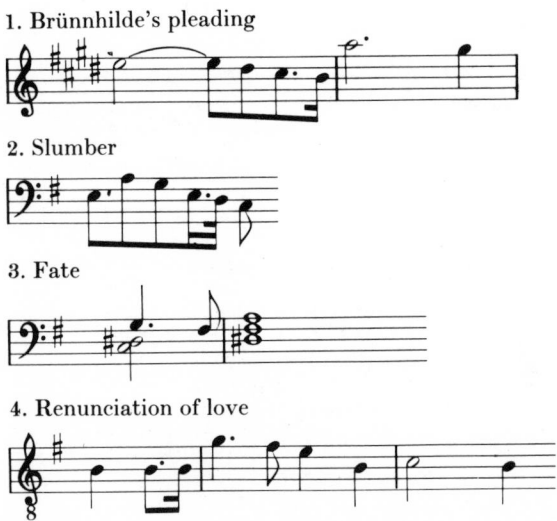

1. Brünnhilde's pleading

2. Slumber

3. Fate

4. Renunciation of love

Brünnhilde, ending in the "Magic Fire Music." In *Siegfried* attention may be drawn to the scene representing the forest murmurs and the song of the bird which guides the young hero to the sleeping Brünnhilde on the mountain, and the effulgence of the awakening and greeting of Brünnhilde. In *Götterdämmerung* there is the famous orchestral depiction of Siegfried's journey down the Rhine to Burgundy, the ominous sound of the crude steer-horns, the heroic tragedy of the funeral music, and the final monologue of Brünnhilde with which the group of operas reaches its conclusion.

EXAMPLE 5-6

WAGNER: "Wotan's Farewell," from *Die Walküre* (END OF ACT III)—
EXCERPT (PIANO REDUCTION OF ORCHESTRA)

The Ring of the Nibelung

EXAMPLE 5-6 (*continued*)

EXAMPLE 5-6 (*continued*)

EXAMPLE 5-6 (*continued*)

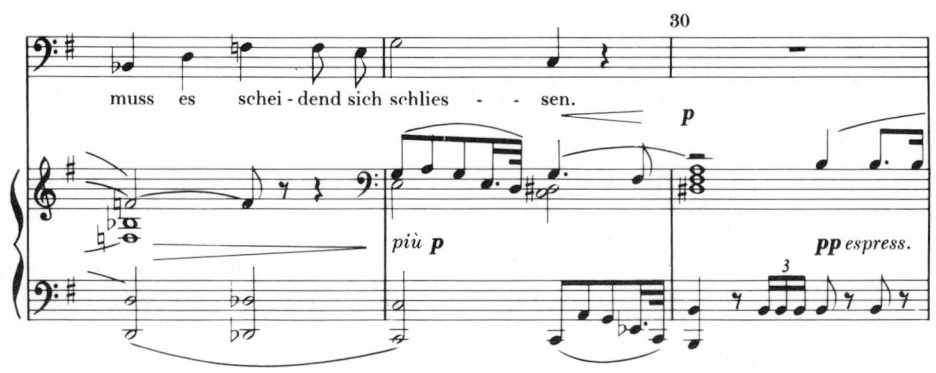

EXAMPLE 5-6 (*continued*)

Denn so kehrt der Gott sich dir ab, so

pp

35

küsst er die Gott - - heit von dir!

ppp

TEXT AND TRANSLATION, WITH AN INDICATION OF THE PRINCIPAL
LEITMOTIVS:

Slumber	Der Augen leuchtendes Paar,	This brightly glowing pair of eyes
	das oft ich lächelnd' gekos't	which, smiling, I have often caressed,
	wenn Kampfeslust ein Kuss dir lohnte,	when you rewarded joy in battle with a kiss,
	wenn kindisch lallend der Helden Lob	when a childishly babbled praise for a hero
	von holden Lippen dir floss:	flowed from your sweet lips:
	dieser Augen strahlendes Paar,	this shining pair of eyes,
	das oft im Sturm mir geglänzt	that often shone on me through the storm
	wenn Hoffnungssehnen das Herz mir sengte,	when hopes had seared my heart
	nach Weltenwonne mein Wunsch verlangte	[and] my wishes demanded the pleasures of the world
	aus wildwebendem Bangen:	out of wildly storming fear:

Example 5-6 (*concluded*)

	zum letzten Mal letz' es mich heut'	for the last time I give them today
	mit des Lebewohles letztem Kuss!	the last kiss of farewell!
	Dem glücklicher'n Manne glänze sein Stern:	Let the star glow for a more fortunate man:
Fate	dem unseligen Ew'gen muss	For the unhappy eternal one
Renunciation of love	es scheidend sich schliessen.	they must close in parting.
	Denn so kehrt der Gott sich dir ab,	And thus the god turns from you,
Slumber	so küsst er die Gottheit	thus he kisses your godhood
Fate	von dir.	away.

It should be noted that in 1857 the composition of *Siegfried* was inter-rupted in the middle of the second act. Work was not resumed until 1865 and not completed until 1871, whereupon Wagner turned to the composition of *Götterdämmerung*, which he finished in 1874. Since he had begun writing the poem of *Der Ring des Nibelungen* in 1848, the work as a whole had occupied him off and on for over twenty-five years, and it is not surprising that the parts written later would be different from those written earlier. Specifically, the last part of *Siegfried* and all of *Götterdämmerung* reveal an attitude rather different from what lay back of *Das Rheingold* and *Die Walküre*. The change involved the role of music, the primacy of which is reasserted in these later works: The vocal tone speech becomes more melodic, the texture of the orchestra becomes denser and more complex, the use of leitmotivs more elaborate and intense. Although this may in part be attributed to Wagner's gradual perfecting of his technique of composition, it may also reflect his increased preoccupation with the work of Schopenhauer, which he read con-stantly after 1854 and in which music is regarded as the supreme art. In letters and essays written after this time, Wagner no longer believed that music should be merely equal to the other arts in his universal artwork; rather, it should be the single most important art. As he wrote in the essay on Liszt in 1857: "Music can never, irrespective of what it is combined with, cease to be the highest, the redeeming art." This attitude lies back of the remaining operas as well: *Tristan und Isolde, Die Meistersinger von Nürnberg*, and *Parsifal*.

The Other Mature Operas

As an especially characteristic example of Wagner's aesthetic theories in action we may take *Tristan und Isolde*, composed between 1857 and 1859 and first performed in 1865. In a number of ways this may be regarded as his most extreme work. Again the subject was taken by Wagner from medieval legend, this time the King Arthur cycle: the story of the doomed love of Tristan, a knight of the Round Table, and Isolde, the princess Tristan is sent to fetch home to be the bride of his overlord, King Mark of Cornwall. Spurred on by a love potion administered by Isolde's lady-in-waiting Brangäne (Isolde herself in the past had been associated with potions and had even healed Tristan, whom she had known only under the pseudonym Tantris), their passionate love knows no bounds until it is broken off by the sudden, shocking entrance of Mark and his followers. After some delay Tristan is mortally wounded by Melot, a knight in Mark's service. In the last act, at his castle, Tristan is awaiting the arrival of Isolde, but she arrives only in time to see him expire; then Mark enters, ready to pardon Tristan, but too late. At the end Isolde, in a fit of ecstatic transport, literally wills herself to death in the famous "Liebestod" ("love-death").

Apart from legend, the opera works with symbols current in German Romantic literature which are combined with Wagner's own brand of philosophy and ethics. Most important is the juxtaposition between day (light) and night (darkness), each of which has its own leitmotiv:. *Day* refers to the everyday, rational world, from which passionate love is excluded; *night,* on the other hand, means the realm of passionate and ecstatic love, and at the same time is the symbol of death, for it is only in death that love can find its true fulfillment. The renunciation of life, then, underlies *Tristan und Isolde* as much as it does most of Wagner's other music dramas.

It is particularly revealing to apply Wagner's conception of the two levels of action in an opera—the inner and the external—to *Tristan und Isolde.* The result is that in this work there is very little external action; there is not much that happens or takes place. Instead, almost all the action is internal, psychological, emotional, which according to Wagner is the proper sphere of musical expression. This is especially clear in the famous love scene between Tristan and Isolde in Act II: We know that they are passionately in love, yet nothing really happens—it is all in the music, so that here the opera becomes all emotion, all music. Thus *Tristan und Isolde* represents the most extreme manifestation in all Wagner's work of Nietzsche's ideal of the Dionysian drama.

Unlike most of Wagner's music dramas, *Tristan und Isolde* operates with a small number of leitmotivs, which are presented with extensive variations. This economy produces an extreme concentration on a small group of themes and results in the overpowering expression of a single emotional mood: love, all-consuming, passionate, reckless, abandoned, ecstatic. The means of achieving this quality of expression is essentially the same as appeared in the Venusberg music of *Tannhäuser,* but is here carried much further: The short melodic motives and patterns are incessantly repeated over and over again, while constantly making the most unexpected modulations, usually very chromatic. This imparts to the music a striving, restless quality—yearning, if one wishes —never arriving at a point of stability but always moving impulsively on. Once a climax is reached, there comes an abatement, then the next climax is reached, and so on.

The Other Mature Operas

All this can clearly be seen in the famous "Liebestod" of Isolde, the monologue that brings the opera to a close. The text makes it plain that death is
conceived as diving into a sort of mystical-sounding, colored misty ocean. The
piece is also a good example of Wagner's style of melodic sprechgesang which
dominates his later works. It should also be mentioned that this extreme use of
chromatic harmonies and the perpetual restless modulating have become known

EXAMPLE 5-7

WAGNER: ISOLDE'S "Love-Death," FROM *Tristan und Isolde* (ACT III)—
EXCERPT*

* Woodwind parts have been omitted.

EXAMPLE 5-7 (*continued*)

EXAMPLE 5-7 (*continued*)

EXAMPLE 5-7 (*continued*)

The Other Mature Operas

EXAMPLE 5-7 (*continued*)

in harmony books as the "Tristan style." The complete text of the love-death scene, with an English version, follows; only a portion of the scene is given in Example 5-7.

Mild und leise	Calm and gently
wie er lächelt,	how he is smiling,
wie das Auge	how he sweetly
hold er öffnet:	opens his eyes:
seht ihr, Freunde,	look, friends,
seh't ihr's nicht?	don't you see it?
Immer lichter	Always brighter,
wie er leuchtet,	how he is shining,
wie er minnig	how he, beautifully,
immer mächt'ger,	always stronger,
sternumstrahlet	surrounded by stars,
hoch sich hebt:	raises himself:
seht ihr, Freunde,	look, friends,
seh't ihr's nicht?	don't you see it?
Wie das Herz ihm	How his heart
mutig schwillt,	swells with courage,
voll und hehr	full and pure
im Busen quillt:	stirs his bosom:
wie den Lippen	how from his lips,
wonnig mild,	wonderfully mild,
süsser Atem	the gentle breath
sanft entweht:	softly comes:
Freunde, seht—	friends, look—
fühlt und seht ihr's	can't you feel and see
nicht?	it?
Höre ich nur	Is it only I that hears
diese Weise,	this melody,
die so wunder-	so wonder-
voll und leise,	ful and quiet,
Wonne klagend,	lamenting in joy,
alles sagend,	saying everything,
mild versöhnend	mildly soothing,
aus ihm tönend	sounding from him,
auf sich schwingt,	[it] whirls around,
in mich dringt,	presses in me,
hold erhallend	sweetly resounding
um mich klingt?	all around me?
Heller schallend	Sounding brighter,
mich unwallend,	surrounding me,
sind es Wellen	are they waves
sanfter Lüfte?	of soft air?
Sind es Wogen	Are they billows
wonniger Düfte?	of joyful fragrance?
Wie sie schwellen	How they billow,
mich umrauschen,	rush around me,
soll ich atmen,	should I breathe them,
soll ich lauschen?	should I listen to them,
soll ich schlürfen,	should I sip them,
untertauchen,	dive within them,
süss in Düften	the sweet perfumes

mich verhauchen?	dissolving me?
In dem wogenden Schwall,	In the billowing wave,
in dem tönenden Schall,	in the sounding noise,
in des Welt-Atems	in the world's breath's
wehendem All—	moving All—
ertrinken—	to drown—
versinken—	to sink under—
unbewusst—	unknowing—
höchste Lust!	highest bliss!

The complete opposite to *Tristan und Isolde*—its perfect complement—is *Die Meistersinger von Nürnberg*, on which Wagner worked at about the same time, completing it in 1867; the first performance took place in 1868. Here we deal, not with old legends, but with sixteenth-century Germany, the guilds of the citizenry of Nürnberg, particularly the organization of the *Meistersinger* (mastersingers) and their most famous member, the poet and shoemaker Hans Sachs (1494–1576). The idea of love-death-redemption is for once not present, although there is renunciation: Sachs renounces his love for Eva so that she may marry the young knight Walther von Stolzing, whom Sachs assists in the composition of a song that eventually wins the prize at the singing competition. The comedy in the opera centers around Beckmesser and his clumsy attempt through his ludicrous singing to win the hand of Eva. But behind all this Wagner has a message concerning art, its relation to society at large, as well as the relation between tradition and progress. Beckmesser represents fanatical and uncreative blind adherence to the rules for their own sake, and Walther the kind of artist who recognizes no rules, who exults in free expression, while Sachs stands as the mediator who, by a judicious application of the most basic rules, a balancing between tradition and innovation, leads Walther to produce a successful composition that will find general acceptance. Unlike most of the mature operas by Wagner, *Die Meistersinger von Nürnberg* contains a number of set pieces, arias, choruses, and other numbers: All the songs of Walther, as well as those of Beckmesser, show the *Barform* characteristic of many old German melodies (see page 95); the opera begins with a hymnlike chorus accompanied by the organ, and toward the end another hymn is used, with words taken verbatim from a poem by the original Hans Sachs. Also worthy of note are the finales to the first two acts: the ridicule that is precipitated by Walther's first appearance before the meistersinger guild, and the great riot based musically on the melody of Beckmesser's serenade, both of which operate on the principle of culmination and acceleration that was characteristic of the finales of the opere buffe of the late eighteenth century. Apart from these there are monologues in the sprechgesang style for Sachs and many other characters. The score employs a large number of leitmotivs, many of which appear in the overture.

With his last opera, *Parsifal*, composed between 1877 and 1882 and performed for the first time at Bayreuth in 1882 (Wagner intended that it be performed only in Bayreuth), Wagner returned to Germanic myth, drawing on the epic of the same title by Wolfram von Eschenbach, a member of the original *minnesinger*. Here Wagner's ideas of death-love-renunciation and redemption appear in a wholly Christian context. The music drama centers around the knights of the Holy Grail, the suffering of their leader, Amfortas, in the power of the evil magician Klingsor, whose spell is broken only by the intervention of the "pure fool" (*der reine Tor*), Parsifal (who appears in the King Arthur legends as Sir Percival). In its style and technique *Parsifal* returns to the procedures of the *Ring of the Nibelung* and *Tristan und Isolde*: the ariosolike sprechgesang, the absence of set pieces, the employment of leitmotivs. The religious atmosphere that pervades the whole is manifested at once in the orchestral prelude, the first theme of which, scored for strings in unison and octaves (the motive of the sacrament), is suggestive of Gregorian chant, and which later uses, as the motive of the Grail itself, the familiar "Dresden Amen" (which actually is nothing more than an embellished plagal cadence). Especially effective is the Good Friday music from Act III.

In Wagner's music the leading ideas of musical Romanticism find perhaps their most complete expression. The typically Romantic yearning for the power and perfection attributed to classic art was fulfilled by Wagner with his gesamtkunstwerk, the universal artwork, unifying music and poetry in one composition. In this fusion of the arts, however, the main role was played by music, to which was imputed the power to express precisely that which words were held unable to express: the dark mysterious world of human passions. The text, its meaning and emotional content, thus controlled the basic aspects of the music, its form, and, by means of the leitmotivs, its thematic material. Accordingly, the traditional musical forms and procedures of opera, the recitative and the aria, were largely abandoned in favor of the sprechgesang and the unbroken continuity of the music, so that, in Wagner's own parlance, the opera had become music drama.

This revolutionary rejection of the traditional forms and procedures of opera is most significant. But perhaps just as important is the conception of the expressive power of music, not merely as the adequate expression of the text, but as a means of making an impression on, even of overpowering, the audience and enhanced by the dramatic situations, the dazzling effectiveness in the handling of the orchestra, the striking execution of the stage designs, and so forth. The opera *Lohengrin*, presenting as it does the pitiable conflict of Elsa between her love of Lohengrin and her curiosity to find out more about him and to ask the forbidden question, has been described as the first work of its kind expressly designed to make special impact on women. All in all this is a most important aspect of Romantic music: the idea of making an impression on the audience, of stimulating an emotional reaction from the audience by means of the musical composition. This Wagner attempted to do by all means at his avail.

The Reaction to Wagner

Wagner's achievement was looked upon at the time as progressive, and even revolutionary. In Germany he and his supporters, along with those of Liszt, were known as the Neo-Germanic group. Among the composers influenced by Wagner we can mention here Anton Bruckner (1824–96), Hugo Wolf (1860–1903), Gustav Mahler (1860–1911), and Richard Strauss (1864–1949). But none of these took over all aspects of Wagner's work: In Bruckner, the influence of Wagner shows itself primarily in the size and composition of the orchestra and in a distinct preponderance of the ceremonial and monumental in his symphonic works. Wolf, for his part, applied certain facets of Wagner's art, especially the characteristic elaborate and coloristic use of harmonies and declamatory melodic writing, to the art song. Mahler drew on the Wagnerian variety of orchestration and the system of leitmotivs, both of which he used in large symphonies with important vocal parts (solo and choral). Strauss adopted the leitmotiv technique and the brilliant use of the orchestra, which he employed in symphonic poems and operas; his operas also show some use of the sprechgesang style of melodic writing.

The work of these composers, and indeed the entire example set by Wagner, did not, however, go unopposed. A most important challenge was the polemical treatise on musical aesthetics by the Viennese critic Eduard Hanslick (1825–1904), *The Beautiful in Music* (1854), which attacked the doctrine of the expressive capacity of music and proposed instead the idea of "absolute music," based on the belief that music is in itself incapable of expressing anything concrete. But there were also composers who by their example opposed the work of the Neo-German group and instead worked within the traditions of the late eighteenth and early nineteenth centuries. Two of these were especially important: Giuseppe Verdi (1813–1901) and Johannes Brahms (1833–1897).

Verdi

Verdi was the foremost exponent of Italian opera in the nineteenth century. As such, the contrast to Wagner could scarcely be more complete, for Verdi maintained the forms and traditions of opera as they had come down from the eighteenth century and employed recitatives, arias, ensembles, and chorus as set pieces. It is only in his last two operas, *Otello* (1887) and *Falstaff* (1893), both based on Shakespeare, that these forms are run continuously together, so that one might get the erroneous impression that Verdi had adopted the Wagnerian "endless melody." Actually the traditional forms are still there, but they are connected so that one goes to the next without a break. Verdi's operas are not based on ancient legends but on contemporary plays, and they present violent and lurid stories taken from history, often dealing with a plot against the life of a duke or king, the intense rivalry of two

Giuseppe Verdi.
Portrait by Bodini.
(COURTESY GALLERIA
NAZIONALE D'ARTE
MODERNA, ROME)

men for the love of a lady, the plight of an exiled people; and they bring in such elements as witches' prophecies, duels, confusion of identity, women dressed as men, and so on. Verdi's melodic style is especially important and characteristic: its use of direct, easily comprehensible and, hence, effective melodic lines, often organized by the repetitions of a brief energetic rhythmic pattern, invariably suited to the dramatic situation. In Verdi the orchestra always provides the accompaniment to the vocal parts, which have the principal melodic lines and thematic interest. This is in sharp contrast to Wagner, where the singer's part, as has been pointed out, is frequently treated as if it were merely another instrument in the orchestra.

As an example, we may briefly consider one of Verdi's most representative and popular operas, *Rigoletto*, composed and performed in 1851. Based on a play by Victor Hugo, *Le roi s'amuse*, the action turns around the lecherous Duke of Mantua, who seduces Gilda, daughter of the hunchbacked court jester Rigoletto, who in revenge plots the murder of the Duke by a hired assassin; but the plot runs awry and it is his daughter that by mistake is killed. In Hugo's play, King François I of France was the intended victim, but since the Italian censors refused to allow royalty to be represented in so unfavorable a light, the Duke of Mantua had to be substituted.

Verdi's procedure in writing an opera is clear from a sequence of numbers at the beginning of Act III. Rigoletto's hired killer, Sparafucille, has lured the Duke to a lonely inn, tempting him with his sister Maddalena, while Rigoletto, hoping to convince his daughter of the Duke's true character, lurks with her outside so that she can see what goes on. The act begins with an instrumental prelude, after which we have recitative between Rigoletto and Gilda. There follows the Duke's celebrated aria (actually a canzone, in this instance a strophic piece of two stanzas), "La donna è mobile," in which Verdi's simple and direct melodic style is readily apparent (see Example 5-8). After more recitative, featuring rapidly moving melodic and rhythmic activity in the orchestra, there comes the famous quartet "Bella figlia dell'amore" in D-flat major, an ensemble essentially like that of the earlier opera buffa, with considerable differentiation among the various voice parts; but here it is the part for tenor (the Duke) that dominates the musical conception, against which come Gilda's anguished exclamations, the coquettish fast-moving phrases of Maddalena, and the more declamatory line of Rigoletto (see Example 5-8). We have, then, at the beginning of Act III, several distinct musical numbers: an instrumental prelude, a recitative and canzone, a recitative and the quartet. The entire opera is constructed in this fashion, so that it may be called a number opera.

EXAMPLE 5-8

VERDI: ACT III OF *Rigoletto*—EXCERPTS (PIANO REDUCTION OF ORCHESTRA)

1. CANZONE, "La donna e mobile"—STROPHE I
2. QUARTET, "Bella figlia dell'amore"—EXCERPT

1.

EXAMPLE 5-8 (*continued*)

Verdi

EXAMPLE 5-8 (*continued*)

EXAMPLE 5-8 (*continued*)

2.

Verdi

EXAMPLE 5-8 (*continued*)

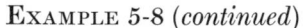

EXAMPLE 5-8 (*continued*)

G. di - to,

Ma. zar.

D. detto, un det - to sol tu

R. ti - - va

TEXTS AND TRANSLATIONS:

1. THE CANZONE

La donna è mobile	Woman is as fickle
Qual piuma al vento,	as a feather in the wind,
muta d'accento	simple in speech
e di pensiero.	and in mind.
Sempre un amabile	Always with a loving
leggiadrovviso,	laughing face,
in pianto o in riso,	but whether laughing or crying
è menzognero.	always a false face.
[First five lines repeated.]	

EXAMPLE 5-8 (*concluded*)

2. THE QUARTET

Duke

Bella figlia dell'amore,	Beautiful daughter of love,
schiavo son de' vezzi tuoi;	I am slave to your charms;
con un detto, un detto sol	with one single, a single word
tu puoi	you can
le mie pene, le mie pene	console all my pains, my pains.
consolar.	
Vieni, e senti del mio core	Come, and feel the beating
il frequente palpitar.	of my heart.
[Last two lines repeated.]	

Maddalena

Ah! ah! rido ben di core,	Ah! ah! my heart is laughing
chè tai baie costan poco;	at all this cheap talk;
quanto valga il vostro gioco	what all this is worth
mel credete, sò apprezzar.	I know too well, believe me.
Son avvezza, bel signore	I am accustomed, dear sir,
ad un simile scherzare.	to jokes like this.

Gilda

Ah! così parlar d'amore!	Ah! to speak of love this way!
a me pur l'infame ho udito!	the wretch used to talk like that to me!
Infelice cor tradito,	Unhappy betrayed heart,
per angoscia non scoppiar.	do not break for sorrow.

Rigoletto (to Gilda)

Taci, il pianger non vale;	Be quiet, it is useless to weep now,
che'ei mentiva or sei sicura.	now you see for sure that he was lying.
Taci, e mia sarà la cura	Be quiet, and I shall begin at once
la vendetta d'affrettar.	to take revenge.
Pronta fia, sarà fatale;	It will be quick, and deadly;
io saprollo fulminar.	I know well how to do it.

Brahms

In the case of Johannes Brahms, the opposition to Wagner is also quite complete. Brahms was widely regarded in his own lifetime as the continuer of the tradition of instrumental music that had been established in the work of Haydn, Mozart, and Beethoven. This immediately becomes plain when one considers the kinds of pieces Brahms composed and those genres that he neglected. Among the forms favored by the Romantics we find in Brahms' work only the song and the character piece for piano. Completely lacking are the more characteristically Romantic forms associated with program music, particularly the symphonic poem; and neither did Brahms compose operas.

Johannes Brahms.
Lithograph by
Von Beckerath.
(COURTESY THE
BETTMANN
ARCHIVE.)

Instead, the main concentration—and it reveals itself early in Brahms' creative work—is on the large forms of instrumental music, precisely those that do not appear in the work of Liszt and Wagner: the traditional piano sonata, the forms of chamber music and the symphony. The most obviously Romantic forms, in which the power of music to express an extramusical content of some sort is assumed, are precisely those which Brahms ignored.

Brahms seemed to agree that he was the principal representative of the older tradition of instrumental music, for he exercised great care in his work as a composer: A number of his pieces exist in more than one version, since he continually revised and reworked his compositions, sometimes even after a number of years. Furthermore, he approached the symphony with hesitation and caution, first working with the piano sonata and the several different types of chamber music, and then producing his first symphony, on which he was engaged for some twenty-two years, at the age of forty-three in 1876. Although both Liszt and Brahms composed piano concertos, in Liszt the form stressed virtuosity and was organized in cyclic form, very much like a symphonic poem, whereas Brahms revived the old concerto-allegro structure (see pages 248–49) characteristic of the first movement in a concerto of the late eighteenth and early nineteenth century. A similar observation can be made with respect to the piano sonatas that both composed.

Furthermore, Brahms was deeply interested in earlier music: He was among the sponsors of the first collected edition of the works of Bach (the edition of the *Bachgesellschaft*); he wrote variations for piano on a theme by Handel, and another set for two pianos (also arranged for orchestra) on a theme by Haydn; his famous *German Requiem* contains several movements that owe much to the brilliant fugal choruses in the work of Bach. Imitative counterpoint generally plays an important part in Brahms' compositions. His preoccupation with earlier music is evident from the last movement of his Symphony in E minor (Op. 98, No. 4), composed in 1884–85, which is an ostinato form similar to Bach's Passacaglia for organ or his Chaconne for unaccompanied violin (Brahms arranged the latter as a piece for piano to be played by the left hand only; see pages 114 and 125–26); the finale of Brahms' *Variations on a Theme of Haydn* likewise employs an ostinato.

As an example of Brahms' conservative orientation and his respect for traditional forms and procedures, we may take the Symphony in F major (Op. 90, No. 3), composed in 1883. This work is disposed in the four-movement scheme that had been characteristic of the symphony since the late eighteenth century: an Allegro con brio in F major, an Andante in C major, a Poco Allegretto in C minor, and a concluding Allegro which begins in F minor but by the end has settled in F major. Since both the first and fourth movements are in the sonata form (in the last movement the development is not present) and the middle movements employ the ternary scheme (along with a sort of development in the second movement), it is only in the keys used that a departure from the old formal plan is evident.

Important in the first movement is a musical theme based on a motto consisting of the notes F, A flat, F, which is supposed to stand for "Frei aber froh" (free but happy); this forms the bass of the three opening chords and then is prominent in the accompaniment to the broad-phrased melody that follows. The principal theme, then, is not constructed with terse motives, but is rather a lyrical melodic line with an elaborate accompaniment. The secondary theme, exceptionally in A major, marked *grazioso*, is likewise lyrical. The composition as a whole is essentially homophonic in conception, although the part-writing in the accompaniment frequently contains a good deal of contrapuntal interest. Significantly, in the development it is the secondary theme that dominates, but its character is transformed by its being put into the minor and by the agitated accompaniment provided for it.

Typical of Brahms' work as a whole is the third movement. Normally this would be a minuet or scherzo, but here it is a simple ternary form in moderate tempo, a sort of lyrical character piece for orchestra. The main features of the first part of the movement are clear enough: The texture is homophonic, an accompanied melodic line, which with its successive phrases moves from one instrument or choir of the orchestra to another, while the accompaniment consists of chords that are intricately broken up, the patterns being changed from phrase to phrase. When one examines the melody itself, one sees that the phrases are disposed according to a specific repetitive pattern, which upon examination turns out to be nothing more nor less than the old rounded binary form with all repetitions written out and no double bars used: *a a b a b a* (Example 5-10 gives the first two statements of *a*). The contrasting middle part of the movement employs the simple ternary plan, after which the entire first part is repeated but with changes in the orchestration. A feature of this piece —and indeed of Brahms' music in general—is density of texture, many notes of the chords being doubled, producing a full and rich sound but often at a subdued dynamic level.

EXAMPLE 5-9

BRAHMS: ALLEGRO CON BRIO, FROM SYMPHONY IN F MAJOR (OP. 90, No. 3)—EXCERPTS

1. PRINCIPAL THEME
2. SECONDARY THEME
3. DEVELOPMENT—BEGINNING

1.

Brahms

EXAMPLE 5-9 (*continued*)

EXAMPLE 5-9 (*continued*)

2.

3.

EXAMPLE 5-9 (*concluded*)

EXAMPLE 5-10

BRAHMS: POCO ALLEGRETTO, FROM SYMPHONY IN F MAJOR (OP. 90, No. 3)—PRINCIPAL THEME (FIRST PART)*

* Flute and bassoon parts have been omitted.

Wagner and the Romantic Age

EXAMPLE 5-10 (*continued*)

Brahms

Example 5-10 (*concluded*)

Wagner and the Romantic Age

Summary

In the music of the nineteenth century, the development of which was to a large extent carried on by German composers, two principal lines may be distinguished: the older forms of what for convenience we will call "absolute" music, the tradition established in the work of Haydn, Mozart, and Beethoven, and the new typically Romantic forms which are rooted in the belief in the expressive power of music and thus exemplify in one way or another the idea of program music, and which most characteristically appear in genres that are new and different. On this basis the opposition between Wagner, on the one hand, and Brahms, on the other, is clear enough, as indeed, on a different basis, is that between Wagner and Verdi. At the same time elements from one tradition appear in the other, and both traditions can be followed by one and the same composer. Berlioz' *Symphonie fantastique* is an early example of such a rapprochement. A most important aspect here is the employment of cyclic form, whereby a few themes in varied forms dominate an entire large-scale composition. Although this procedure was most closely associated with the symphonic poem, it was also used in, for example, Robert Schumann's Symphony in D minor (Op. 120, No. 4) of 1841 (revised in 1851) as well as in the well-known Symphony in D minor by César Franck and many other works by French composers of the second half of the nineteenth century. Furthermore, in the "absolute" works of nineteenth-century composers like Mendelssohn, Schumann, and Chopin, there may be found a certain tendency away from strict thematic development and instead more reliance on homophonic texture, simple lyric melodic lines, harmonic surprises and orchestral color, all of which are characteristic of the newer Romantic forms. Nonetheless the basic opposition of the two traditions seems clear enough. And the central figure in the new Romantic music, whose example, by virtue of both those who followed it as well as those who violently opposed it, was clearly Wagner.

Chapter Six

Stravinsky and the New Music of the Twentieth Century

*W*ith the advent of the twentieth century, forces that had long been at work began to produce the most profound changes in all aspects of the life of Western man. His views of the universe and of his own nature were completely changed under the impact of radically new ideas, among them Einstein's theory of relativity, Planck's quantum theory of matter, Heisenberg's uncertainty principle, and Freud's concept of the unconscious mind, to name but a few. These changes were reflected in art, and again, elements that had been regarded as basic and essential in art were reexamined and often rejected. As a result, phenomena such as nonrepresentational or abstract painting and sculpture as well as literary works in which the writer experimented with new and often ungrammatical combinations of words and phrases, came to dominate the scene.

The art of music was profoundly affected by these new orientations. Here, too, the basic assumptions on which the art had rested were challenged and new solutions worked out, tested, and applied. But most of these new solutions had their roots in nineteenth-century music. Three movements in the late nineteenth and early twentieth centuries are of particular significance: nationalism, impressionism, and dodecaphonic serialism.

Nationalism

The term *musical nationalism* refers to the use of the music of a particular country in a musical composition: dances, songs, instrumental tone colors, characteristic rhythmic and melodic patterns, and so on. To some degree this was by no means new, since it can be traced far back into the history of music; and there were, for example, well-known adumbrations of Hungarian music in Haydn and of Russian music in Beethoven. What was new and important here was that the use of one's own national music in a composition was connected with national feeling, with patriotism, with the desire for the establishment of one's own country as a nation in its own right. Thus this type of music came to the fore in those countries that were politically dependent upon another larger and more powerful country. Both Chopin and Liszt had employed forms indigenous to the music of their native countries, as in Chopin's Polonaises and Mazurkas and Liszt's Hungarian Rhapsodies.

The first important group of nationalistic composers emerged in Bohemia (what is now Czechoslovakia), represented primarily by two composers, Bedřich Smetana (1824–1884) and Antonín Dvořák (1841–1904). Representative is Smetana's symphonic poem *The Moldau*, part of a group of symphonic poems called *My Country*, composed between 1874 and 1879. *The Moldau*, adopting the typical aesthetic of nineteenth-century music, takes as its subject matter the course of Bohemia's great river as it rises in the mountains, flows down the valleys, past villages and towns, growing bigger and bigger as it goes, until it majestically moves past the city of Prague and is lost in the distance. Themes resembling Bohemian folk songs and peasant dances are used in the work, which reaches its culmination in a mighty brass choir. Smetana's opera *The Bartered Bride* (1866) deals with life and love among the peasants of Bohemia. Dvořák, for his part, frequently employed Bohemian folk melodies or themes modeled on them in his symphonic compositions.

Another national school existed in Scandinavia, with Edvard Grieg (1843–1907), a Norwegian, as its most important figure in the nineteenth century. A Spanish school developed mainly in the twentieth century.

By all odds the most important national school in nineteenth-century music was the Russian, which was centered in St. Petersburg, shortly after the middle of the century, dominated by a group known as "The Five": Mily Balakirev (1837–1910), Alexander Borodin (1833–1887), César Cui (1835–1918), Modest Mussorgsky (1839–1881), and Nicholas Rimsky-Korsakov (1844–1908). Here we see not only the attempt to draw on native Russian folk music in artistic compositions but also the strident rejection of Western music, especially as represented by German Romanticism. In some ways the most interesting member of the group was Mussorgsky, two of whose works gained wide renown: the opera *Boris Godunov* and a set of piano pieces, *Pictures at an Exhibition* (both composed in 1874). Rimsky-Korsakov, apart from a number of operas, composed the popular and colorful symphonic poem *Scheherazade*. Alone among his colleagues he became a professionally trained musician and finally a professor at the Conservatory of Music in St. Petersburg. Somewhat apart from this group stands Peter Ilyich Tchaikovsky (1840–1893), who generally remained true to the Western forms of musical composition even though he now and then made use of Russian folk melodies in his works.

An important result of this movement was that it made composers and musicians generally conscious of the folk music of their own countries, which frequently displayed types and principles of organization considerably different from what was exemplified in the traditional art music of the West. Among these would be the use of different scales, sometimes related to the modes of Medieval and Renaissance music (the Lydian mode, like a major scale except for the raised fourth degree, is not unusual), occasionally using intervals smaller than the semitone and employing unusual melodic turns; different harmonies, often quite dissonant; and irregular metric and rhythmic patterns. Whereas in the nineteenth century composers generally modified the folk-types so that they would accord with the traditional norms of art-music, at the end of the century and in the twentieth century it became recognized that such differences from the tradition were valuable in themselves and could contribute to an entirely new kind of music.

Impressionism

An important breakthrough may be seen in the impressionism of the French composer Claude Debussy (1862–1918). In a way Debussy did for music what the impressionistic painters did for painting: He sought out new media and techniques. As the impressionistic painters portrayed mood and atmosphere by avoiding clear, precisely articulated designs and relying instead on colors, shades, and textures, so Debussy in a variety of ways began to undermine the main force for definiteness and coherence in music: tonality, the idea of a tonic, a central note from which all other notes of the piece take their orientation. Debussy did this in at least three principal ways: first, by using seventh and ninth chords (see page 17) built on all degrees of the scale, with the result that notes added above the triad tended to weaken its function (i.e., tonic, dominant, subdominant, etc.) in the tonality, especially in the case of the tonic; second, by using chords in new and unusual progressions, such as moving them stepwise diatonically or chromatically instead of from tonic to dominant or in other conventional progressions; third, by using the chromatic, the whole-tone and pentatonic scales, the tonal implications of which are less definite, to say the least, than with the diatonic major and minor scales. In actual compositions we often find these procedures associated with meandering and fragmentary musical phrases, often presented with characteristic coloristic effects: In orchestral music the use of muted strings, the solo wind instruments, the flute in particular, and the harp is most characteristic; in piano music, effects created by the damper and sostenuto pedals are used extensively.

As an example we may take the first of the three *Nocturnes* for orchestra, entitled "Clouds," completed in 1899. The idea of composing a piece suggesting the incessant changing of something as insubstantial and ephemeral as clouds is in itself highly impressionistic. Here we can observe many of the features mentioned above: The muted dynamic, the parallel chords moving by step in the strings, the suggestive melodic fragment in the solo oboe, all contribute to the aura of vagueness and ceaseless changing (see Example 6-1).

As a whole, Debussy's work as a composer was characterized by the implicit rejection of the German Romantic tradition of music in general.

Impressionism: Houses of Parliament, Westminster, *by Claude Monet.*
(COURTESY OF THE ART INSTITUTE OF CHICAGO)

Debussy sought models and inspiration elsewhere: from earlier Western music, in particular the French harpsichord music of the eighteenth century, as well as the national music of different countries. In the first, he deliberately took over forms and procedures from earlier music. This may be seen in his *Pour le piano*, composed between 1896 and 1902, a suite for piano, the three movements of which employ forms suggestive of Baroque music (prelude, sarabande, and toccata). Music of this kind, which came to be known as *neoclassic*, took on great significance as the twentieth century wore on. Implicit in neoclassicism was a certain objectivity in the conception of the musical artwork: It was not regarded as existing for the effect it had on the listener, but was simply there of, for, and in itself. This attitude was in sharp contrast to the Romantic conception of the musical artwork, in which the emphasis was put on expression.

Claude Debussy. Portrait,
artist unknown. (THE
BETTMANN ARCHIVE.)

We can see the influence of at least three different national musics in Debussy's work: the Spanish dance (as in "An Evening in Granada," from the suite *Estampes* for piano), the exotic sound of the Balinese *gamelan* (gong orchestra) which he heard during the Paris International Exposition of 1899 (as in "Pagodas," also from *Estampes*), and American minstrel-show music (as in the "Golliwog's Cake-Walk," from the *Children's Corner*, or "Minstrels," from the *Preludes* for piano, Book I). It is by no means unlikely that the experience of coming into contact with the music of these and other countries had an important effect on Debussy's whole conception of music. In any case, both the neoclassic and the national and exotic musical styles are of profound significance for twentieth-century music generally.

EXAMPLE 6-1

DEBUSSY: "Clouds," FROM *Nocturnes* FOR ORCHESTRA—BEGINNING

Impressionism

EXAMPLE 6-1 (*continued*)

Dodecaphonic Serialism

Other composers became more daring in their rejection of the traditional system of tonal relationships. Béla Bartók (1881–1945), a Hungarian, immersed himself in the folk music of his native country, which then was allowed to permeate his own original compositions. Similarly, the use of typically American musical forms and styles characterizes the music of Charles Ives (1874–1954). On the other hand, Paul Hindemith (1895–1963), whose music in many respects went back to the German Baroque, developed a theoretical basis for his art which allowed both for complete chromaticism and for relating the various notes to any given tonic by their relative positions in its overtone system.

But by far the most drastic change may be observed in the work of the Viennese composer and theorist Arnold Schoenberg (1874–1951). Unlike the nationalistic composers and Debussy, Schoenberg had begun his work as a

*Arnold Schoenberg.
Portrait by Oskar
Kokoschka, 1924.*
(THE BETTMANN
ARCHIVE.)

composer very much in the tradition of Wagner, so that he regarded his innovations as evolutionary in nature, as logical steps beyond the music of Wagner.
Thus, as a development from the perpetual modulating used by Wagner,
Schoenberg declared that one should not be restricted to the use of the notes of
whatever key one happened to be in, but should be able to use any of the
twelve notes freely. One should have available, as he put it, "the total
resources of chromaticism." Furthermore, in consequence of Wagner's use of
extremely chromatic chords, Schoenberg declared that consonance and dissonance were antiquated concepts and that any combination of notes, no
matter how dissonant by conventional standards, should be acceptable. This
he referred to as "the emancipation of the dissonance." He felt all this neces-

Expressionism:
The Scream,
by Edvard Munch,
1895. (COLLECTION,
THE MUSEUM OF
MODERN ART, NEW
YORK. MATTHEW
T. MELLON
FOUNDATION FUND.)

sary in order to achieve a completely new means of expression, a new musical language, in which the conventional rules governing the relationships between tones as well as those governing consonance and dissonance were eliminated at one stroke. Since the main point was the abandonment of the idea of a tonic, the tone to which all others are oriented, this music came to be called, not wholly with Schoenberg's approval, *atonal*.

These innovations have been associated with Schoenberg's desire to express something on the order of the chaotic and irrational turmoil of fears and lusts in the Freudian *id*, and this may in turn be linked with the literary and artistic movement known as *expressionism*. In any case, some very problematical compositions resulted, among them the five *Pieces for Orchestra* (Op. 16) of 1909, and *Pierrot Lunaire* (Op. 21) of 1912. The latter work is wholly representative. It is the musical setting of a group of symbolist-expressionistic poems by the Belgian Albert Guiraud as translated into German by Otto Erich Hartleben, scored for recitation and a small group of solo instruments. All the chords used are dissonant by traditional standards, but the texture is light and essentially contrapuntal. Especially noteworthy is the effect created by the recitation, which Schoenberg called *Sprechstimme*, in which the reciter is to speak syllables at precise musical pitches and in strict rhythm. As an example we may take the first piece in the cycle, "Mondestrunken" ("Moon Drunk"), for recitation (Sprechstimme), flute,

EXAMPLE 6-2

SCHOENBERG: "Mondestrunken," FROM *Pierrot Lunaire*—BEGINNING

EXAMPLE 6-2 (*continued*)

Au-gen trinkt, gießt nachts der Mond in Wo - - - gen nie-der,

und ei - ne Spring - flut ü - ber -

EXAMPLE 6-2 (*concluded*)

violin, violoncello, and piano. The speechsong of the recitation is declamatory. In the accompaniment each instrument is given thematic material of differing character: the filigree arpeggios of the piano, the pizzicato of the violin, the rhapsodic line of the flute (the violoncello does not enter until bar 29, not represented in the example), although in bar 11 the flute takes over the figuration of the piano. The harmonies are chromatic and dissonant throughout. The atmosphere produced by all these factors in combination could not be more striking, at least from the standpoint of the nineteenth-century tradition.

Dodecaphonic Serialism

From 1915 to 1923 Schoenberg composed but little. After a few years in the Austrian army he turned to teaching and to conducting as well as to reflecting and theorizing. It is almost as if he realized that his developments and innovations had reached an impasse and that some new principle was needed before he could progress further. But by around 1922 he had developed such a new principle, which he reported to a colleague would insure the supremacy of German music for the next hundred years. He referred to this new principle as a *method of composition with twelve tones,* and it is usually known as the *twelve-tone system* or as *dodecaphonic serialism,* the meaning of which will become clear as the procedure is explained. Schoenberg felt the need for a new principle or system which would control the combination and succession of musical tones, one that could replace the old conventional system but which would at the same time incorporate his ideas on the use of chromaticism and dissonance.

According to this newly developed principle, as a first step in composition the composer must arrange the twelve tones of the chromatic scale in a particular sequence, known as the *series, row,* or *basic set.* This series determines the succession and combination of musical tones in the composition, according to the rule that no tone of the series may be employed again until all the others have been used. Hence, all the notes are equally important. Chords may be constructed in accordance with the succession of notes in the series, which is generally read upward from the bass note of each chord. The set thus becomes the basis of the composition. It is with this idea that Schoenberg sought to replace the idea of tonality, which he had already discarded. The term *dodecaphonic serialism,* then, refers to music based on a series consisting of the twelve tones. But the use of the basic set, or series, is not restricted to its original form: Variations are possible, indeed almost mandatory. The intervals of the set may be inverted (turned upside-down), the set may be reversed (retrograde), it may be both turned upside-down and reversed (retrograde inversion), and it may be transposed in any of these forms.[1] With all these possibilities, there are some forty-eight different forms the set may take. There are other procedures for varying the set, among them segmenting it, assigning some tones to the melody and the rest to the accompaniment, then perhaps interchanging the two, and so forth.

As an example we may take the Trio from Schoenberg's Suite for Piano (Op. 25), composed in 1924. The basic series (ϕ) is as follows:

E	F	G	D flat	G flat	E flat	A flat	D	B	C	A	B flat
1	2	3	4	5	6	7	8	9	10	11	12

---

[1] The following symbols are used in the analysis of this music: ϕ—basic set in its original form at its original pitch; R—retrograde form; I—inverted form; hence, RI—retrograde inversion; transpositions are indicated by subscripts: e.g., I_9—inverted form in its ninth transposition.

This appears at the outset in the left hand, answered by the right hand, which gives the inversion of the sixth transposition

(I_6):	B flat	A	G	D flat	A flat	B	F sharp	C	E flat	D	F	E
	1	2	3	4	5	6	7	8	9	10	11	12

which is arranged so as to constitute a canon in inversion at the interval of a tritone with the left-hand part. The left hand continues with the inverted form of the basic series (I), which is answered in the right hand by the basic series in its sixth transposition (ϕ_6), still arranged so as to constitute a canonic imitation by inversion with the left hand. In the second ending, the notes of the basic series (ϕ) are somewhat redistributed in the left-hand part. It may be mentioned that contrapuntal procedures are of basic importance in this system of composition.

EXAMPLE 6-3

SCHOENBERG: TRIO, FROM SUITE FOR PIANO (OP. 25)—BEGINNING

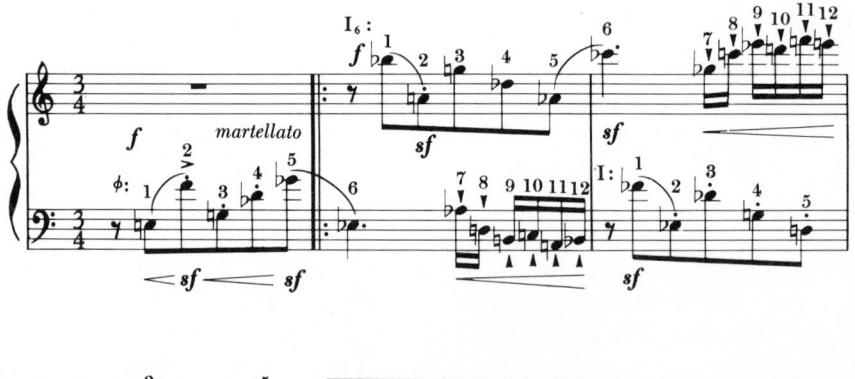

We have thus summarized the main currents in music in the earlier years of the century. These trends remain dominant: the development of new systems of tonal relations, as seen in musical nationalism, impression, and the dodecaphonic serialism of Schoenberg, as well as the emergence of neo-classicism. But they are by no means mutually exclusive. At the same time a number of composers have been less concerned with innovations and more interested in simply composing music in something approaching the traditional forms and in the traditional tonal system, even though they now and then avail themselves of some of the new sounds.

Stravinsky's Life

In Igor Stravinsky we have a composer who has represented in one way or another and at one time or another all of the important progressive trends in contemporary music. He was born in 1882 of a well-to-do family, his father being a bass singer in the St. Petersburg opera. Although Stravinsky first studied law, he soon turned to music and became a pupil of Rimsky-Korsakov, who, as has been seen, was important among the pioneers of Russian nationalistic music. In 1908 Stravinsky, having come into contact with Sergei Diaghilev (1872–1929), the director of the famous *Ballet russe*, decided to move to Paris. There he set about composing his first important works, all of which were ballets for Diaghilev's company: *The Firebird* (*L'Oiseau de feu*) of 1910, *Petrushka* of 1911 and *The Rite of Spring* (*Le sacre du printemps*) of 1913. The last-named work has, with Schoenberg's *Pierrot Lunaire*, become one of the most important landmarks of early twentieth-century music. During World War I Stravinsky lived in Switzerland and in consequence of the Bolshevik revolution he returned to Paris after the war, which remained his home until 1939. After 1923 he was active as composer, pianist, and conductor, but never as a teacher. His work as a composer established him among the foremost musical figures of the time. In 1939–40 he was appointed to the Charles Eliot Norton Chair of Poetics at Harvard University. Since the outbreak of World War II he has been living in the United States, mainly in California, where he continues to make his home. Apart from composition he has interested himself in philosophical questions concerning music, how it works, what it does or does not express, and so on. Throughout his career his work has been dominated by a constant search for new techniques of composition, and as a result works composed at different stages of his career may differ sharply from works composed at other times. The following periods in his career as a composer may be distinguished: the early nationalistic works (up to 1919), the neoclassic works (1919–51) and the serial works (since 1952). Our discussion will correspond to this threefold periodization.

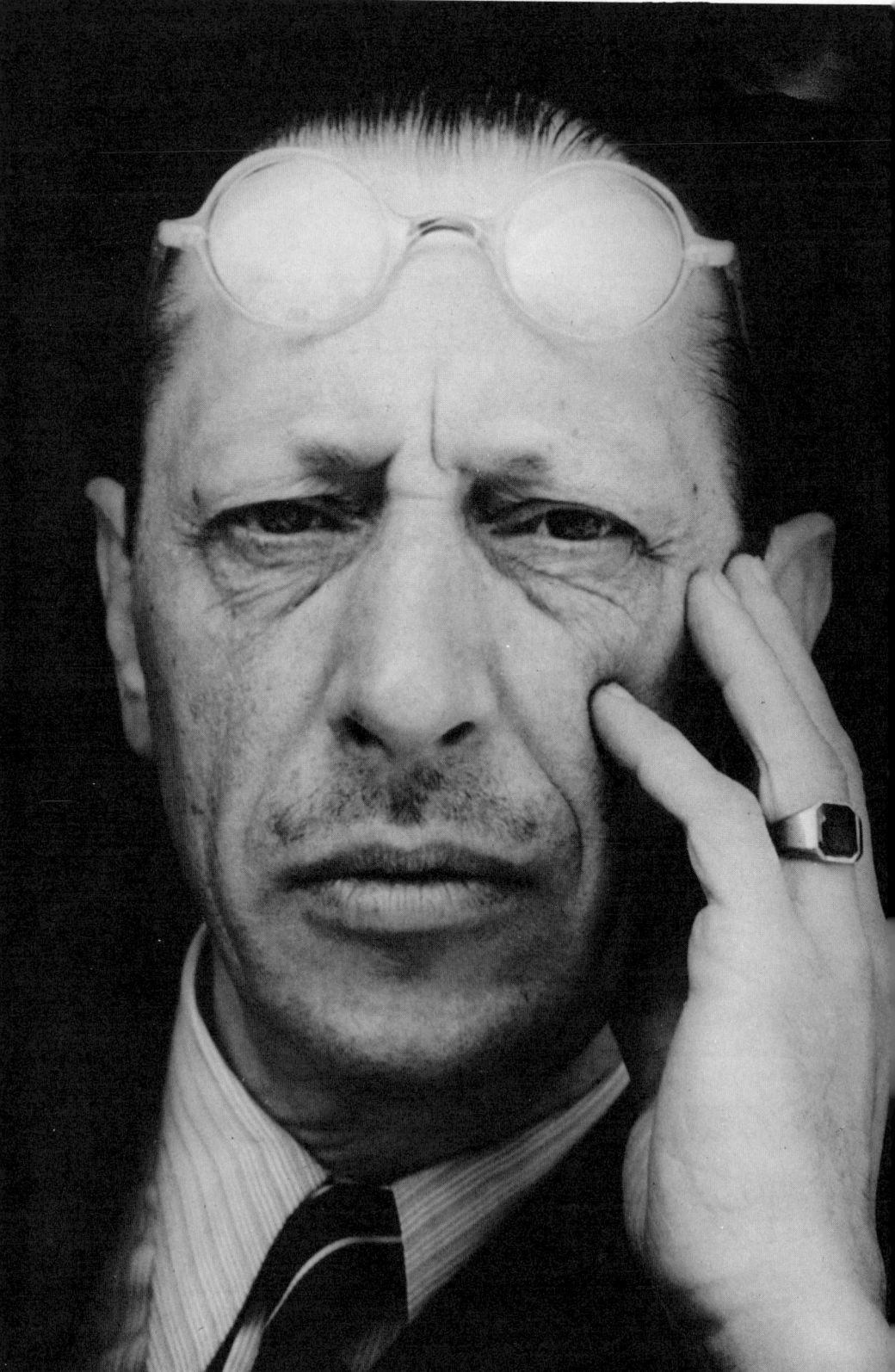

The Nationalistic Works

In view of his studies with Rimsky-Korsakov, it is not surprising that nationalistic music was dominant in the earlier work of Stravinsky. All three of the famous early ballets show this influence. But equally decisive for Stravinsky's development was his direct and early exposure to the musical world of Paris in the early years of the century: He thus absorbed the full impact of the experimentation and innovations of Debussy, in particular the new freedom in the handling of dissonance.

The Firebird, the first of the ballets, is based on the Russian fairy tale of the maidens held captive by the evil Kashchei, who transforms all would-be rescuers into stone, and the young prince, who from the magic firebird learns how to destroy Kashchei's power by smashing the secret egg which holds his soul. Many tunes of pronounced Russian character are employed in this ballet, the instrumentation of which can only be called brilliantly effective. As an example, we may take the beginning of the "Khorovode," or round dance, for the princesses, the melody of which is the well-known Russian folk song "In the Garden." Stravinsky's striking instrumentation is in the tradition of the Russian nationalistic composers: The coloristic use of the oboe and other wind instruments, with accompaniment by the harp, after which the melody is continued in the strings.

The Firebird was followed by *Petrushka*, the story of three puppets brought to life by an old magician to enact a tragedy: Petrushka, the ugly puppet in love with the ballerina, is slain by the vindictive Moor. The action is set during carnival season, and the crowd scenes at the beginning and end provide opportunity for much color. In this work Stravinsky has made extensive use of popular and folk melodies, hurdy-gurdy tunes, Russian dances, and even Viennese waltzes. The prominence of the piano in *Petrushka* is explained by the fact that Stravinsky made use of music originally intended as a concert piece for piano and orchestra.

The fullest fruit of this combination of Russian nationalism and French impressionism is to be seen in the ballet *The Rite of Spring* of 1913, which on its premiere was greeted by a storm of controversy. According to Stravinsky's *Autobiography* (1936), the epoch-making work had its origin in a "fleeting vision": "I saw in imagination a solemn pagan rite: sage elders, seated in a circle, watched a young girl dance herself to death. They were sacrificing her to propitiate the god of spring" (page 31). The ballet as a whole is divided into a number of short sections, each one going without pause into the next, but organized into two large parts, "The Adoration of the Earth" and "The Sacrifice." The subject dictated the musical style; and just as Debussy used

EXAMPLE 6-4

STRAVINSKY: "Khorovode," FROM *The Firebird*—BEGINNING

By permission of the Copyright Owners, J. & W. Chester Limited, London E.C.1.

EXAMPLE 6-4 (*continued*)

EXAMPLE 6-4 (*concluded*)

Oriental scales or American ragtime rhythms in accordance with what he wanted to suggest, so Stravinsky in this work made use of elements of primitive music. Important here are the fiercely pounding and often irregular rhythms in an orchestra in which the brass, woodwinds, and percussion are dominant, along with violently dissonant harmonies.

Two principal elements are to be noted: the vertical combinations (the harmonic aspect) and the rhythm. The harmonies used are intended to have what we might call percussive color, in keeping with the nature of the subject matter. In this work Stravinsky often has combined two triads, the roots of which are a half-step apart, as at the beginning of "The Auguries of Spring" (just after the Introduction), where an E major chord (actually written F-flat major) is heard simultaneously with an E-flat major chord (see Example 6-5). Here the traditional concept of tonality has been modified to comprise two elements, in this case the major triads on E and E-flat. Thus an interplay or tension between two tonal centers is produced. This principle has been called *polarity.* A chord that consists of the combination of two or more triads is known as a *polychord.* Although both triads and the concept of tonality (a

EXAMPLE 6-5

STRAVINSKY: *The Rite of Spring*—EXCERPTS

1. INTRODUCTION—BEGINNING

2. AUGURIES OF SPRING—BEGINNING

3. ROUND DANCES OF SPRING—BEGINNING

1.

EXAMPLE 6-5 (*continued*)

EXAMPLE 6-5 (*continued*)

2.

EXAMPLE 6-5 (*continued*)

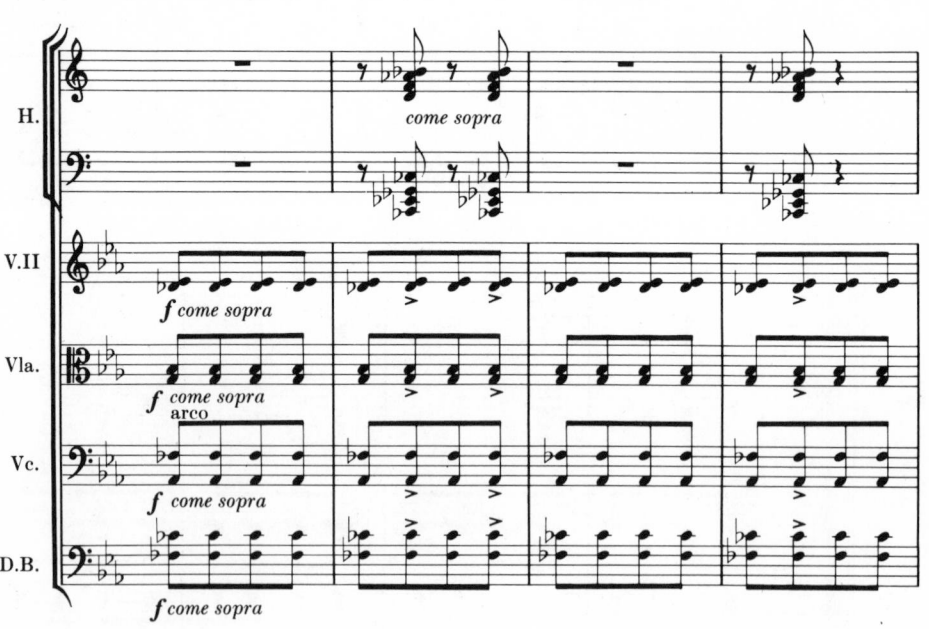

EXAMPLE 6-5 (*concluded*)

3.

tonal center of some sort) have been retained, the principle of organization, the way of confirming the tonality, is entirely new and different. In his *Poetics of Music* (1947, page 37) Stravinsky puts great stress on the need for ordering in some fashion the tones used in a piece of music:

> The tuning of an instrument, of a piano for example, requires that the entire musical range available to the instrument should be ordered according to chromatic steps. Such tuning prompts us to observe that all these sounds converge towards a center which is the *a* above middle *c*. Composing, for me, is putting into an order a certain number of these sounds according to certain interval-relationships. This activity leads to a search for the center upon which the series of sounds involved in my undertaking should converge.

As far as the treatment of rhythm is concerned, we may observe in *The Rite of Spring* the constantly shifting accents along with a constant changing of the time signature, even though the unit of beat remains the same. Both aspects mark a striking departure from the practice of nineteenth-century music.

At the very beginning of *The Rite of Spring* one senses a complete departure from what one might expect in a ballet: the long, high-pitched rhapsodic bassoon solo (actually a Lithuanian folk song) later joined by other instruments, but with the woodwinds predominating, the whole passage characterized by short thematic fragments, continuously repeated and varied. Then, after the bassoon solo has been heard once again, the pounding relentless rhythms of "The Auguries of Spring" begin with dissonant percussive chords in the strings and harsh irregular accentuations supplied by the horns and percussion (see Example 6-5). In the section of the first part of the ballet called "Round Dances of Spring," a rhythmic pattern set up in the strings provides the accompaniment; it is repeated over and over again, the harmony remaining unchanged, then suddenly it is stated fortissimo as the percussion is added. The organization of this passage is typical of the work as a whole, except that here, because of the relative regularity of the rhythmic pattern (see Example 6-5, No. 3) one can see a clear link to Russian ballet music in general, that of Tchaikovsky, for instance, whose ballets Stravinsky admires.

Much of the same procedure may be found in the Introduction to the second part of the ballet (a passage which originally bore the title "Pagan Night"), except here several distinct entities, each with its individual thematic motive, instrumental color, and particular character, are presented in succession: the soft, densely scored chromatic chords, the melancholy melodic fragment repeated over and over in the horn, and the duet passage for the trumpets. As would be expected, frenetic pounding rhythms come to dominate the concluding part of the ballet, representing the sacrificial dance of the chosen maiden. Here Stravinsky not only constantly changes the time signature, often every bar being in a different meter, but also disregards the normal accentuation pattern of the various meters he employs.

The Nationalistic Works

Another important work of this period is *The Soldier's Story* (*L'Histoire d'un soldat*). The piece was composed in 1918 during Stravinsky's stay in Switzerland to take refuge from the war. It is a theatrical work using narration along with music and dancing, based on Russian folk tales which were adapted by Stravinsky's friend, the Swiss writer C. F. Ramuz. The plot has to do with a soldier returning home on leave, with his violin; he is accosted by the devil, who lures the soldier into his power by deception and gives him a book that enables him to read tomorrow's stock market report, thus making him rich.

EXAMPLE 6-6

STRAVINSKY: *The Soldier's Story*—EXCERPTS

1. THE ROYAL MARCH—BEGINNING

2. TANGO—BEGINNING

3. WALTZ—BEGINNING

4. LITTLE CHORALE

1.

Stravinsky and the New Music of the Twentieth Century

EXAMPLE 6-6 (continued)

EXAMPLE 6-6 (*continued*)

2.

EXAMPLE 6-6 (*concluded*)

4.

niente
Enchainez

The Neoclassic Works

After posing as a military doctor who is able to cure the princess whom he then marries, the soldier eventually returns home, in defiance of the devil's threats, and in the end the devil gets him.

The constitution of the orchestra here is most rationalistically worked out. Since his financial resources were limited and the size of the instrumental ensemble for the work had to be kept to a minimum, Stravinsky elected to have each of the choirs represented by two instruments, the highest and the lowest: thus, for the strings, violin and double bass; for the woodwinds, clarinet and bassoon; for the brass, cornet and trombone; and percussion, with two side drums, bass drum, triangle, tambourine, and cymbals. As in *The Rite of Spring*, where Stravinsky drew on primitive music to be true to the subject matter, so in *The Soldier's Story* certain characteristic types of music are used. Most prominent is the march, which is heard at the beginning and at other parts of the work; especially noteworthy is the brilliant triumphal march as the soldier enters the royal palace to cure the princess. Having cured the princess, the two engage in a set of three dances—a tango, a waltz, and a ragtime—each of which preserves its characteristic elements in Stravinsky's stylized version. At the same time, Stravinsky's new methods of harmonic and rhythmic organization are readily apparent: the unusual chord combinations and progressions involving the free use of dissonance, all of which is organized around tonal centers, and the constant changing of meter. Yet another hallowed form is treated in this composition, the hymn or chorale in congregational style as we have seen it, for example, in the cantatas of Bach. Stravinsky preserves the melodic, rhythmic, and harmonic style along with some of the chord progressions, but the use of dissonant and chromatic chords in combination with the unusual nature of most of the chord progressions creates a striking impression.

The Neoclassic Works

Around 1919 Stravinsky made the decisive turn to neoclassicism, which, as we have already pointed out, became a powerful current in France as well as elsewhere at the time. Stravinsky himself has denied the validity of the term *neoclassic* in reference to his work. But in 1925 he was quoted in a remark that became a slogan: "back to Johann Sebastian Bach, whose universal mind and enormous grasp upon musical art has never been transcended." "Back to Bach" indeed became the catchword of the neoclassic movement. Furthermore, it is undeniable that many of the works Stravinsky composed from 1919 to 1951 are inspired by models from earlier periods in the history of Western music: *Pulcinella* of 1920, from Pergolesi (see later); the Serenade in A for Piano of 1925, which in his *Autobiography* Stravinsky described as "in imitation of the *Nachtmusik* (night music or serenade) of the eighteenth century"; and the Concerto in E-flat major (the *Dumbarton Oaks Concerto*) of 1938, which is closely related to the *Brandenburg Concertos* of Bach (see later).[2] This is, incidentally, continued in his most recent work; there are the arrangements of Bach's canonic variations on *Von Himmel hoch*, originally for organ, which Stravinsky scored for wind ensemble and chorus of mixed voices (1955–56), as well as two pieces based on madrigals and motets by Gesualdo (1959–60).

Other works, however, seem indebted not to any individual composer of the past, but to Baroque music in general, its unity of expressive character, the prevalence of the fortspinnung type of melodic writing, propulsive rhythms, instrumental fugues, and so forth. Many compositions display these features, among them the Octet for Winds (1923), the Concerto for Piano and Orchestra of Wind Instruments and the Sonata for Piano (both 1924) the *Symphony of Psalms* (1930, see later), the Duo Concertant for Violin and Piano (1932), the Concerto for Violin and Orchestra in D (1931), the Concerto for Two Solo Pianos (1931–35), the Symphony in C (1940), the Symphony in Three Movements (1945), and Ode (1943). His operas are also modeled on eighteenth-century types: *Mavra* (1922) and *The Rake's Progress* (1951, see later), and much the same applies to the opera-oratorio *Oedipus Rex* (1927, see later).

Another important aspect of the neoclassic orientation involves Stravinsky's attitude toward music and its purpose. In his *Autobiography* and *Poetics of Music* we note a strong reaction against the views that had dominated the nineteenth century, when music was regarded as the art that can "speak the unspeakable." This power of music is vehemently denied by Stravinsky: "I consider that music is, by its very nature, essentially powerless to *express* anything at all. . . . *Expression* has never been an inherent property of music," in his *Autobiography* (page 53). Much later, in his *Expositions and Developments* of 1962, Stravinsky returns to this idea: "That overpublicized bit about expression (or non-expression) was simply a way of saying that music is supra-personal and super-real and as such beyond verbal meanings and verbal descriptions. . . . I stand by the remark, incidentally, though today I would put it the other way around: music expresses itself" (pages 114–15).

What music really does, according to Stravinsky, is quite different (*Autobiography*, page 54):

> Music is the sole domain in which man realizes the present. . . . The phenomenon of music is given to us with the sole purpose of establishing an order in things, including, and particularly, the coordination between *man* and *time*. To be put into practice, its indispensable and single requirement is construction. Construction once completed, this order has been attained, and there is nothing more to be said. . . . It is precisely this construction, this achieved order, which produces in us a unique emotion having nothing in common with our ordinary sensations and our responses to the impressions of daily life.

Stravinsky's definition of music—a speculation in sound and time—has

---

[2] The ballet *The Fairy's Kiss* (*Le Baiser de la fée*), however, is based on the music of Tchaikovsky.

already been taken up when we approached the fundamentals of the art. Since music, thus, is a chronological art, fundamental importance is assigned to what Stravinsky calls *musical time*, "an exclusively musical experiencing of time." Stravinsky makes a distinction—and here he follows closely an essay by his friend Pierre Souvchinsky—between real or clock time (which Stravinsky also calls "ontological time") and psychological time, or time as perceived by an individual human being, the rate of passage of which varies with his particular feelings and states of mind. The two kinds of time exist simultaneously and in combination in the concept of *musical time*: "What gives the concept of musical time its special stamp is that this concept is born and develops as well outside of the categories of psychological time as it does simultaneously with them." On this basis two types of music are recognized: one that develops "parallel to" the stream of real time and one that runs either ahead of or behind it. "Music that is based on ontological time is generally dominated by the principle of similarity. The music that adheres to psychological time likes to proceed by contrast." Stravinsky's own music, according to him, proceeds according to the principle of similarity:[3]

> Contrast produces an immediate effect. Similarity satisfies us only in the long run. Contrast is an element of variety, but it divides our attention. Similarity is born of a striving for unity.

Whatever one may think about these ideas—and their validity as pronouncements on aesthetics has been widely debated—they at least shed light on Stravinsky's artistic beliefs and intentions. The musical artwork is viewed as something objective, as a construction, in which unity is sought through coherence, through order and logic or, in Stravinsky's terms, "the principle of similarity," and in which personal subjective expression is irrelevant. Contrast is avoided except as a means of attaining unity. It is thus entirely consistent that most of the nineteenth-century tradition be denied and that Stravinsky's music harks back to earlier points of view.

Symbolic of the nineteenth-century tradition, in Stravinsky's eyes, is Wagner, who is subjected to a scathing attack in the *Poetics of Music*, his music dramas being castigated as containing "continual bombast." More important, however, is Stravinsky's view that Wagner's music is more improvised than composed (*Poetics of Music*, page 62):

> Wagner's work corresponds to a tendency that is not, properly speaking, a disorder, but one which tries to compensate for a lack of order. The principle of the endless melody perfectly illustrates this tendency. It is the perpetual becoming of a music that never had any reason for starting, any more that it has any reason for ending. Endless melody thus appears as an insult to the dignity and to the very function of melody which, as we have said, is the musical intonation of a cadenced phrase.

[3] This discussion is found in the *Poetics of Music* (1947), pages 30–32.

Design for Pulcinella, *by Picasso* (*1917*). (COURTESY OF THE ART INSTITUTE OF CHICAGO AND MR. AND MRS. MORTON G. NEUMANN, CHICAGO.)

Hence it is not surprising that Stravinsky comes out strongly in favor of Verdi's music, as opposed to that of Wagner, and this stand is based on the concept of melody as a "cadenced phrase." Thus, when Stravinsky takes over Nietzsche's dichotomy of Apollonian and Dionysian art, he comes down firmly in favor of Apollo (*Poetics of Music*, pages 80–81):

> What is important for the lucid ordering of the work—for its crystallization— is that all the Dionysian elements which set the imagination of the artist in motion and make the life-sap rise must be properly subjugated before they intoxicate us, and must finally be made to submit to the law: Apollo demands it.

In other words, Wagner is rejected in favor of Bach.

The Neoclassic Works

The most characteristic features of Stravinsky's music are direct consequences of this attitude. Paramount is the stress on melody and the way this important element is conceived—as a "cadenced phrase." Stravinsky's music, the earlier works as well as those of the neoclassic period and the later serial compositions, is compounded of terse cadenced phrases, repeated incessantly (the principle of similarity) but with variations that are rhythmic (shifting of accents, changing the durations), melodic (changing of intervals), and harmonic. It has been suggested that these short phrases, with their pronounced rhythmic qualities, may ultimately go back to the ballet, where Stravinsky scored his first successes as a composer. In any case, Stravinsky's *order* consists of the arrangement of such small melodic particles.

Stravinsky's first venture with this kind of music was the ballet *Pulcinella*, composed in 1919–20 for Diaghilev with stage sets and costuming designed by Pablo Picasso. The characters in the ballet are taken from the stock types of the eighteenth-century commedia dell'arte: Pulcinella (the dwarf), Fourbo (the magician), and Pimpinella. The action may be summarized as follows: frustrated by the circumstance that all the girls are in love with Pulcinella, the other young men plot to kill him; they dress themselves to look like him, go to see their sweethearts and then pounce upon him; but Pulcinella's place has been taken by Fourbo, who pretends to succumb to the attack; then Pulcinella reappears dressed as Fourbo, whom he revives, and then, after arranging marriages for all the young men, marries Pimpinella himself.

Since the commedia dell'arte was at its height in early eighteenth-century Italy, it is to be expected that Stravinsky would take a model from Italian Baroque music. Indeed, this was Diaghilev's intention in commissioning the work, since he had just scored a success with *The Good-Humored Ladies*, with music by Ottorino Respighi based on compositions by the eighteenth-century Italian composer Domenico Scarlatti. Stravinsky's model was provided by Giovanni Battista Pergolesi (1710–1736), a composer who represented the early galant type of music and who worked chiefly with the opera buffa, but who also wrote a good deal of chamber music. Stravinsky's procedure with respect to Pergolesi was, however, not what one might expect: that is, he did not simply orchestrate Pergolesi's music (as Respighi did with that of Scarlatti); rather he recomposed it, usually retaining Pergolesi's soprano and bass lines but altering the harmonies by adding biting dissonances, and frequently bringing in variations of his own. Generally in *Pulcinella*, the chords—in accordance with the spirit of the subject matter—are kept simple and remain essentially in the tradition of tonally oriented harmony. The orchestra used is small: The strings contain a solo group and a *ripieno* (after the fashion of the Baroque concerto grosso), there are no clarinets in the woodwinds, and percussion is completely lacking. Some of the numbers taken over by Stravinsky from vocal pieces by Pergolesi are sung, but the remainder—the majority—of the ballet are purely instrumental. Modern touches in the instrumentation are by no means lacking, as the trombone glissando in the Vivo section demonstrates.[4] Several eighteenth-century forms are represented in *Pulcinella*: the *sinfonia*, the short festive opening piece; the toccata (originally a keyboard piece by Pergolesi); a gavotte with two *doubles* (variations); and a minuet.

As an example we may take the minuet, which Stravinsky has adapted from an aria in Pergolesi's opera *Lo Fratre inammorato*. The passage, which is primarily homophonic, operates with a lyrical theme that is cast in the familiar *a a b* formal plan; the use of such a repetitive plan, incidentally, is characteristic of neoclassic works. The theme begins with a melodic phrase, seven bars in length, played by the horn and accompanied by another horn and two bassoons; this is then restated by the first violins accompanied by the remaining string instruments and the bassoon, and the theme then concludes with a passage featuring a descending chromatic phrase in the flute that is repeated by the oboe and continued in the horns. The entire theme is now stated again, with the melody first in the trombone, then in the trumpet and horns, and the concluding portion featuring the flute and solo violin. In the first presentation of the theme the harmonies are Pergolesi's, however much the instrumentation is Stravinsky's. But in the second statement of the theme (from bar 25) the harmonies have been changed, spiced with dissonances, as is clearly seen from the chords in the violoncello that accompany the presentation of the melody in the trombone. Thus we see how Stravinsky has adapted Pergolesi for his own particular purposes.

In 1962 Stravinsky himself testified to the importance of this work in his development: "*Pulcinella* was my discovery of the past, the epiphany through which the whole of my late work became possible." It was followed by many others. One of the largest and most impressive of these is the opera-oratorio *Oedipus Rex* of 1927. Here the treatment of the text is characteristic. Since Stravinsky's intention at the outset was to compose a "sublime" work, he felt it necessary to select something old and hallowed. Thus he took the tragedy of Oedipus and had its text—originally adapted from Sophocles in French by his friend Jean Cocteau (1891–1963)—translated into Latin, "a medium not dead, but turned to stone and so monumentalized as to have become immune from all risk of vulgarization," as he put it in his *Autobiography* (page 125). At the beginning of each act a narrator summarizes in French[5] the action that is to take place. Although the work was to be staged, Stravinsky envisioned a static form of presentation, with the chorus seated in a single row in the background, the singers up front, masked, standing on raised platforms, motionless except

---

[4] Glissando: the playing of scale passages by sliding from note to note, not articulating each note separately and clearly.

[5] An English version of this narration has been made by the poet E. E. Cummings.

EXAMPLE 6-7

STRAVINSKY: MENUETTO, FROM *Pulcinella*—BEGINNING

Example 6-7 *(continued)*

The Neoclassic Works

EXAMPLE 6-7 (continued)

EXAMPLE 6-7 (continued)

The Neoclassic Works

EXAMPLE 6-7 (continued)

EXAMPLE 6-7 *(concluded)*

for their arms and heads: "They should give the impression of living statues." The disposition of the score is in kind: It reverts to the old idea of the "number opera," and presents a succession of closed pieces, arias, ensembles, and choral pieces, each of which represents a single stage in the dramatic action; thus each piece manifests the unity of character that was found in the arias of Baroque operas. At the same time, there are portions of *Oedipus Rex*, such as Jocasta's large aria ("Nonn'erubescite") that show in many details the influence of Verdi. As would be expected, there is no sign of any influence from the music dramas of Wagner.

Another work in the neoclassic style but of a totally different sort is the *Symphony of Psalms* (*Symphonie des psaumes*), composed in 1930, a commission for the fiftieth anniversary of the Boston Symphony Orchestra. Scored for mixed chorus and a symphony orchestra without violins, each of the work's three movements is the setting of a psalm, in whole or in part: Psalm 38 (Vulgate) or 39 (King James Version), Verses 13 and 14; Psalm 39 (Vulgate) or 40 (King James Version), Verses 2–4; and Psalm 150, the whole psalm. Stravinsky describes the three movements as presenting, in succession, prayer, testimony, and praise (the descriptive titles originally given the three movements—Prelude, Double Fugue, and Allegro symphonique—were dropped). The nineteenth-century symphonic tradition, characteristically, is rejected: Stravinsky's aim, instead, was "to create an organic whole without conforming to the various models adopted by custom, but still retaining the periodic order by which the symphony is distinguished from the suite" (*Autobiography*, page 161). Furthermore, the work was to be essentially contrapuntal, the vocal and instrumental elements kept "on an equal footing."

The austere character of the *Symphony of Psalms* appears at the outset: the loud chords in an irregular rhythm, followed by evenly moving figuration in thirds in the woodwinds, which becomes the accompaniment to the chorus' singing of a melodic line consisting at first of two notes a second apart. There ensues a gradual intensification. The second movement consists of two fugues, first one for the instruments alone, with which the movement begins; this instrumental fugue then provides the accompaniment for a second fugue assigned to the chorus. Largest and most elaborate is the third movement, the text of which has often been set to music, since this psalm enumerates ways in which God may be praised: "Praise him with the sound of the trumpet, praise him with the psaltery and harp. Praise him with the timbrel and dance; praise him with stringed instruments and organs. Praise him upon the loud cymbals; praise him upon the high sounding cymbals." The movement falls into three principal sections: first, slow, setting the words, "Alleluia, laudate Dominum" (Alleluia, praise the Lord), then a passage in an almost barbaric vein, reminiscent of *The Rite of Spring*, loud, with sharp, insistently repeated rhythmic patterns, interrupted in the middle by a brief return to the material of the opening section; then there is a sustained lyric passage, the

Stravinsky and the New Music of the Twentieth Century

melodie line of which moves within the compass of a major third, over an ostinato bass; at the very end the "Alleluia, laudate Dominum" of the opening is heard.

Especially indebted to Baroque music in general and to the music of Bach in particular is the Concerto in E-flat major for fifteen instruments of 1937–38 (known as the *Dumbarton Oaks Concerto*). The work is closely modeled on the concerto grosso of the early eighteenth century; Stravinsky himself has described it as "a little concerto in the style of the *Brandenburg Concertos*." The external form, in three movements (Tempo giusto, Allegretto, Con Moto),

EXAMPLE 6-8

STRAVINSKY: THIRD MOVEMENT, FROM *Symphony of Psalms*—EXCERPTS

1. BEGINNING*

2. MIDDLE SECTION—BEGINNING

3. CONCLUDING SECTION—BEGINNING

1.

* Wind, brass, and percussion parts omitted.

Example 6-8 *(continued)*

2.

Stravinsky and the New Music of the Twentieth Century

EXAMPLE 6-8 (concluded)

shows this association obviously enough. Beyond this, many other features linking the piece with Baroque music may be noted: Most characteristic is the fortspinnung type of melodic formation, with a short rhythmic thematic motive reiterated over and over again, with regularly recurring accentuations,

The Neoclassic Works

thus producing those driving rhythms found in much Baroque music; the melodic line itself frequently takes on the character of figuration; passages in fugal style abound: finally, the relation of the various instrumental groups (choirs) of the orchestra to one another, the way they alternate and contrast

EXAMPLE 6-9

STRAVINSKY: TEMPO GIUSTO, FROM CONCERTO IN E FLAT—BEGINNING

EXAMPLE 6-9 (*continued*)

EXAMPLE 6-9 (*continued*)

EXAMPLE 6-9 (*continued*)

Example 6-9 (*continued*)

EXAMPLE 6-9 (*concluded*)

with each other, has a specific resemblance to Bach's *Brandenburg Concerto No. 3 in G major* (see Example 1-34).

In 1947–48 Stravinsky composed a setting of the Ordinary of the Mass. He reports that he was influenced—albeit negatively—by Masses of Mozart in the eighteenth-century galant style, which made him determined to compose what he calls a "real" Mass—i.e., suited in all respects for liturgical use. The result was a concise work scored for chorus of mixed voices and soloists, accompanied by a wind ensemble (oboes, English horns, bassoons, trumpets in pairs, and three trombones). As a whole, the Mass is, in Stravinsky's words, "almost without ornament." The Credo, as the longest movement ("there is much to

The Orgy, *from* The Rake's Progress, *by Hogarth.* (BY PERMISSION OF THE TRUSTEES OF SIR JOHN SOANE'S MUSEUM, LONDON.)

believe"), stands in the center. Here the text is declaimed for the most part in chords with much use of repeated chords, thus suggesting the recitation formulas of Gregorian chant (see pages 41–44); the dynamic level is soft throughout. Although this style is prominent throughout, in the other movements elements of variety are introduced here and there, such as the more melodic quality of the Kyrie, the contrast between soloists and chorus in the Gloria, or the fugue at "Pleni sunt coeli" in the Sanctus; but on the whole, the austere functional character is maintained. This work has invited comparison with the Mass by Guillaume de Machaut (see pages 57–61).

Although practically all of the works Stravinsky composed in the years 1919 to 1951 are related to some extent to the neoclassic outlook in the broad meaning assigned the term here, his largest effort was his last: This was the opera *The Rake's Progress* of 1951, to a libretto by W. H. Auden and Chester

Kallman, founded on a series of eight etchings by the eighteenth-century English artist William Hogarth that depict the stages in the downward path of a rake from affluence to poverty, disgrace, and ultimately insanity. But a number of other elements are brought in: the old idea of a pact with the devil, here represented by Nick Shadow, who offers the hero Tom Rakewell his services for a year, during which three wishes are to be granted—for wealth, happiness, and the power to save humanity—for which, as it turns out in the effective graveyard scene, the wages are to be Tom's soul; the episode with the Bearded Lady, Baba the Turk, whom Shadow, by means of a neat piece of existentialistic sophistry, persuades Tom to marry (the wish for happiness); Tom's devoted sweetheart Ann, left behind when he went off with Shadow to the city, who through her love at the last minute robs the devil of Tom's soul. At the end a note from classical mythology is sounded, when Bedlam becomes the underworld and Ann and Tom represent Venus and Adonis, respectively. As in the great operas of Mozart, in *The Rake's Progress* comedy and tragedy appear side by side: the fierce gaiety of Mother Goose's brothel; the crass deception of Shadow's machine for turning stones into bread (the fulfillment of Tom's wish to save humanity); the brilliant trio for Ann, Baba, and Tom; the aria for the gossiping Baba, whom Tom turns off by throwing a cape over her head, the aria being resumed in the following scene as Baba is about to be auctioned off as "an unknown object" with all her possessions; the grim terror of the graveyard scene as Tom and Shadow play a game of chance for Tom's soul; and the affecting lyricism of the final scene in Bedlam.

We have already mentioned Stravinsky's profound opposition to the works and principles of Wagner. This opposition is plainly demonstrated in *The Rake's Progress* which, according to Stravinsky, is in the "Italian-Mozartian" tradition of opera. It is, then, a "number opera," in Stravinsky's words "is, emphatically, an opera—an opera of arias and recitatives, choruses and ensembles. Its musical structure, the conception of the use of these forms, even to the relations of tonalities, is in the line of the classical tradition." In keeping with the eighteenth-century atmosphere, the orchestra is kept small and a harpsichord is used to accompany the secco recitative.

As an example of Stravinsky's melodic style at its most lyrical, we may refer to Tom's cavatina (literally, small aria) in the brothel scene (Act I, Scene 2). Here the resemblance to Mozart, or even Verdi, is striking: the melodic line, holding the center of attention, is organized by balanced phrases and a constantly repeated rhythmic pattern, over the subdued accompaniment of the orchestra. Somewhat the same thing, but with comic effect, is Shadow's aria persuading Tom of the advantages to his marrying Baba the Turk.

A striking use of old forms may be seen in Act I, Scene 3. Here Ann, worried about Tom who has left for the city and about her duty to her father, ultimately decides to go to London after Tom. Here we find first a recitative

("No word from Tom"), then an aria of longing ("Quietly night"), followed by a second recitative in which she makes the decision to go to London, and finally by a second aria, this time a heady cabaletta expressing resolution, in

EXAMPLE 6-10

STRAVINSKY: "Quietly night," from *The Rake's Progress* (ACT I, SCENE 3)
—BEGINNING (ORCHESTRAL ACCOMPANIMENT ARRANGED FOR PIANO)

EXAMPLE 6-10 (*continued*)

bright C major ("I go, I go to him"). In constructing the scene this way, Stravinsky and his librettists are working within a tradition of nineteenth-century Italian opera: a seriously expressive aria, followed by a recitative passage in which there is a change of heart on the part of the protagonist that is expressed in a vigorous second aria, a cabaletta. Again the voice part dominates the conception while the orchestra provides the accompaniment, consisting of chords in a repeated rhythmic pattern. Ann's first aria, in B minor, falls into two strophes which roughly parallel one another, except that the close is in recitative style. The phrases are clearly separated from one another, and there is some repetition of music associated with repetitions in the text. The declamation includes numerous melismatic passages. The cabaletta is organized in three parts, of which the third is a varied version of the first, while the second provides contrast. The cabaletta as a whole is characterized by wide leaps and sharp accents in the vocal part, and running scale figuration in the orchestra; a brilliant melismatic cadenza comes at the end.

Typical of the old ensemble is the trio (Act II, Scene 2) for Ann, Baba, and Tom, as Ann, unexpectedly arrived from the country, meets Baba and Tom, who are returning home from their wedding. The dramatic situation affords an opportunity for conceiving and combining sharply contrasting musical themes representing the emotions of the three characters: Ann's shocked sadness, Baba's haughtiness (she sits in the sedan chair by herself while Tom and Ann are outside), Tom's conflict and remorse.

Finally, attention may be drawn to the graveyard scene (Act III, Scene 2), the reckoning between Shadow and Tom. This is cast in continuous recitative accompanied to a large extent by only the solo harpsichord, but the scene is introduced by a somber piece for string quartet; the orchestra as a whole is not used until the end of the scene, when Ann's loyal love deprives Shadow of his victim (she sings, "A love that is sworn to me before Thee can plunder hell of its prey," actually using a phrase from her arioso in Act II), in retaliation for which Shadow, in an aria of rage, strikes Tom insane. In the last scene of the opera the melodic writing becomes intensely lyric.

An important aspect of Stravinsky's work is that he often composes not autonomous and independent compositions, but rather compositions for specific purposes, occasions, and even individual persons. This means that he has to work with something external to music, and this in turn often provides the point of departure for the musical composition. Thus he has often been in contact with the leading writers, artists, and so forth, of the time. His collaborations with Diaghilev, Picasso, Cocteau, and Auden have been discussed. Among the others we can mention André Gide (*Perséphone*, 1934), George Balanchine (a number of works, among them the ballet *Orpheus*, 1948), and Dylan Thomas, with whom Stravinsky planned to compose an opera, the work cut short by Thomas' death. But Stravinsky's contacts have not been exclusively among what might be called the "highbrow" artists: There is a ballet for Billy Rose's revue *Seven Lively Arts* (the *Scènes de ballet,* 1944),[6] a piece for Woody Herman's dance band ("Ebony Concerto," 1945), and even a polka for the elephants composed for the band of Ringling Brothers, Barnum and Bailey Circus ("Circus Polka," 1942). He has also composed a short piece based on the song "Happy Birthday to You" ("Greeting Prelude," 1955). But he never gave his approval to Walt Disney's use of portions of *The Rite of Spring* in the movie *Fantasia.* In 1941, during World War II, Stravinsky made an arrangement of "The Star-Spangled Banner," but in Boston the authorities balked when they heard it in rehearsal and secured a court order forbidding its public performance on the grounds that it constituted "tampering" with national property; he still is convinced that his is the best setting of this in some ways rather problematic song. Among his more recent works are memorial compositions for Dylan Thomas, John F. Kennedy, Aldous Huxley and T. S. Eliot.

The Serial Works

By 1950 Stravinsky had long been recognized as perhaps *the* outstanding composer of the time. Apart from his early work up to *The Rite of Spring* he was regarded as the leading representative of the neoclassical tradition. Throughout his career his opposition to the music and the system of Schoenberg (see pages 369–71) had been clearly and repeatedly expressed. In his *Autobiography* (page 43) he said of *Pierrot Lunaire,* "I did not feel the slightest enthusiasm about the aesthetics of the work," although he valued its instrumentation. By 1963 his attitude on this work and its creator had changed completely: He then called *Pierrot Lunaire* "the solar plexus as well as the mind of early twentieth-century music." This change of heart represented a most startling transformation. Actually, although what Stravinsky embraced represented the Schoenbergian system, the principal artistic influence came from one of Schoenberg's disciples and colleagues, Anton Webern (1883–1945), whose music is characterized by the use of very short melodic phrases, often consisting solely of intervals, in an extremely thin texture in which tone color itself was an important formal element.

The first work of Stravinsky's in which this change may be seen is the Cantata on anonymous fifteenth- and sixteenth-century Elizabethan lyrics (texts apparently taken from Auden's *Anthology of English Verse*) of 1952. This work, scored for soprano, tenor, a chorus of female voices, and a small ensemble of woodwinds and violoncello, consists of a choral piece ("The Lyke-Wake Dirge") that is repeated, in ritornello fashion; between its repetitions come two ricercars, the first for soprano and the second for tenor, and then a

---

[6] On the pre-Broadway tour Rose telegraphed to Stravinsky: "Your music great success stop could be sensational success if you would authorize Robert Russell Bennett retouch orchestration stop Bennett orchestrates even the works of Cole Porter." Stravinsky's reply: "Satisfied with great success." Needless to say, Billy Rose did not use Stravinsky's score in its entirety.

duet. Although the term *ricercar* here does not designate a fugal composition, as it did in the Renaissance and Baroque, these movements nonetheless are essentially contrapuntal and make use both of imitation and of canon. The second of these ricercars, for solo tenor and instrumental ensemble, is at once the central and principal movement of the cantata and is also the piece that reveals the first appearance in Stravinsky's work of the serial method of composition. The text is a strophic poem presenting an allegorical narrative of Christ's life and death, the Christian religion being referred to in the refrain as his "dance." Stravinsky's series, stated in unison and octaves right at the beginning, departs from Schoenberg's norms in that it does not use all twelve notes; furthermore, it contains notes that are used more than once, and it is clearly oriented around C as the tonic:

EXAMPLE 6-11

BASIC SET USED IN RICERCAR II OF STRAVINSKY'S CANTATA

The basic set moves within a very limited range, that of a diminished fifth, and is characterized by the alternation between E and E flat, the major and minor third above C. In the setting, the strophic and refrain form of the poem determines the form of the music. It is in the strophes, and not in the refrains, that the basic set of notes is used. Indeed, it can be said that the entire melodic material in the strophes consists of nothing but statements of the series in some form or other, either the regular (original form, φ), the inversion (I), the retrograde (R), the retrograde inversion (RI), or some transposition of these variations. In the score Stravinsky has placed brackets to mark the various presentations of the series in the vocal part. At times the series appears in the instrumental accompaniment as well. Although always based on the series, the music for the different strophes is varied, usually in accordance with the meaning of the poem—as, for instance, when mention is made of Jesus' betrayal by Judas, the tonic is abruptly shifted and the accompaniment becomes agitated. The beginning of the movement appears in Example 6-12.

Other works composed shortly after the Cantata reveal a similar use of the serial technique: the three Shakespeare Songs and the Septet (both of 1953) and the *In Memoriam Dylan Thomas* for tenor and brass instruments (1954). The *In Memoriam* consists of a setting of Thomas' poem "Do not go gentle into that good night" for tenor and strings, flanked by a prelude and postlude for small brass ensemble. The villanelle structure that characterizes the poem is respected in the musical setting.[7] The basic set in this composition consists of but five notes, all within the range of a major third. The pitch organization of the entire piece is rigorously derived from this set and its permutations. At the same time the setting of Thomas' elegy is powerfully

EXAMPLE 6-12

STRAVINSKY: RICERCAR II, FROM CANTATA—BEGINNING

[7] A villanelle is a poetic form consisting usually of five three-line strophes with a single four-line strophe at the end. It makes use of but two rhymes, and the first and third lines of the opening three-line strophe recur in alternation as the last lines of the remaining three-line strophes, and together in the four-line strophe. Thus, if *a* and *b* stand for the two rhymes, and *A* and *A'*, for the repeated lines, the following typical scheme for a villanelle results:

A b A'   a b A   a b A'   a b A   a b A'   a b A A'

EXAMPLE 6-12 (*continued*)

EXAMPLE 6-13

STRAVINSKY: SONG, FROM *In Memoriam Dylan Thomas*—BEGINNING

EXAMPLE 6-13 (*continued*)

Ten. Old age should burn and rave at close of day; Rage, rage a - gainst the dy -

- ing of the light.   Though wise men

The Serial Works

EXAMPLE 6-13 (*concluded*)

expressive (see Example 6-13). The instrumental prelude and postlude are called by Stravinsky "dirge-canons": They are canons by virtue of their use of some form of the basic set in each voice part.

As Stravinsky continued to work with the serial method he came more and more to adopt the full system of dodecaphonic serialism, as is clear from the *Canticum sacrum* (1955), *Threni,* a setting of the Lamentations of Jeremiah (1958), the ballet *Agon* (also 1958), and the Movements for Piano and Orchestra (1961), and subsequent compositions.

An example of those compositions in which the method of dodecaphonic serialism is completely manifested may be seen in the cantata *A Sermon, a Narrative, and a Prayer* of 1961. The texts used were taken from the Epistles of St. Paul (Romans, Chapter 8, Verse 24; Hebrews, Chapter 11, Verse 1, and Chapter 12, Verse 29; Romans, Chapter 8, Verse 25), the Acts of the Apostles, Chapter 6, Verses 2–15 and Chapter 7, Verses 1, 51–60, with some changes and deletions), and the seventeenth-century English writer Thomas Dekker. In the center is the *narrative* of the stoning of St. Stephen, the first Christian martyr, preceded by a *sermon* on hope and followed by a personal *prayer* for being granted entrance into heaven after death. At the very end is an "Alleluia" which in tone resembles the conclusion of the *Symphony of Psalms*. Not only is the basic set of twelve notes rigorously applied throughout all parts of the

EXAMPLE 6-14

BASIC SET USED IN *A Sermon, a Narrative, and a Prayer*

cantata, but the musical style is very up-to-date: There is constant changing of time signature with great irregularity of accentuation, a melodic style without phrases in the conventional meaning of the term, abounding in wide leaps, grace notes, sudden bursts of ornamentation, and in the instrumentation much use of harmonics, sudden changing from *arco* (with the bow) to *pizzicato* (plucking) in the string parts, rapid shifting from one instrument to another, and so on. Stravinsky evidently felt that the unity afforded by rigorous use of the basic set was sufficient to sustain such seeming variety in other aspects of the composition.

By way of example we may take the portion of the *Narrative* describing Stephen's works for the newly founded church. This opens with a brief instrumental passage for violoncello, flute, and at the end, clarinet, employing the basic set in the forms ϕ, R and RI$_9$. After the sentence for the speaker, the alto, entering (the word "Stephen" is spoken and sung simultaneously), presents the set in the R form while the accompanying instruments present it in the ϕ form, some notes being used more than once. As the narrator goes on to describe Stephen's works (bars 5–8), two trumpets in canon present the basic set (ϕ), except that the first trumpet omits the eighth note and the second trumpet the seventh and twelfth; in the next passage, for the alto accompanied by three solo violoncellos, the alto part consists first of a disarranged presentation of ϕ (bars 9–11), and then a strict presentation of R (bars 12–15), while the three violoncellos respectively present RI$_9$, ϕ and R. It is clear, then, that Stravinsky does not invariably follow Schoenberg's methods all the way.

One work in this idiom by Stravinsky that has attracted particular attention is *The Flood*, conceived with George Balanchine for television performance; it had its premiere on June 14, 1962. The libretto was compiled by Stravinsky's associate Robert Craft from several sources: Genesis and English

EXAMPLE 6-15

STRAVINSKY: *Narrative*, FROM *A Sermon, a Narrative, and a Prayer*—
EXCERPT

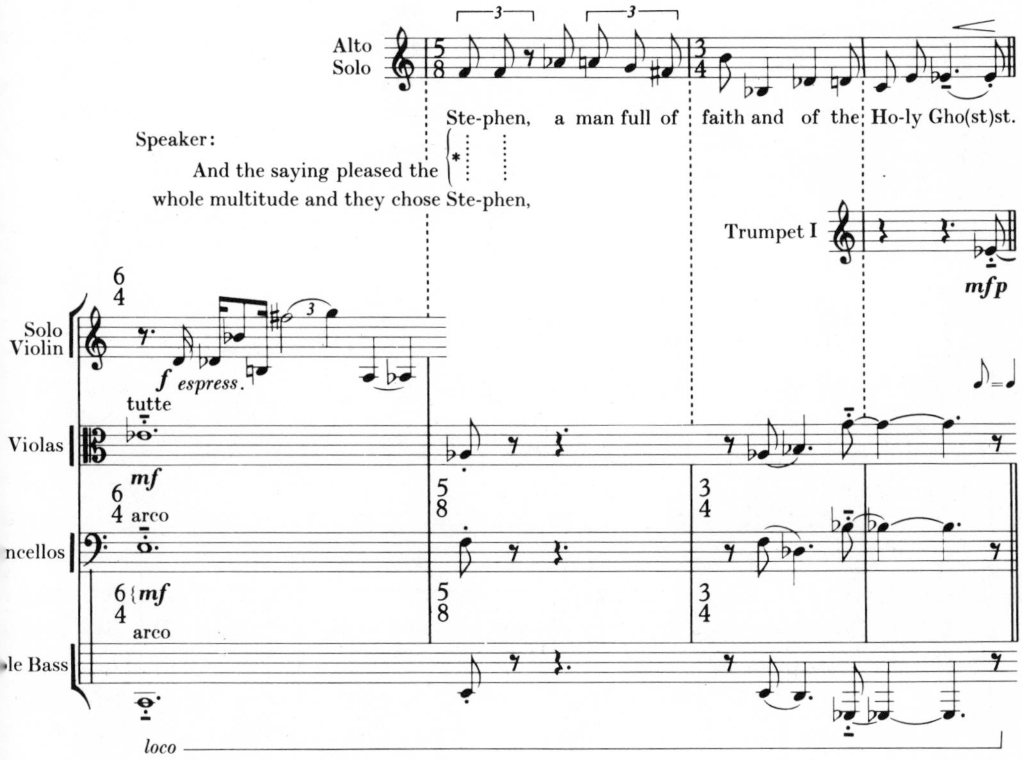

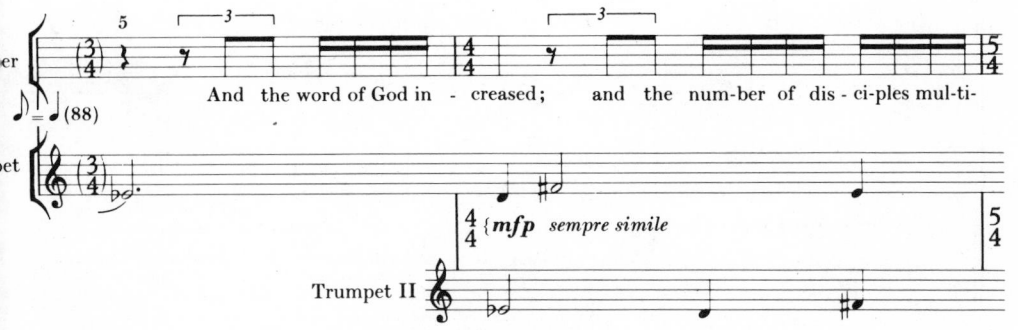

* The two voices must co-ordinate exactly

EXAMPLE 6-15 (*continued*)

EXAMPLE 6-15 (*continued*)

Speaker: Then   there   arose   certain   of   the   synagogue,   disputing   with   Stephen.

And   they   were   not   able   to   resist   the   wisdom   and   the   spirit   by   which   he   spake.

Then   they   suborned   men,   which   said,   we   have   heard   him   speak

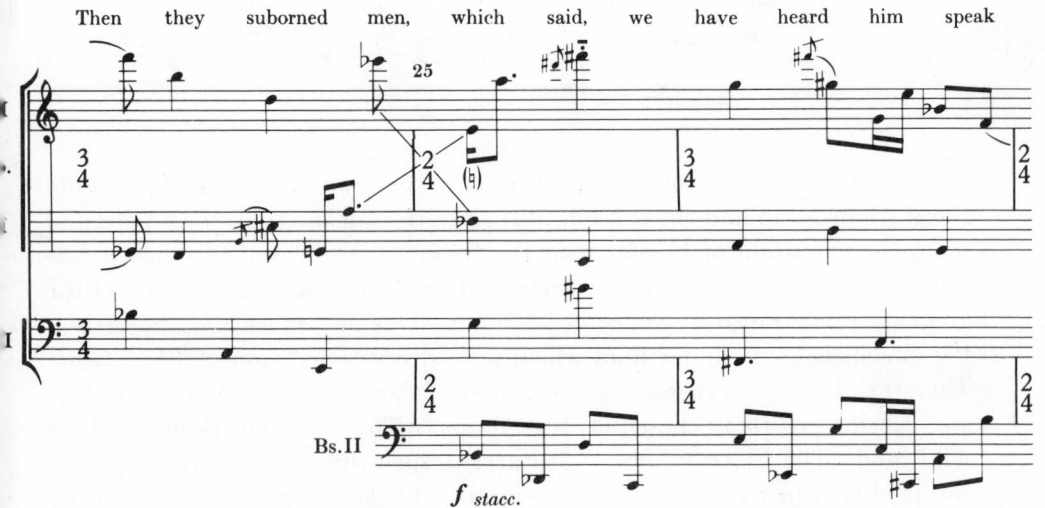

EXAMPLE 6-15 *(concluded)*

blasphemous words against Moses, and against God. And they stirred up

the people, and the elders, and the scribes, and came upon him, and brought him to the council.

medieval miracle plays found in York and Chester. *The Flood* recounts not only the story of Noah and the ark but also gives the background, the creation of man, the expulsion of Lucifer, and the temptation of Eve. Stravinsky conceived television as a medium entirely different from the stage because of the great speed in transition it makes possible: "This new musical economy was the one specific of the medium which guided my conception of *The Flood.*" This work thus is arranged as a succession of short scenes, episodic in nature and varying greatly in character. It contains two ballets ("The Building of the Ark" and "The Flood"), along with arias (especially for Lucifer-Satan), the words of God being set in a sort of recitative for two basses accompanied by timpani, choral passages (near the beginning and the end), and much spoken narration, along with a comedy, as Noah's wife refuses to enter the ark and a catalogue of the animals in the style used by an auctioneer. Thus while the work covers a good deal of ground and contains great variety in the music, it lasts less than half an hour. Other recent works by Stravinsky in this vein are *Abraham and Isaac* (1963), a piece based on Old Testament texts, thus forming a counterpart to *A Sermon, a Narrative, and a Prayer*, the texts of which come for the most part from the New Testament, three short memorial pieces, "Elegy for John F. Kennedy" (1964), "Variations" (1964), and "Introitus" (1965), and finally the *Requiem Canticles* (1966).

Stravinsky's career as a composer, as we have seen, ranges from the early nationalistic ballets through the long succession of neoclassic compositions up to the late works which use the serial method of composition. In many cases Stravinsky's work has been that of a pioneer. Because of this very comprehensiveness, the study of Stravinsky provides in itself a good overview of the central trends in the music of our time. It is clear that his work will constitute a powerful legacy to those who will follow.

Epilogue

At the beginning of this book the artwork in general was defined as a man-made object or representation which is made from materials of one sort or another. The manner in which these materials are put together is subject to the exercise of human reason. On this basis the musical artwork becomes a representation in which sounds or tones are deployed in time; or, in Stravinsky's words, a musical composition is "a speculation in sound and time." Although the quality of the speculation, the terms with which it operates, and its purposes have varied from age to age, one leading idea—perhaps *the* leading idea, which runs like a red thread through the history of Western music—has involved a close association between music and human emotions. The exact forms in which this idea has manifested itself in actual musical compositions have changed from epoch to epoch. These principal changes have been the subject of the foregoing discussion, in which four composers—Bach, Beethoven, Wagner, and Stravinsky—have been taken as representatives of what has been characteristic of the art of Western music since the Renaissance. It may be well, in conclusion, to look once more briefly at the idea that music represents human emotions in order to see how the continually changing interpretations of it have caused changes in the art of music from age to age.

With the concept of *ethos*, the ancient Greeks established the idea of the musical artwork as expressive of human characters and emotions. We have seen how, having had but secondary importance during the Middle Ages, the idea rose to prominence in the Renaissance, in, for example, the motets of Josquin des Prez, ultimately leading to the extreme contrasts that characterize the madrigals of Gesualdo. The idea continued to dominate the music of the Baroque, from the very inception of the recitative style down to the operas of the early eighteenth century, the oratorios of Handel and most of the music of Bach. But an important change had taken place: Reason had entered the picture, imposing an organization both on the conception of the emotions themselves and on their musical expression. This made possible a sort of abstract representation of the passions based on a stockpile of previously conceived and generally recognized musical forms and procedures—in short, what we call the theory of the affections, in accordance with which a piece of music

426

should properly manifest one and only one emotional character all the way through.

With the second half of the eighteenth century, still another change took place: The new art of instrumental music brought with it compositions that depended upon contrasting emotional characters; Beethoven stands as perhaps the principal representative of this music. Then in the nineteenth century the idea of expression took on dominant importance for the art of music, which was conceived as a sort of mysterious language capable of expressing the innermost essence of human feeling, an idea that found its most characteristic manifestation in the music of Wagner. In our own time, however, there has come a strong reaction against this: from Stravinsky, a vehement denial that music is an expressive art at all, that instead it should be viewed in wholly objective terms. Stravinsky's attitude seems closer to that of the Middle Ages, or to the intellectualized approach of the Baroque, than to the music of the nineteenth century.

As a convenient illustration we may consider briefly the history of the Mass as a large form of musical composition. Omitting the repertory of the Gregorian chant, we may take first the polyphonic setting of the Ordinary of the Mass by Guillaume de Machaut (fourteenth century). Here the primarily mathematical orientation of Medieval music is clear from the elaborate rhythms (particularly seen in the use of isorhythm) and the functional importance attributed to the perfect consonances in the harmonic organization. With the coming of the Renaissance, in the Masses of, for example, Josquin or Palestrina, this has changed: The ear-pleasing secondary consonances are now dominant, as is the principle of contrapuntal imitation; but more important is the design of the musical themes used to set the text, which frequently reflects the desire to express, or at least to enhance, the words. Music has become an expressive art. But in the hands of Bach, the Mass expanded to a very large form in which each few lines of text became the basis for an extended piece (an aria, duet, or chorus) that expressed but a single emotional character. This rigid and entirely rationalistic separation of different emotional states in musical composition disappeared by the time of Beethoven, whose Mass displays constant contrasting in characters in a dynamic ebb and flow. Since Wagner composed no Masses, it is unprofitable to speculate on what he might or might not have done. But it is clear that Stravinsky's Mass reveals a position considerably different from what had prevailed since the Renaissance: In place of expression comes a functional austerity that recalls the Middle Ages. To quote Leonard B. Meyer, we have reached "the end of the Renaissance."

These changes in the art of music, all of which may be viewed in terms of the expressive character imputed to or denied the art, may be interpreted as products of the conditions prevailing in the various historical periods. In the Middle Ages, when thought was dominated by the rigid and abstract procedures of scholasticism, music was regulated and judged primarily according to mathematical principles. But in the Renaissance, with the advent of humanism and a new interest in man and his environment, music became the vehicle for the gratification of the ear and for the expression of human emotions. After 1700, in the Baroque, which was also the age of reason (as typified by Bacon, Descartes, and Spinoza), the musical expression of the passions became intellectualized. Then after 1750, along with the new stress on the importance of individuality in the artwork, which thus became the personal expression of the artist, the musical composition, with its dynamic risings and fallings, its accelerations and decelerations, its tensions and releases, came to be looked upon as a sort of analogue to the life process itself, so that music became the expressive art *par excellence*. Finally, after 1900, a reaction set in against this, and the values of reason and objectivity became once more the arbiters of excellence in art. We see, then, that to study music is simply a way to study man.

Appendix One

Notes and Comments

CHAPTER ONE: Music as an Art

Among the best general reference works on music in English are *Grove's Dictionary of Music and Musicians*, 5th edition, edited by Eric Blom, 9 vols. (London, 1954), along with the supplementary volume edited by Eric Blom and Denis Stevens (1961) and Willi Apel's *Harvard Dictionary of Music* (Cambridge, 1944; 2nd edition, 1969).[1] Also recommended is *Baker's Biographical Dictionary of Musicians*, 5th edition, edited by Nicholas Slonimsky (New York, 1958, with the Supplement added in 1965).

On the conception of the artwork in general and the musical artwork in particular, the following are suggested: Suzanne K. Langer, *Philosophy in a New Key* (Cambridge, 1942; reprint, New York, 1948; 3rd ed., 1957) and *Feeling and Form* (New York, 1953); Henri Bergson, *Time and Free Will* (New York, 1910); Igor Stravinsky, *Poetics of Music* (Cambridge, 1947; reprint, New York, 1956); Paul Hindemith, *A Composer's World: Horizons and Limitations* (Cambridge, 1952; reprint, Garden City, New York, 1961); Aaron Copland, *Music and Imagination* (Cambridge, 1952); Leonard B. Meyer, *Emotion and Meaning in Music* (Chicago, 1956); and two books by Victor Zuckerkandl, *Sound and Symbol: Music and the External World* (New York, 1956) and *The Sense of Music* (Princeton, 1959).

On the physics of music and the derivation of the scale systems used in Western music, see especially Sir James Jeans, *Science and Music* (Cambridge, 1937; many reprintings); J. Murray Barbour, *Tuning and Temperament: A Historical Survey* (East Lansing, 1951, 2nd edition, 1953); and Llewellyn S. Lloyd, *Intervals, Scales and Temperaments* (London, 1963).

There are a number of books presenting the notational, scalar, metric, and harmonic systems of Western music. A good introductory work is Howard Boatwright, *Introduction to the Theory of Music* (New York, 1956). Two standard texts by prominent American composers may be mentioned: Walter Piston, *Harmony* (New York, 1941; 3rd edition, 1962); and Roger Sessions,

---

[1] Useful and inexpensive is the shorter version, Willi Apel and Ralph Daniel, *Harvard Brief Dictionary of Music* (Cambridge, 1960), also available in paperback form.

Harmonic Practice (New York, 1951). Concerning rhythm and meter, see Curt Sachs, *Rhythm and Tempo: A Study in Music History* (New York, 1953) and Leonard B. Meyer and Grosvenor Cooper, *The Rhythmic Structure of Music* (Chicago, 1960). On musical instruments, see Curt Sachs, *The History of Musical Instruments* (New York, 1940); Karl Geiringer, *Musical Instruments* (New York, 1945); and Robert Donington, *The Instruments of Music*, 3rd edition (New York, 1945). On orchestration, see, among others, Walter Piston, *Orchestration* (New York, 1955) and Kent Kennan, *The Technique of Orchestration* (New York, 1952).

Concerning the elements of form in music, the following may be suggested: J. Smits van Waesberghe, *A Textbook of Melody* (1955); Grosvenor Cooper, *Learning to Listen* (Chicago, 1957); Bence Szabolcsi, *A History of Melody* (New York, 1965); Wallace Berry, *Form in Music* (Englewood Cliffs, N. J., 1966); Douglass Marshall Green, *Form in Tonal Music* (New York, 1965); and Robert E. Tyndall, *Musical Form* (Boston, 1964).

CHAPTER TWO: The Historical Background

Among many general works dealing with the history of music in the West as a whole, we may here mention some of the more recent: Donald Jay Grout, *A History of Western Music* (New York, 1960); Beekman Cannon, Alvin Johnson, and William G. Waite, *The Art of Music* (New York, 1960); Homer Ulrich and Paul A. Pisk, *A History of Music and Musical Style* (New York, 1963) and Richard L. Crocker, *A History of Musical Style* (New York, 1966). Among the older surveys we list Paul Henry Láng, *Music in Western Civilization* (New York, 1941) and Curt Sachs, *Our Musical Heritage* (Englewood Cliffs, N.J., 1948; 2nd edition, 1955). An extremely compressed but brilliantly conceived overview is Alfred Einstein, *A Short History of Music* (New York, 1937; 4th edition, 1954).

Two larger multivolume works are the *Norton History of Music* (published by the W. W. Norton Company, New York) and the *New Oxford History of Music* (published by the Oxford University Press, London). Individual volumes from these sets will be mentioned under the appropriate headings below. Both *Grove's Dictionary* and Apel's *Harvard Dictionary* contain information on the history of music

Among a number of books dealing with individual forms and genres of musical compositions we can mention Donald Jay Grout, *A Short History of Opera* (New York, 1947; 2nd edition, enlarged, 1965); Ulrich Weisstein (editor), *The Essence of Opera* (New York, 1964); Joseph Kerman, *Opera as Drama* (New York, 1956; reprint, 1959); Homer Ulrich, *Symphonic Music* (New York, 1952; 2nd edition, 1961); Abraham Veinus, *The Concerto* (Garden City, New York, 1945; reprint, 1964); Homer Ulrich, *Chamber Music* (New York, 1948; 2nd edition, 1966); Walter Willson Cobbett, *Cyclopedic Survey of*

Notes and Comments

Chamber Music, 2 vols. (London, 1929; 2nd edition, with supplement edited by ꞌColin Mason, 3 vols., London, 1963); Denis Stevens (editor), *A History of Song* (London and New York, 1960); Elwyn Wienandt, *Choral Music of the Church* (New York, 1965); Friedrich Blume, *History of Protestant Church Music* (New York, in preparation); Willi Apel, *Masters of the Keyboard* (Cambridge, 1947; many later printings); John Gillespie, *Five Centuries of Keyboard Music* (Belmont, 1965); F. E. Kirby, *A Short History of Keyboard Music* (New York, 1966). Finally we should mention the collection of excerpts from treatises on music and philosophical works dealing with music, Oliver Strunk (editor), *Source Readings in Music History* (New York, 1950; reprint, 5 vols., 1965).

Of great importance are the several historical anthologies of early music, among which we may list Arnold Schering, *A History of Music in Examples* (New York, 1950); Archibald T. Davison and Willi Apel, *Historical Anthology of Music*, 2 vols. (Cambridge, 1946–50); Carl Parrish and John F. Ohl, *Masterpieces of Music Before 1750* (New York, 1951); Carl Parrish, *A Treasury of Early Music* (New York, 1958);[2] William J. Starr and George F. Devine, *Music Scores Omnibus*, 2 vols. (Englewood Cliffs, N.J., 1964); Roger Kamien, *The Norton Scores: An Anthology for Listening* (New York, 1968); finally, there is an extensive set of recordings covering the entire history of Western music, with accompanying handbooks which discuss and often reproduce, in whole or in part, the compositions: *The History of Music in Sound*, 10 vols. (RCA Victor Records and Oxford University Press).

On ancient Greek music: Curt Sachs, *The Rise of Music in the Ancient World, East and West* (*Norton History of Music*, I; New York, 1943); Egon Wellesz (editor), *Ancient and Oriental Music* (*New Oxford History of Music*, I; London, 1957); Edward A. Lippman, *Musical Thought in Ancient Greece* (New York, 1964); and Warren D. Anderson, *Ethos and Education in Greek Music* (Cambridge, 1966).

On Medieval music in general: Gustave Reese, *Music in the Middle Ages* (*Norton History of Music*, II; New York, 1940); Anselm Hughes (editor), *Early Medieval Music Up to 1300* (*New Oxford History of Music*, II; London, 1954); and Albert Seay, *Music in the Medieval World* (Englewood Cliffs, N.J., 1965). Other books to be mentioned here are Willi Apel, *Gregorian Chant* (Bloomington, 1958); Willi Apel, *The Notation of Polyphonic Music, 900–1600*, 5th edition (Cambridge, 1949); Carl Parrish, *The Notation of Medieval Music* (New York, 1957); William G. Waite, *The Rhythm of Twelfth-Century Polyphony* (New Haven, 1954); Hugo Riemann, *History of Music Theory* (Lincoln, Neb., 1962); and Nan C. Carpenter, *Music in the Medieval and Renaissance Universities* (Norman, Okla., 1958).

[2] The compositions contained in these last two books have been recorded *in toto* by the Haydn Society, each set respectively bearing the same title as the corresponding book, the succession and numbering of the pieces being the same. A complete recording of the Davison-Apel *Historical Anthology of Music* has begun to appear, issued by Southern Illinois University Press.

Appendix One

On Renaissance music in general: Gustave Reese, *Music in the Renaissance* (*Norton History of Music*, III; New York, 1954; revised edition, 1959); Anselm Hughes (editor), *Ars nova and Renaissance, 1300–1540* (*New Oxford History of Music*, III; London, 1960); Gerald Abraham (editor), *The Age of Humanism: 1540–1630* (*New Oxford History of Music*, IV; London, 1968); and Friedrich Blume's article "Renaissance Music," in his *Renaissance and Baroque Music, a Comprehensive Survey* (New York, 1967). An important book is Alfred Einstein, *The Italian Madrigal*, 3 vols. (Princeton, 1949).

On Baroque music, the standard work is Manfred F. Bukofzer, *Music in the Baroque Era* (*Norton History of Music*, IV; New York, 1947); more up-to-date but considerably less detailed is Claude V. Palisca, *Baroque Music* (Englewood Cliffs, N.J., 1968); see also Friedrich Blume's article "Baroque Music," in his *Renaissance and Baroque Music* (see above). On individual composers, see Leo Schrade, *Monteverdi: Creator of Modern Music* (New York, 1950; reprint, 1969); Hans Joachim Moser, *Heinrich Schütz, His Life and Work* (St. Louis, 1959); and Franklin B. Zimmerman, *Henry Purcell, 1659–1695: His Life and Times* (London, 1967).

The compositions discussed in the chapter are available in standard recordings as follows:[3]

1. Antiphon, *Laus Deo patri* and Psalm 113, *Laudate pueri* (Music Example 2-3)—*MM*, No. 1.
2. Gradual, *Viderunt omnes* (Music Example 2-4)—Angel 35116.
3. Kyrie *Cunctipotens genitor* (Music Example 2–5)—Vanguard BGS 5045 and Nonesuch H-71184 (in conjunction with Machaut's Mass).
4. Hymn, *Exsultet orbis* (Music Example 2-6)—*HMS* II 2 ii.
5. Gace Brulé: *Je ne puis pas si loing* (Music Example 2-7)—*HMS* II 2 iv (c).
6. *Worldes blis* (Music Example 2-8)—*HMS* II 3 i (a).
7. Parallel organum, *Sit gloria Domini* (Music Example 2-9)—*HMS* II 3 iii.
8. St. Martial Organum, *Benedicamus Domino* (Music Example 2-10)—*MM*, No. 8.
9. Perotin: *Viderunt omnes* (Music Example 2-12)—Vanguard BGS 5045 (Leonin's setting is recorded on Decca DL 9400, *TEM*, No. 9 and Experiénces anonymes EA 21).
10. *En non Diu—Quant voi—Eius in oriente* (Music Example 2-13)—*MM*, No. 10.
11. Conductus, Perotin: *Salvatoris hodie*—Experiénces anonymes EA 35.

---

[3] Abbreviations: *HMS, History of Music in Sound* (in citing this collection, Roman numerals indicate the volume, Arabic numerals the record side, lower-case Roman numerals the band); *MM, Masterpieces of Music before 1750*, by Carl Parrish and John F. Ohl; and *TEM, A Treasury of Early Music*, by Carl Parrish.

12. Machaut: Sanctus, from *Mass of Notre Dame* (Music Example 2-15). Three complete recordings of the Mass exist: DGG ARC 3032, Vanguard BGS 5045, and Nonesuch H-71184; the Agnus is recorded in *MM*, No. 13.
13. Josquin des Prez: *De profundis* (Music Example 2-16)—Vanguard BGS 620.
14. Palestrina: Kyrie, Gloria, and Credo, from *Mass Assumpta est* (Music Example 2-17)—DGG ARC 73241.
15. Gesualdo: *Moro lasso* (Music Example 2-18)—*TEM*, No. 33 and DGG ARC 3073.
16. Gabrieli: *Sonata pian' e forte*—Several recordings exist: DGG ARC 73154, Esoteric ES 503 and Vanguard BGS 5037.
17. Gabrieli: *In ecclesiis*—*HMS* IV 3 ii, RCA Victor LM 1721 and Angel S-36443.
18. Monteverdi: "Tu se' morta," from *Orfeo* (Music Example 2-19)—*MM*, No. 31. There is one complete recording of the opera: DGG ARC 3035-6. An excerpt from Act IV is in *HMS* IV 4 iii.

CHAPTER THREE: Bach

The standard critical collected edition of Bach's work is that published in the late nineteenth century by the Bach Society (*Bachgesellschaft*) in Leipzig: *Werke*, 47 vols. (Leipzig, 1851–99, and 1926; reprint, 46 vols., Ann Arbor, 1946). It is gradually being replaced by a completely new edition: the *Neue Ausgabe sämtlicher Werke*, planned in approximately 86 vols. (Kassel, in progress since 1954). Reliable editions of individual compositions or groups of compositions exist in far too great abundance to be included here. An important aid in the study of Bach is the thematic catalogue, a listing of all his works, quoting the beginning of each composition and giving all the essential bibliographical information: Wolfgang Schmieder, *Thematisch-systematisches Verzeichnis der musikalischen Werke von Johann Sebastian Bach* (Leipzig, 1950); in this work each composition is assigned an "S" or "BWV" number for exact identification. The standard English-language collection of documents relating to Bach is Hans T. David and Arthur Mendel, *The Bach Reader* (New York, 1945; revised edition with a supplement, 1966).

The most recent and up-to-date survey of Bach, and the only one available at this time in English to incorporate recent discoveries concerning the chronology of his works, is Karl and Irene Geiringer, *Johann Sebastian Bach: The Culmination of an Era* (New York, 1966). But the older standard works still retain their basic importance: Philipp Spitta, *Johann Sebastian Bach: His Work and Influence on the Music of Germany*, 3 vols. (London, 1899; reprint, 2 vols., New York, 1951) and Albert Schweitzer, *J. S. Bach*, 2 vols. (New York, 1911; reprint, 1962). Among other general books on Bach, we can mention here Paul Hindemith, *Johann Sebastian Bach: Heritage and Obligation* (New Haven, 1952) and Leo Schrade, *Bach: The Conflict Between the Sacred and the Secular* (New York, 1955; also in *Journal of the History of Ideas*, VII [1946], pp. 151–94). See also Karl Geiringer, *The Bach Family: Seven Generations of Creative Genius* (New York, 1954).

On individual compositions and types of compositions: W. Gillies Whittaker, *The Cantatas of Johann Sebastian Bach, Sacred and Secular*, 2 vols. (London, 1959; reprint, 1964); the edition of the cantata *Christ lag in Todesbanden* (S. 4), edited by Gerhard Herz (New York, 1968) includes good historical and analytical essays; Henry S. Drinker, *Texts of the Chorale Works of Johann Sebastian Bach in English Translation* (New York, 1941); Hermann Keller, *The Organ Works of Bach* (New York, 1967); Harvey Grace, *The Organ Works of Bach* (London, 1922); Robert L. Tusler, *The Style of J. S. Bach's Chorale-Preludes* (Berkeley, 1956; reprint, New York, 1968); Erwin Bodky, *The Interpretation of Bach's Keyboard Works* (Cambridge, 1960); and Hans T. David, *J. S. Bach's Musical Offering: History, Interpretation, and Analysis* (New York, 1945).

On tuning and temperament, see the books by Jeans, Barbour, and Lloyd listed for Chapter One. On fugue in general, see Alfred Mann, *The Study of Fugue* (New Brunswick, 1958; reprint, 1965) and Imogene Horsley, *Fugue: History and Practice* (New York, 1966).

Among the compositions by Bach discussed and otherwise mentioned in the chapter, the following are to be found in *HMS, MM, MSO* (*Music Scores Omnibus*), and *NS* (*Norton Scores*):

Cantata, *Wachet auf* (S. 140): *NS*, 121–75.

Cantata, *Ein' feste Burg* (S. 80): *MSO* I, 152–82.

Cantata, *Christ lag in Todesbanden* (S. 4); two movements, *MM*, Nos. 46 and 48.

St. Matthew Passion: excerpt from Part II, *MSO* I, 117–25; also *MM* No. 49.

From the Mass in B minor: Crucifixus: *NS*, 176–79.

From the *Little Organ Book:*
   Christ lag in Todesbanden: MM, No. 47.
   In dulci jubilo: HMS VI 2 iv (b).
   Durch Adams Fall: HMS VI 2 iii (b).

From *The Well-Tempered Clavier*, Book I:
   Prelude and Fugue in C major (No. 1),
   Prelude and Fugue in C minor (No. 2),
   Prelude and Fugue in E-flat minor (No. 8) in *MSO* I, 182–87.

Partita in D major (No. 4): *MSO* I, 138–47.

Concerto grosso in F major (*Brandenburg Concerto No. 2*): *MSO* I, 126–37 and *NS*, 73–108.

From *The Art of Fugue:* Contrapunctus III: *MM*, No. 50.

CHAPTER FOUR: Beethoven and the New Instrumental Music

There is as yet no comprehensive account of late eighteenth-century music in English; in preparation is Friedrich Blume, *The Music of the Classic Era* (*Norton History of Music*, V); a short interpretation is given by Reinhard Pauly, *Music of the Classic Period* (Englewood Cliffs, N.J., 1965). On Handel, see Paul Henry Láng, *George Frideric Handel* (New York, 1966) and Otto Erich Deutsch, *Handel: A Documentary Biography* (New York, 1955); see also Robert Manson Myers, *Handel's Messiah, a Touchstone of Taste* (New York, 1948) and Jens Peter Larsen, *Handel's Messiah* (New York, 1957).

On composers of the late eighteenth century, see Karl Geiringer, *Haydn: A Creative Life in Music* (New York, 1946; 2nd edition, paperback, 1963; reprint, 1967); W. J. Turner, *W. A. Mozart, The Man and His Works* (New York, 1938; reprints, 1954 and 1966); and two books by Alfred Einstein, *Mozart: His Character, His Work* (New York, 1945; reprint, 1965) and *Gluck* (New York, 1936; reprint, 1962).

With Beethoven, as with Bach, there is an old standard critical collected edition of his works and a new one in progress, as well as a thematic catalogue: *Werke. Vollständig kritisch durchgesehene überallberechtigte Ausgabe*, 24 vols. (Leipzig, 1862–88; reprint, Ann Arbor, 1949); *Werke*, published by the Beethoven-Archiv in Bonn (Munich, in progress since 1961); and Georg Kinsky and Hans Halm, *Das Werk Beethovens. Thematisch-bibliographisches Verzeichnis seiner sämtlichen vollendeten Kompositionen* (Munich, 1955). For the letters of Beethoven, see Emily Anderson (editor and translator), *The Letters of Beethoven*, 3 vols. (New York, 1961). There is as yet no complete edition of Beethoven's sketchbooks, some of which have been published individually, mainly under the sponsorship of the Beethoven-Archiv in Bonn; the older and up-to-now standard discussions of Beethoven's compositions based on the sketchbooks are by Gustav Nottebohm: *Beethoveniana* (Leipzig and Winterthur, 1872) and *Zweite Beethoveniana* (Leipzig, 1887), both in German. There is also no complete edition of Beethoven's conversation books: The most complete attempt has been that of Georg Schünemann, *Beethovens Konversationshefte*, 3 vols. (Berlin, 1941–43), which covers the years 1818–23, and which is now being continued. This may be supplemented by the selection published in French by J. G. Prod'homme, *Les cahiers de conversation de Beethoven* (Paris, 1946). A convenient selection from Beethoven's letters, notes and sketchbooks in English is Michael Hamburger (editor and translator), *Beethoven: Letters, Journals and Conversations* (London, 1951; reprint, Garden City, N.J., 1960). See also Paul Nettl, *Beethoven Encyclopedia* (New York, 1956).

General works on Beethoven: The standard biography remains Alexander Wheelock Thayer, *The Life of Ludwig van Beethoven*, especially in its new edition by Elliot Forbes, 2 vols. (Princeton, 1964); the original English edition (the work was first published in German) is that of Henry E. Krehbiel, 3 vols. (New York, 1921; reprint, Carbondale, 1961). Also recommended are

Appendix One

Paul Bekker, *Beethoven* (London and New York, 1925); Walter Riezler, *Beethoven* (London and New York, 1938); Romain Rolland, *Beethoven the Creator* (London, 1929; reprint, New York, 1964) and *Goethe and Beethoven* (London and New York, 1931). Finally, of great importance is the biography of Beethoven by Anton Schindler, the third edition of which has just been published in English under the editorship of Donald W. MacArdle, *Beethoven as I Knew Him* (Chapel Hill, 1966). Concerning individual types of Beethoven's compositions, see Joseph Kerman, *The Beethoven Quartets* (New York, 1967) and Eric Blom, *Beethoven's Pianoforte Sonatas Discussed* (London, 1938; reprint, New York, 1968).

CHAPTER FIVE: Wagner and the Romantic Age

The standard work on Romantic music is Alfred Einstein, *Music in the Romantic Era* (*Norton History of Music*, VI; New York, 1947). On the different composers of the early nineteenth century, the following are suggested: Alfred Einstein, *Schubert: A Musical Portrait* (New York, 1951); Jacques Barzun, *Berlioz and the Romantic Age*, 2 vols. (Boston, 1950), or in its shortened version, *Berlioz and His Century* (New York, 1956); Arthur Hedley, *Chopin* (London, 1947; New York, 1962); and Humphrey Searle, *The Music of Liszt* (London, 1954).

There are a number of different editions of Wagner's music dramas, both in full orchestra scores and with reduction of the orchestra for piano (piano-vocal scores); there is no standard critical collected edition of his works. The prose writings have been translated, collected and edited: *Prose Works*, 8 vols. (London, 1893–99; reprint, 1967). Other writings available separately include his autobiography, *My Life*, authorized translation (London 1911; New York, 1911; many later editions) and *Beethoven*, 3rd edition (New York, 1883). There are also anthologies of his prose writings, of which [Richard Wagner] *Art, Life and Theories*, edited by E. L. Burlingame (New York, 1875) has long been standard; more recent is *Wagner on Music and Drama: A Compendium of Richard Wagner's Prose Writings*, edited by A. Goldman and E. Sprinchorn (New York, 1965). An extensive excerpt from *The Art-Work of the Future* is included in Strunk's *Source Readings in Music History* (New York, 1950), pp. 876–903.

Reference should also be made to two writers who exerted great influence on Wagner: Arthur Schopenhauer, *The World as Will and Representation*, 2 vols. (Indian Hills, Colorado, 1958) and Friedrich Nietzsche, *The Birth of Tragedy from the Spirit of Music* (Garden City, N.Y., 1956).

On Wagner's life and work, see C. F. Glasenapp, *Life of Richard Wagner*, 6 vols. (London, 1900–8); Ernest Newman, *Life of Richard Wagner*, 4 vols. (New York, 1942–46) and *Wagner as Man and Artist* (London, 1914; New York, 1924; reprint, 1952); Paul Bekker, *Richard Wagner: His Life in His*

Notes and Comments

Work (New York, 1931); Chappell White, *An Introduction to the Life and Work of Richard Wagner* (New York, 1967); Jack M. Stein, *Richard Wagner and the Synthesis of the Arts* (Detroit, 1960); Robert Donington, *Wagner's "Ring" and Its Symbols: The Music and the Myth* (London, 1963); and Elliott Zuckerman, *The First Hundred Years of Wagner's Tristan* (New York, 1964). Of the innumerable guides to Wagner's operas, identifying the various leitmotivs, we may mention here (apart from Donington's book, which concerns itself only with the *Ring*) Gustave Kobbé, *Wagner's Music-Dramas Analysed* (New York, 1890).

On followers of Wagner in the late nineteenth century: Hans Ferdinand Redlich, *Bruckner and Mahler* (London and New York, 1955); Norman del Mar, *Strauss: A Critical Commentary on his Life and Works*, 2 vols. (London, 1962 and 1969); Frank Walker, *Hugo Wolf, a Biography* (New York, 1952); Eric Sams, *The Songs of Hugo Wolf* (London, 1961).

See also: Francis Toye, *Giuseppe Verdi, His Life and Works* (London, 1931; New York, 1946; reprint, 1959); Frank Walker, *The Man Verdi* (New York, 1962); Walter Niemann, *Brahms* (New York, 1929; reprint, 1945); Karl Geiringer, *Brahms: His Life and Work* (New York, 1936; 2nd edition, 1961); and Eduard Hanslick, *The Beautiful in Music* (New York, 1957).

CHAPTER SIX: Stravinsky and the New Music of the Twentieth Century

On the various nationalistic groups of composers of the late nineteenth and early twentieth centuries, see, among others, Gerald Abraham, *A Hundred Years of Music* (London, 1938; 3rd edition, Chicago, 1964); Paul Stefan, *Antonin Dvořák* (New York, 1941); Rosa Newmarch, *The Music of Czechoslovakia* (New York, 1942); Bence Szabolcsi, *A Concise History of Hungarian Music* (Budapest, 1964); John Horton, *Scandinavian Music: A Short History* (London, 1963); Gerald Abraham, *Studies in Russian Music* (London, n.d.); Boris Vladimirovích Asafiev, *Russian Music from the Beginning of the Nineteenth Century* (Ann Arbor, 1953); Richard Anthony Leonard, *A History of Russian Music* (New York, 1957); James Bakst, *A History of Russian-Soviet Music* (New York, 1966); and Gerald R. Seaman, *History of Russian Music, Vol. I: From its Orgins to Dargomyzhsky* (New York, 1967); Eric Blom, *Music in England* (London, 1942; revised, 1947); Martin Cooper, *French Music from the Death of Berlioz to the Death of Fauré* (London, 1951; reprint, 1961); Gilbert Chase, *The Music of Spain* (New York, 1941; 2nd edition, 1959) and *America's Music* (New York, 1955; 2nd edition, revised, 1966); Wilfrid H. Mellers, *Music in a New Found Land* (New York, 1965); and Paul Henry Láng (ed.), *One Hundred Years of Music in America* (New York, 1961).

On twentieth-century music in general, see the prize-winning new standard work, William Austin, *Music in the Twentieth Century* (*Norton History of*

Music, VII; New York, 1966). Among other general surveys are Adolfo Salazar, *Music in Our Time* (New York, 1946); Paul Collaer, *A History of Modern Music* (New York, 1961); Nicholas Slonimsky, *Music Since 1900* (New York, 1937; 3rd edition, revised, 1949); Joseph Machlis, *Introduction to Contemporary Music* (New York, 1961); and Eric Salzman, *Twentieth-Century Music: An Introduction* (Englewood Cliffs, N.J., 1967). Finally, attention may be drawn to the provocative viewpoint expressed in Leonard B. Meyer, *Music, the Arts and Ideas: Patterns and Predictions in Twentieth-Century Culture* (Chicago, 1967).

On Debussy, see particularly two books by Edward Lockspeiser: *Debussy, His Life and Mind,* 2 vols. (New York and London, 1962–65), a large biographical study, and *Debussy* (New York, 1936; 4th edition, revised, 1963), a good general work; see also Leon Vallas, *The Theories of Claude Debussy* (London, 1929; reprint, New York, 1967).

On Schoenberg, see Dika Newlin, *Bruckner, Mahler, Schoenberg* (New York, 1947); René Leibowitz, *Schoenberg and His School* (New York, 1949); H. H. Stuckenschmidt, *Arnold Schoenberg* (New York, 1959); and George Perle, *Serial Composition and Atonality* (Berkeley, 1962; 2nd edition, 1967). A critical collected edition of Schoenberg's works, under the general editorship of Joseph Rufer, commenced in 1966; Rufer has also prepared a catalogue of Schoenberg's works: *The Works of Arnold Schoenberg* (New York, 1963). A new critical biography of Schoenberg with studies of his compositions by Dika Newlin is in preparation.

On Bartók and Ives see Halsey Stevens, *The Life and Music of Béla Bartók* (New York, 1953; 2nd edition, 1964) and Henry and Sidney Cowell, *Charles Ives and His Music* (New York, 1955).

Of Stravinsky's musical works there is as yet no standard critical collected edition, but the compositions he has published are available in editions which he himself has approved. The two principal literary works are *Chronicle of My Life* (London, 1936) or *Autobiography* (New York, 1936; reprinted, 1958 and 1962); and *Poetics of Music in the Form of Six Lessons* (Cambridge, 1947; reprint, 1956). Then there is the series he has done in collaboration with Robert Craft: *Conversations with Igor Stravinsky* (Garden City, New York, 1959), *Memories and Commentaries* (Garden City, New York, 1960), *Expositions and Developments* (Garden City, New York, 1962), *Dialogues and a Diary* (Garden City, New York, 1963) and *Themes and Episodes* (New York, 1966). It should also be mentioned that Stravinsky has recorded his own performances of his principal compositions; the documentary importance of these recordings is not to be overestimated.

Of books written on Stravinsky and his work, the following may be mentioned here: the most recent encyclopedic study, Eric Walter White, *Stravinsky: The Composer and His Works* (Berkeley, 1966), as well as White's earlier *Stravinsky: A Critical Survey* (London, 1947, and New York, 1948);

Notes and Comments

Rollo H. Myers, *Introduction to the Music of Stravinsky* (London, 1950); Alexandre Tansman, *Igor Stravinsky: The Man and His Music* (New York, 1949); Theodore Strawinsky, *The Message of Igor Strawinsky* (London and New York, 1953); Heinrich Strobel, *Stravinsky: Classic Humanist* (New York, 1955); Roman Vlad, *Stravinsky* (London and New York, 1960; 2nd edition, 1967); Edwin Corle (editor), *Igor Stravinsky* (New York, 1949); and Paul Henry Láng (editor), *Stravinsky: A New Appraisal of His Work* (New York, 1963). Of great interest is the recent edition of *Petrushka*, edited by Charles Hamm (New York, 1968), which includes analytical and descriptive essays on the work.

The Ordinary of the Mass: Text and Translation

KYRIE

Kyrie eleison.	Lord, have mercy upon us.
Christe eleison.	Christ, have mercy upon us.
Kyrie eleison.	Lord, have mercy upon us.

GLORIA

Gloria in excelsis Deo.	Glory be to God on high.
Et in terra pax hominibus bonae voluntatis.	And on earth peace to men of good will.
Laudamus te, benedicimus te, adoramus te, glorificamus te.	We praise Thee, we bless Thee, we adore Thee, we glorify Thee.
Gratias agimus tibi propter magnam gloriam tuam.	We thank Thee for Thy great glory.
Domine Deus, rex coelestis, Deus pater omnipotens.	Lord God, heavenly king, God the Father almighty.
Domine fili unigenite, Jesu Christe.	O Lord, the only begotten Son, Jesus Christ.
Domine Deus, agnus Dei, filius patris.	Lord God, Lamb of God, Son of the Father.
Qui tollis peccata mundi, miserere nobis.	That takest away the sins of the world, have mercy upon us.
Qui tollis peccata mundi, suscipe deprecationem nostram.	Who taketh away the sins of the world, hear our prayer.
Qui sedes ad dexteram patris, miserere nobis.	Thou that sittest at the right hand of the Father, have mercy upon us.
Quoniam tu solus sanctus, tu solus dominus, tu solus altissimus, Jesu Christe.	For Thou only art holy, Thou only art the Lord, Thou only Christ, art most high.
Cum sancto spiritu in gloria Dei patris. Amen.	With the Holy Ghost in the glory of God the Father. Amen.

CREDO

Credo in unum Deum.	I believe in one God.
Patrem omnipotentem, factorem coeli et terrae, visibilium omnium et invisibilium.	The Father almighty, Maker of heaven and earth and all things visible and invisible.

440

Et in unum dominum, Jesum
Christum, filium Dei
unigenitum.
Et ex patre natum ante omnia
saecula.
Deum de Deo, lumen de lumine,
Deum verum de Deo vero.
Genitum, non factum, consub-
stantialem patri, per quem
omnia facta sunt.
Qui propter nos homines et
propter nostram salutem
descendit de coelis.
Et incarnatus est de spiritu
sancto ex Maria virgine, et
homo factus est.
Crucifixus etiam pro nobis, sub
Pontio Pilato, passus et
sepultus est.
Et resurrexit tertia die
secundum scripturas.
Et ascendit in coelum, sedet ad
dexteram patris.
Et iterum venturus est cum
gloria judicare vivos et
mortuos, cuius regni non
erit finis.
Et in spiritum sanctum, dominum
et vivificantem, qui ex patre
filioque procedit.
Qui cum patre et filio simul
adoratur, et conglorificatur,
qui locutus est per prophetas.
Et unam sanctam catholicam et
apostolicam ecclesiam.
Confiteor unum baptisma in
remissionem peccatorum.
Et expecto resurrectionem mortuorum.

Et vitam venturi saeculi.
Amen.

And in one Lord, Jesus Christ,
the only begotten Son of
God.
And born of the Father before
all ages.
God of God, light of light, true
God of God.
Begotten, not made, being of one
substance with the Father,
by Whom all things were made.
Who for us men and our salvation
came down from heaven.

And was incarnated by the Holy
Ghost of the Virgin Mary, and
was made man.
And was crucified also for us under
Pontius Pilate, suffered and
was buried.
And the third day He rose again
according to the Scriptures.
And ascendeth to heaven, and sitteth
on the right hand of the Father.
And He shall come again with glory
to judge the living and the dead,
Whose kingdom shall have no
end.
And in the Holy Ghost, the Lord and
giver of life, who proceedeth
from the Father and the Son.
Who with the Father and the Son
together is worshipped and glorified,
who spake by the prophets.
And in one holy Catholic and
apostolic church.
I acknowledge one baptism for the
remission of sins.
And I look for the resurrection of the
dead.
And for the life of the world to come.
Amen.

SANCTUS

Sanctus, sanctus, sanctus, dominus
Deus sabaoth,
Pleni sunt coeli et terra
gloria ejus.
Osanna in excelsis.
Benedictus qui venit in nomine
Domini.
Osanna in excelsis.

Holy, holy, holy, Lord God of hosts,

Heaven and earth are full of
Thy glory.
Hosanna in the highest.
Blessed is He who cometh in the name
of the Lord.
Hosanna in the highest.

Appendix Two

AGNUS DEI

Agnus Dei, qui tollis peccata mundi, miserere nobis.
Agnus Dei, qui tollis peccata mundi, dona nobis pacem.

O Lamb of God, that takest away the sins of the world, have mercy upon us.
O Lamb of God, that takest away the sins of the world, give us peace.

Index

Index

INDEX COMPILED BY ROBERT J. PALMER.